Field Guide
to
EDIBLE
WILD
PLANTS

Field Guide
to
EDIBLE
WILD
PLANTS

BRADFORD ANGIER

Jacket and book plant illustrations by
Arthur J. Anderson

Stackpole Books

FIELD GUIDE TO EDIBLE WILD PLANTS
Copyright© 1974 by
Bradford Angier
Illustrations Copyright© by
Arthur J. Anderson

First printing, August 1974
Second printing, December 1974
Third printing, June 1975
Fourth printing, March 1976
Fifth printing, August 1977
Sixth printing, May 1979

Printed in the U.S.A.

Library of Congress Cataloging in Publication Data

Angier, Bradford.
    Field guide to edible wild plants.

    1. Plants, Edible—Identification. I. Title.
QK98.5A1A53   581.6'32   73-23042
ISBN 0-8117-0616-8
ISBN 0-8117-2018-7 (pbk.)

For Carol Gooderham, my prettiest editor,
who thought of it.

NOTE TO THE READER

OTHER BOOKS BY BRADFORD ANGIER

Being Your Own Wilderness Doctor
  with E. Russell Kodet, M. D.
Feasting Free on Wild Edibles
Field Guide to Medicinal Wild Plants
How to Live in the Woods on Pennies a Day
Introduction to Canoeing
  with Zack Taylor
The Master Backwoodsman
One Acre and Security

DIRECTORY OF WILD FOODS

A

Aaron's Rod, 132
Acorn, 24
Ague Tree, 194
Ahklingqualk, 64
Alaska Blueberry, 40
Alaska Pine, 166
Alexanders Angelica, 232
Algerita, 28
Allegheny Sloe, 244
Alpine Bearberry, 120
Alpine Bistort, 122
Alpine Dandelion, 70
Alpine Sorrel, 146
Amaranth, 88
Amatokoro, 122
American Arum, 110
American Aspen, 172
American Bamboo Shoots, 122
American Barberry, 28
American Beech, 32
American Bistort, 122
American Coffee Bean, 118
American Crab, 230
American Crab Apple, 230
American Cranberry, 66
American Elder, 76

American Elderberry, 76
American Hazelnut, 98
American Mandrake, 136
American Mint, 142
American Mountain Ash, 144
American Pennyroyal, 142
American Red Currant, 68
American Red Raspberry, 182
American White Birch, 34
American Wild Plum, 244
Angelica, 232
Arberry, 120
Arctic Dandelion, 70
Arctic Dock, 72
Arctic Raspberry, 182
Argentine, 204
Arizona Grape, 86
Arrowhead, 26
Arrowleaf, 26
Arrow Saltbush, 156
Asarabacca, 238
Ashleaf Maple, 134
Ash-Leaved Rose, 186
Aspen, 172
Aspen Sunflower, 220
Asperge, 80
August Plum, 244
Australian Saltbush, 156
Austrian Pine, 166

F

G

T

U

V

INTRODUCTION

Few of the American and Canadian Indians had gardens when Columbus rediscovered the New World, instead regularly supplementing their meat and fish with wild fruits, nuts, roots, tubers, greens, seeds, beverages, and the like which they gathered free from the land. We can have the satisfaction of doing the same thing today, for these edible wild plants still grow everywhere.

You needn't be any kind of an expert, even in this day of space travel and split atoms, to begin eating what remains unspoiled and free. If you will positively identify everything before you gather it—made easy at long last by this field guide with its detailed descriptions and its illustrations in full color—you will never have any trouble.

Wild foods have long been important on this young continent. Acorns probably rated the top position on the long list of edible wild vegetation depended upon by the Indians, acorn soup or mush being the chief daily food of more than three-fourths of the native Californians. Too, when Cortez and his conquistadores advanced through the dry, open Southwest, they found the Indians of that region using the tiny brown, grey, and white seeds of the chia for food, a teaspoonful of them being regarded as sufficient to sustain a brave for a day on a forced march.

Indians long used the seeds of the lamb's quarter, 75,000 of which have been counted on a single plant, for cereal and for grinding into meal. Although the purslane that today grows wild from one coast to the other does not become large, 52,300 seeds have been found on a single plant, and the Indians in our Southwest used these for making bread and mush. They made a nutritious meal from the roasted seeds of the shepherd's purse. Incidentally, the green leaves of all three of these plants are delectable.

If you've ever sat down to a well prepared meal that included wild vegetables, maybe you've noticed that many of them seem to taste better than domesticated varieties from the store. I'll let you in on a trade secret. They *are* better.

Green leafy vegetables, to give just one example, deteriorate very rapidly. Even when purchased as fresh as obtainable from the finest nearby market, they'll already have lost a sizable proportion of vitamins. Some of the food values of greens diminish as much as one-third during the first hour after picking. But gather them fresh from nature's own garden and eat them while they're at their tastiest, and you'll enjoy the best they have to offer.

When the Forty-Niners stampeded up California's streams and into the deserts and mountains for gold, the lack of fresh food brought crippling and killing scurvy to not a few of the camps. The Indians helped some of these argonauts cure the vitamin-deficiency disease by introducing them to the succulencies of miner's lettuce. The more than a dozen docks thriving on this continent from the Arctic coast southward throughout the United States provide hearty greens which were widely eaten by the Indians, some of whom used the abundant seeds in grinding meal.

Indians used the bark of the slippery elm for food, some of them boiling it with the tallow they rendered from buffalo fat. They used to preserve serviceberries by drying them by the thousands of bushels, spreading them in the sun and later beating some of them into a mash which was molded into cakes and dried. Mulberries, which can be gathered by the gallon just by shaking a heavily laden branch over an outspread cloth, were also a standby.

Instead of potatoes, carrots, radishes, parsnips, beets, and turnips as we now know them, Indians often relied on wild roots and tubers, especially in those parts of the arid West where the lack of rainfall made any vegetable raising virtually impossible. When pioneers, prospectors, and others later began daring the plains and deserts, many of them starved amidst abundance because they didn't know what to eat or how to prepare it.

The prairie turnip, for example, was a mainstay of such tribes as the Sioux. Indians from the Atlantic to the Pacific ate the potatolike roots of the arrowhead, usually either boiling them or roasting them in the hot ashes of campfires. Jerusalem artichokes, distinctively flavored tubers of a native wild sunflower, were relished by the redmen. Indians along the eastern seaboard relied on the potatolike groundnut which, after they'd shown them to the Pilgrims, saw these latter to a large extent through their first rugged winter in Plymouth.

Wild onions, including the leeks, the chives, and the garlics, grow wild all over North America except in the far northern regions. Indians used them extensively, not only for the provocative taste they impart to blander foods but also as a main part of the meal. Some of the tribes regularly used wild ginger roots for seasoning. Many Indians relied on the dried and powdered roots of the familiar jack-in-the-pulpit for flour.

The picturesque cattails, now too often neglected except by nesting birds, once provided many important Indian foods. The two native varieties of wild rice, tagged with surprisingly high prices when they are available today, have long been notable Indian delicacies. Walnuts, butternuts, hazelnuts, beechnuts, and especially hickory nuts were eaten in great quantities by the Indians. The pinon and its cousins, such as the Parry pine and the Digger pine, have long been important foodwise to the Indians in the Southwest.

The Indians depended largely on edible wild plants such as spearmint, oswego tea, some of the wild coffees, sweet fern, sassafras, spicebush, Labrador tea, sumac, the birches, and the pines for their beverages. When the first settlers arrived, and for centuries afterward when they were pushing their way westward, they followed suit. If these wild drinks had not been rich in Vitamin C, a vitamin which the body cannot store and which is necessary for the prevention and cure of scurvy, many pioneers would not have lived to open our frontiers.

When it comes to the maple, even the seeds are edible, some Indians formerly hulling the larger of them and then boiling them. The various species of broad-leaved, tendril-clinging, high-climbing or trailing wild grapes were long an Indian mainstay throughout much of the continent. The Senecas were among the Indians roasting wild sunflower seeds, after the highly edible kernels had been extracted, and pouring hot water over them to produce a coffeelike beverage.

Wild plums were great favorites among the Indians. A few of the tribes used to dry and grind juniper berries and use them for cakes and mush. Both the Indians and the early settlers dried barberries for winter use, making an agreeably cooling drink from them, and turning much of the rest into pleasantly tart sauces. Indians used to devour tremendous amounts of buffalo berries, gathering them by the bushel and often making a pudding of them and the flour of the aforementioned prairie turnip.

Milkweed, growing from coast to coast, was long used by the Indians. The Indians found pokeweed, one of the first wild greens of the spring, delicious, and some of the first European adventurers on these shores were in such agreement that they took the seeds back to France and southern Europe, where the vegetable became popular. And so it went.

Today gourmets, campers, and stay-at-home cooks alike will find pleasure in harvesting their meals from the wild lands where nature is the farmer and where nothing is ever due at any checkout counter.

ACORN *(Quercus)*

FAMILY - Beech *(Fagaceae)*

OTHER NAMES - Red Oak, Black Oak, Scarlet Oak, Yellow Oak, Turkey Oak, Georgia Oak, Northern Pin Oak, Chestnut Oak, Chinquapin Oak, Laurel Oak, Bluejack Oak, Live Oak, Oglethorpe Oak, Durand Oak, Shingle Oak, Scrub Oak, Water Oak, Bur Oak, Post Oak, Valley Oak, Gambel Oak, Blackjack Oak, Low Oak, Swamp-White Oak, Basket Oak, Mossycup Oak, Spanish Oak, Oregon White Oak, California Black Oak, etc.

DESCRIPTION - Acorns were likely tops on the long list of wild foods relied upon by the Indians. For example, acorn soup or mush was probably the main daily food of more than three-fourths of the native Californians. The eastern settlers were early introduced to the goodness of acorns, too. During 1620 when they spent their first hungry Massachusetts winter in Plymouth, the Pilgrims were lucky enough to find baskets of roasted acorns that the Indians had buried in the ground. In parts of Mexico today, as well as in Europe, many of the natives still eat acorns in the old ways.

Oaks give us about half of the hardwood lumber now produced in the U.S. A major proportion of our eastern hardwood forests is oak. Not only that, but oaks are among the most popular shade and ornamental trees along our streets and about our dwellings.

Oaks have single, not compound, leaves that grow alternately on the trees. In the North they all have deciduous leaves, although some of the dead leaves cling and clatter for a long while. In the winter the twigs ordinarily have small clusters of buds at their ends, a characteristic shared by only a very few other plants. The leaves of some of the southern oaks are evergreen.

Flowers appear in the early springtime when the new branches are just starting to develop. The male blossoms grow in slender, drooping, spikelike clusters in which they have no petals but are borne in close circular rows on a slim stalk. The feminine blossoms are small and inconspicuous, coming forth in the angles of the leaves on the seasons's new growth. The pollen is dispersed by the wind. The fruits, the principal distinguishing feature, are nuts that are partially enclosed with scaly cups and which are found on no other tree.

The oaks are divided into two huge groups, each of which has its own distinctive properties.

The acorns of the white oaks mature in one growing season, the inner surfaces of the shells being smooth and the kernels sweet. The leaves, never tipped with bristles, typically have rounded lobes. The grey bark is characteristically scaly.

The acorns of the red oaks do not mature until the finish of the second growing season, the shells' inner surfaces generally being coated with woolly hair and the kernels ordinarily being bitter. The leaves have bristles. The bark is typically dark and furrowed.

All acorns are good to eat. Some are less sweet than others, that's all. But the bitterness that is prevalent in differing degrees is due to tannin, the same ingredient that gives tea its bitterish characteristic. Although tannin is not digestible by humans in large amounts, it is very readily soluble in water. It follows, therefore, that even the bitterest acorns can be made sweet enough to eat without any great effort.

Indians leached their bitter acorns in a number of ways. Sometimes the acorns would be buried in the mud of a swamp for a year, after which they would be retrieved for roasting and eating whole. Other tribes let their shelled acorns mold in baskets, then buried them in clean freshwater sand. When they had turned black, they were sweet and ready to use.

Incidentally, we think of antibiotics as modern developments, but some of the Indian tribes used to let their acorn meal accumulate a mold. This was scraped off, kept in a damp place, and used to treat sores and inflammations.

Some groups ground their acorns by pounding them in stone mortars, such as those I occasionally find today, then ran fresh water through the meal by one method or another for often the greater part of a day until it was sweet. The meal might be placed in a specially woven basket for this purpose, or it might just be buried in the sandy bed of a stream.

It's an easy matter to leach your bitter acorns at home today. Just shell the nuts and boil them whole in a kettle of water, changing the fluid when it yellows. You can shorten the time necessary for this to as little as a couple of hours if you keep a teakettle of water always heating on the stove while this process is continuing. The acorns can then be dried in a slow oven whose door has been left ajar, to let the steam escape, then either eaten as is or ground into coarse bits for use like any other nuts, or into a fine meal, best blended with either cornmeal or wheat flour.

DISTRIBUTION - Our some eighty-five species of oaks are found throughout the continuous States except in the northern prairies, thriving at various altitudes and in various types of soil. Oaks grow throughout southern Canada.

EDIBILITY - Acorns, being so abundant and substantial, are probably also our wildlife's most important sustenance. The relatively tiny acorns of the willow oak, pin oak, and water oak are often obtainable near

© AJA

Acorns. Top—Red; Bottom—White

streams and ponds where they are relished by mallards, wood ducks, pintails, and other waterfowl. Quail devour such small acorns and peck the kernels out of larger nuts. Pheasants, grouse, pigeons, doves, and prairie chickens enjoy the nuts as well as the buds. Wild turkeys gulp down whole acorns regardless of their size. Squirrels and chipmunks are among the smaller animals storing acorns for off-season uses. Deer, elk, peccaries, and mountain sheep enjoy the nuts and also browse on twigs and foliage. Black bears grow fat on acorns.

Indians used acorns both by themselves and in combination with other foods. For instance, the Digger Indians roasted their acorns from the Western white oak *(Quercus lobata),* hulled them, and ground them into a coarse meal which they formed into cakes and baked in rude ovens. In the East, the acorns of the white oak *(Q. alba)* were also ground into meal but were then often mixed with the available cornmeal before being shaped into cakes and baked. Roasted and ground white oak nuts provide one of the wilderness coffees.

To make the Indians' familiar somewhat sweetish gruel or mush, all that is necessary is to heat the meal in water. The Indians generally used no seasoning. As a matter of fact, until the white man came they ordinarily had no utensils better than closely woven baskets. These were flammable, of course, and the heating was sometimes done by putting rocks warmed in the campfires. Still showing how little one can get along with, the tribes then ate from common baskets, using their fingers.

Bread, cupcakes, and flapjacks made in the home today from a combination of acorn meal and store flour are richly dark and pleasantly nutty.

ARROWHEAD *(Sagittaria)*

FAMILY -Water Plantain *(Alismataceae)*

OTHER NAMES -Duck Potato, Arrowleaf, Swan Potato, Wapatoo, Katniss, Swamp Potato, Tule Potato.

DESCRIPTION - Indians from the Atlantic to the Pacific knew and relished this ½-to-3-foot-tall member of the water plantain family. In spite of the name, however, all the leaves are not in the shapes of arrowheads, although there are generally enough of these for identification purposes. They all grow in clusters from long stems at the base of the plant, from about 2 to 9 inches long and from ⅓ to ½ of this measure in breadth. Some are long and uniform in width, while others, considering the stems, resemble lances. They are frequently seen floating, depending on the stage of water.

The flowers, appearing from July to September, grow prettily in coils near the tops of their individual stalks. They are delicately three-petaled. Beneath each conspicuous but gossamery white petal is a green floral leaf, the three feminine members of each trio. The blossoms are 1 to 1½ inches broad, and although the green components persist, the rounded white petals fall after a few days. The resulting fruits produce flat, double-winged, rounded-headed seeds.

All bearing edible tubers, some thirty species of *Sagittaria* enliven wet, fresh-water corners of this continent, about seven of these bearing large starchy bulbs. The differences in the plants are generally minor, and there is no need to try to separate them as all are edible.

DISTRIBUTION - The picturesque arrowheads are found in swamps, marshes, along the edges of ponds and sluggish rivers, and in other shallow waters from the southern half of Canada, throughout most of the United States, to deep into Mexico. Related species are even more enjoyed these days in Europe and especially Asia where some Orientals cultivate them along the damp rims of rice paddies, where I've seen them not only furnishing food but holding the land in place.

EDIBILITY - The starchy and nutritiously important parts of the arrowhead are the tubers that form at the ends of the often long, narrow roots, frequently several feet beyond the plant. Mature after midsummer and in the autumn, these are also nourishing throughout the winter. You'll need a lot of them as the larger are only an inch or two in diameter, but fortunately they grow abundantly nearly everywhere they appear, and even those no larger than peas are crunchy and good.

Where they grow underwater, wading Indians used either their toes or long sticks to dislodge the tubers which, once freed of roots and mud, readily float. You can also accomplish the same thing, perhaps in boots, with a vigorously wielded fork or hoe. Such activity, incidentally, advantageously thins out and helps extend the distribution of the plants.

This was a favorite food of the North American Indians. Lewis and Clark, as well as other explorers on this continent, were pleasantly introduced to it by friendly tribes. When the early Chinese, largely imported for low-cost labor, moved into California, they quickly adopted this wild plant, known here as the tule potato, and brought it commercially to some of the local markets.

The tubers, which have a milky juice, are edible raw. They then have somewhat of a bitterness which, however, is dissipated by cooking. Roasted, baked, boiled, creamed, French-fried, or scalloped, they can be handled like new potatoes, although their united sweetness and smoothness gives them more of a water chestnut flavor. They are the better for peeling, and they peel more easily after the more common forms of cooking than they do when raw.

BARBERRY *(Berberis)*

FAMILY - Barberry *(Berberidaceae)*

OTHER NAMES - Oregon Grape, Mountain Holly, Creeping Barberry, Mahonia, California Barberry, Algerita, Mountain Grape, American Barberry, Blue Barberry, Jaundice Berry, Piprage, Sourberry, Berbery.

DESCRIPTION - Barberries become redolent expanses of golden blossoms in the springtime, shiny and opulent green masses during the summer, and bright scarlets and bronzes in the nippy weeks of autumn. Berries range from crimson and orangish and blackish-purple to the fine blue of such species as the so-called Oregon grape and the pretty California barberry. The wood, a particularly lovely yellow, is sometimes used for jewelry.

There are about 15 species of barberry in this country at the present time, one of those that are typical of the genus being the *Berberis vulgaris* which got its start in Asia and in Europe where it is sometimes grown in gardens for its fruit. This shrub grows some eight or nine feet tall along fences, in dusty thickets, in New England gardens where it was originally introduced here, in stony pastures, and along the rims of rocky woodlands; generally in upland situations and in well-drained loam.

The leaves, growing from 1 to 1½ inches long in the springtime, hang from slimly arched or sagging grey branches. Rounded at their tops and narrowing at their bases, they are sawtoothed along their green edges, a roughness that is further carried out by a bristly surface. They grow either alternately or in clusters. Tri-pointed spines grow instead on some of the younger shoots.

Long clusters of flowers, each about ¼ inch across, appear in drooping clusters, mainly yellow but sometimes ranging through other hues from white to black.

The berries of this particular bushlike herb are for the most part red. Oval-shaped, not unlike fairy footballs, they are rather dry, acidulous, and rich in the antiscorbutic Vitamin C.

All inner parts of the wood, particularly the roots, are a definite yellow color which was widely sought by our pioneer ancestors as a dye. This can be extracted by boiling.

DISTRIBUTION - The barberries grow from coast to coast.

EDIBILITY - Partly because efforts have been made in the East to eradicate the barberry because of its part in acting as a host for one phase of wheat rust, the shrubs are mainly valuable as a wildlife food in the West where the soft-mouthed deer nibble at them despite the thorniness of some, and so do mountain sheep and goat and the wary elk. Varying hares and other members of the rabbit family look to them for food. Ring-necked pheasants and ruffed grouse are among the game birds consuming the fruit. Black bears like them, too.

Parched hikers find chewing a few of the agreeably acid, younger leaves refreshing.

You can make a pleasantly cooling drink from the berries or turn them into appetizingly tart sauces, jams, purees, and preserves. The jelly rivals that of the so-called highbush cranberry which, to me at least, is the best made. It requires no addition of pectin. Also, home cooks still add barberries to blander, sweeter fruits to lend them authority. The berries are also sometimes candied or, on the other hand, pickled in vinegar.

BAYBERRY *(Myrica)*

FAMILY - Sweet Gale *(Myricaceae)*

OTHER NAMES - Wax Myrtle, Bay, Candleberry, Common Wax Myrtle, Black Bayberry, Dwarf Wax Myrtle.

DESCRIPTION - The bark of these evergreen shrubs and small trees, sometimes 30 or more feet high with a trunk diameter of from 3 to 30 inches, is grey. The narrowly oblong or more or less egg-shaped leaves, from 1 to 4 inches long, are occasionally slightly toothed.

The attractive fruit, actually a nutlet, is based on a hard stone which encloses a two-seeded kernel. On the outside of the stone are gunpowderlike grains. Over these is a dryish, pleasantly scented crust of granular, green-white wax that once smelled will never be forgotten. When bruised the leaves, too, give off a memorable aroma.

Male and female blossoms grow on separate plants, and therefore only some of them produce bayberries. The staminate catkins are conspicuous in the springtime, especially when the breezes are carrying their dusty pollen.

Some stores feature bayberry candles and soaps, but you'll enjoy these even more if you make them yourself. The details, beyond the scope of this book, are given along with hundreds of wild-food recipes in my *Feasting Free on Wild Edibles.*

DISTRIBUTION - The bayberry is essentially a seaboard small tree and stocky shrub, although it follows the broad St. Lawrence River inland to the beginning of the Great Lakes. Seven species are native to this country and southern Canada, one along the Pacific Coast and the other six in the East. Too, bayberries are widely planted as a part of landscape gardening.

This wax myrtle, as it is also called, thrives in moist woodlands and along the rims of swamps and ponds, but only on sandy, never muddy, soils. It often grows in large clumps and in thickets.

EDIBILITY - The myrtle warbler lives up to its name by consuming great amounts of bayberries in the areas where these grow. Along the Atlantic coast, the tree swallow moderates its diet of insects with this fruit. Duck and rails also eat it, as do grouse, quail, and wild turkey. It should not be given pen-raised quail, incidentally, as its excessive waxiness disturbs their digestion. Bluebirds, flickers, grackles, meadowlarks, scarlet tanagers, white-eyed vireos, and a host of other songbirds also devour the berries, as does the grey fox. Deer browse on the twigs and foliage.

The winy evergreen leaves of the bayberry, used in moderation and removed before the dish is brought to the table, have been doing wonderful things for soups, broths, stews, and steaming chowders since Colonial times.

If bayberries grow near your home, you may therefore choose to pick several leaves whenever you're cooking one of these dishes. The leaves can also be satisfactorily preserved for use out of season. Just gather the shiniest and greenest of them, perhaps during the summer or early fall vacation at the seashore, and bring them home in a bag. Then spread them out to dry in the kitchen or attic. Finally, pack them in tightly closing jars. Store them in a handy, dark cabinet. They're apt to become one of your favorite spices.

Growing as it does from Newfoundland to Florida, the bayberry was one of the earliest North American plants used for medicine by the settlers venturing up and down the eastern seaboard of the New World. The dried bark of the root, preferably gathered just before winter, was pounded into powder and stored, tightly enclosed, in a dark place. A teaspoonful to a cup of boiling water, drunk cold one or two cupfuls a day, was used to quiet diarrhea. Pioneers also sniffed the powder with reported good results for catarrh and nasal congestion. It was also occasionally applied in poultices to cuts and inflammations.

©AJA

BEECH *(Fagus)*

FAMILY - Beech *(Fagaceae)*

OTHER NAMES - American Beech, Red Beech, White Beech.

DESCRIPTION - Our single native beech is one of four recognized species and is a big, handsome tree with vivid green leaves that turn coppery in the autumn. Its distinctively smooth, light grey, tight, often mottled bark invites carved initials and arrowed hearts. Wildlife vie with man for its important nut crop which, as Indians and early settlers well knew, is one of the most flavorful products of our northern woodlands.

Interestingly, the now largely cleared beechnut forests of our Middle West were once the gathering places of the also departed passenger pigeons which subsisted to a large extent on the nuts. In fact, as was the case with other once plentiful game, it is likely that the circling in of civilization rather than any overhunting by itself was the real reason for the decimation of much of our wild life. Where, for example, is there any room now for buffalo except in places such as our government parks, and even here their numbers have to be kept under rigid control.

Towering well over 100 feet in some instances, beeches usually lift from 50 to 80 feet into the air, with 2- and 3-foot, sometimes 4-foot diameters. When a beech grows in the open, its crown is high, symmetrically conical, and thick. In heavy stands, the trunk shoots up tall and bare and is topped with a both narrow and shallow head.

Slender, cone-shaped, sharply-tipped buds about five times longer than they are wide, and covered with up to some twenty reddish-brown scales, distinguish the beech. In the winter, these buds, about an inch long, cannot be mistaken for those of any other native tree.

The stiff and elliptic to egg-shaped leaves, with straight veins and roughly sawtoothed edges, are also distinctive, especially as they are also pointed, single entities, and alternate. They are almost twice as long as they are wide, with a papery texture, smoothly emerald-green above and yellowed beneath. Their short stems, ¼ to ½ inch long, have a somewhat hairy silkiness.

Both the male and female blossoms appear, on the same tree, in April and May. The former, pollen-bearing flowers grow in balls that dangle on long stems. The latter pistillate blossoms appear in pairs where the upper leaves meet the twigs, developing into small, four-part burs, softly bristling with recurved hairs. Easily opened by the thumbnail when they mature in September and October, these contain two triangular, somewhat concave, brown, little nuts that are nutritious and sweet.

DISTRIBUTION - Our single native species of beech grows from the Maritime Provinces to Ontario and Wisconsin, south to Texas and Florida. Occurring on fertile bottom lands and uplands, it prefers moist, cool, shady areas. It is also well known as an ornamental and as a shade tree.

EDIBILITY - Wood ducks, blackbirds, chickadees, finches, grackles, grosbeaks, jays, nuthatches, sapsuckers, and several of the woodpeckers eat the nuts. Such upland game birds as grouse, pheasants, and wild turkeys devour the buds as well. Black bears, foxes, raccoons, squirrels, and chipmunks seek the nuts, while the white-tailed deer eats these, the twigs, and the foliage. Beavers and porcupines, not to be outdone, gnaw the nutritious wood.

Beechnuts are so small and delicious that a large proportion of them are enjoyed raw, but they are good cooked, too. Some roast and grind them for a substitute coffee. The young leaves can be cooked as a green in the spring. The inner bark, dried and pulverized for bread flour in times of need, is an emergency food to remember. Too, beech sawdust can be boiled in water, roasted, and then mixed with flour for bread.

©AJA

BIRCH *(Betula)*

FAMILY - Birch *(Betulaceae)*

OTHER NAMES - Canoe Birch, Lady Birch, Paper Birch, Northern Birch, Black Birch, Red Birch, Cherry Birch, Mahogany Birch, River Birch, Sweet Birch, Gray Birch, Oldfield Birch, Poverty Birch, Poplar Birch, Water Birch, Yellow Birch, Silver Birch, Golden Birch, Wirefield Birch, American White Birch, European White Birch, European Weeping Birch, Blueleaf Birch, Virginia Birch, Newfoundland Dwarf Birch, Tundra Dwarf Birch, Minor Birch, Swamp Birch, Mountain Paper Birch.

DESCRIPTION - The familiar birches have alternate, single, egg-shaped or triangular with a broad base, green, conspicuously-veined leaves with sawtooth and sometimes lobed edges. On the second-year trees they are distinctively arrayed in pairs on brief, spurlike branches. The twigs themselves are slim, generally with very noticeable pores by means of which air can penetrate to the interior. Although there are no terminal buds, partially developed staminate flowers, the ones bearing the grains of pollen are often manifestly present. The bark on the younger trees and branches is smooth, more or less resinous, and very distinctly marked with horizontally long, open pores.

The flowers of these trees bloom in the early springtime, in advance of the leaves. The ones bearing the pollen grow in spikelike flower clusters in which the blossoms have no petals but appear in close circular rows on a slender stalk, as in the alder, willow, and poplar. The central organs of the flowers containing the ovules appear in smaller, more or less erect catkins of the same sort on growth of the previous season. Both the male and female blossoms, as each is in turn, appear on the same tree, from which they are pollinated by the wind.

When the fruits mature, they appear in tiny conelike structures, consisting of a long central axis to which numerous dry scales are affixed. These scales are five-lobed and look like miniature fleur-de-lis. Each seed boasts a pair of partly rounded, thin, lateral wings and, again, is eventually wind-borne.

The bark of many species is, as we've already considered, marked by numerous cross streaks and horizontally long perforations, and distinctively tends to peel readily into papery sheets. In fact, such thin sheets can be your woodland paper. Two general varieties of the trees, in fact, grow across the continent, the black birch and those similar to it, and the familiar white birches whose cheerful foliage and softly gleaming bark lighten the northern forests.

However, native birches with dark bark might be confused with some of the wild cherries if it were not for the following differences. Birches differ in that broken twigs may have a strong wintergreen odor in contrast to the bitter-almond smell of cherry twigs, bud scales are fewer, the leaf stems do not have glands, and the bark of numerous birches can be separated into paperlike sheets.

DISTRIBUTION - The trees and shrubs of the birch family are distributed over most of the United States and Canada except for the lower Pacific Coast, the Southwest, and a broad strip down the west central part of the U.S. Some of our native species are typically northern, however, except for the river birch *(Betula nigra)* which grows on flood plains and river shores as far south as Texas and Florida. They prefer rich moist ground but also spring up in gravelly organic soil amid rocks and on silty-loam bottom lands.

EDIBILITY - Grouse and prairie chicken feast on the catkins, buds, and seeds, while such songbirds as the chickadee, finch, redpoll, sapsucker, siskin, and sparrow confine themselves more to the seeds. Moose, elk, and deer browse on the twigs and foliage.

The inner bark of the birches is edible and in emergencies has kept many from starving. Dried and then ground into flour, this has been used by Indians and frontiersmen for bread. It is also cut into strips and boiled like noodles in stews. But you don't even need to go to that much trouble. Just eat it raw.

You can drink the refreshing sap just as it comes from the trees in springtime or boil it down into syrup. About half as sweet as maple sap, it flows much faster and can easily be harvested by the methods suggested in the section on maple.

A particularly tasty tea can be made from the red inner bark of the black birches, that from the roots being less disfiguring to the trees. A teaspoon to a cup of boiling water, set off the heat and allowed to steep for five minutes, makes a beverage that is delicately spicy. Milk and sugar make it even better in the estimation of many. As a matter of fact, any of the birches make good tea even if you use only the young twigs.

This tea is brisk with wintergreen. In fact, when the commercial oil of wintergreen is not made synthetically, it is distilled from the twigs and bark of the black birch. This oil is exactly the same as that from the little wintergreen plant, described elsewhere.

© AJA

Black Birch

BITTERROOT *(Lewisia)*

FAMILY - Purslane *(Portulacaceae)*

OTHER NAMES - Rock Rose, Spatlum, Tobacco Root, Redhead Louisa, *Racine-amere, Rediviva,* Sand Rose.

DESCRIPTION - The numerous leaves of the bitterroot sprout greenly from a surprisingly large root with the receding of the snows, generally wrinkling and decaying before the conspicuous flowers burst forth. Lifting and bending from a big root crown in a verdant rosette, the narrow and spoon-shaped oblong leaves are from one to two inches long and are still eagerly awaited by some of our Indians. They are fleshy rather than flat.

The pinkish to snow-white flowers appear nakedly on single, short stems from late April into July, depending on the altitude. They are the only prominent blossoms of the sort in their usually mountainous realms that seem to be unaccompanied by leaves. Although conspicuous, each blossom, lifting on a stem seldom longer than three inches, is only one or two inches across its wheel-like showiness which is silken in its beauty. About a half-dozen petal-like sepals back up the 6 or 7 to about 18 elliptical petals which the sunshine brings open. Numerous stamens decorate the center of each blossom. Buds, like slim long cones, often nod nearby on fellow stalks.

The prominent, white, large, starchy roots, which can be uncovered with a sharp stick, are the important parts of this particular member of the purslane family.

DISTRIBUTION - The towering range of mountains between the green and grey wildernesses of Montana and Idaho, a trout-teeming river, and a valley are named for this nourishingly valuable bitterroot whose blossom is the state flower of the country's fourth largest state, Montana.

This wild edible was first collected and brought back to civilization in 1806 from Bitterroot Valley of western Montana by Captain Meriwether Lewis, of the Lewis and Clark Expedition, in whose honor it was named. The other part of its Latin cognomen, *Lewisia rediviva,* takes note of the fact that it can be uprooted, transported, dried for many months, and then successfully replanted.

It is commonly found in the dry and stony valleys, arid interior, plains, on rocky slopes and ridges, and on mountain tops up to some eight thousand feet high from its most intensive habitat of Montana to south-central British Columbia, Mexico-ward to Colorado and Southern California.

EDIBILITY - These succulent roots are best located in the early springtime, when the frost is barely out of the ground, by their green tufts of long leaves. They are then tenderest and most nourishing, before the flowers use up part of the stored starch.

The outer rind of the roots, whose bitterness gives the perennial its most common name, will slip off easily if the parts are first cleaned in boiling water. But if you're camping, rub it off the younger roots between the hands or remove it with a sharp knife.

A fleshy white core is thus exposed that can be boiled to a jellylike deliciousness with a somewhat tobaccolike aroma. The cores are also baked or roasted, as well as sometimes being dried and powdered. Stored by the bagful for winter use, the dried roots often lent consistency to Indian soups and stews. On today's reservations, some of them still do.

©AJA

BLACK WALNUT *(Juglans)*

FAMILY - Walnut *(Juglandaceae)*

OTHER NAMES - Common Black Walnut, Walnut Tree, Texas Walnut, California Walnut, Walnut.

DESCRIPTION - The black walnut is a strong and durable tree, often 50 to 100 feet and sometimes 150 feet high and bringing the top prices of any native wood, with a close-grained trunk from 2 to 5 feet across. The prominently furrowed bark is a dark, rich brown, the ridges being dull instead of shiny.

The large, compound leaves, 12 to 24 inches long, are composed of from about 13 to 23 leaflets apiece. Crushed, they emit a spicy odor. These somewhat ovally lancehead-shaped leaflets, from two to four inches long and about half as wide, have sharply sawtoothed rims and pointed tips. Yellowish green on top, they are lighter colored and ordinarily hairy underneath.

The black walnut is sometimes mistaken for its cousin, the butternut. One difference is that the butternut has, instead, 11 to 17 leaflets to each compound leaf. The bark is grey. The pitch, light brown in the black walnut, is dark brown in the butternut. Too, walnuts are round with a smooth husk. Butternuts are elongated with a hairy and sticky husk. The terminal bud in the walnut is as broad as it is long. In the butternut, it is longer than it is wide. A hairy fringe is visible above the leaf scar in the butternut, although none occurs in the black walnut.

During the warm days of summer the nuts of the black walnut, covered with a warty and greenish husk, become two to three inches in diameter. Incidentally, although certainly unsporting and illegal, these bruised nut husks can be used to kill fish for food, something to remember if starvation is ever imminent in a survival situation.

Growing alone and in pairs, the nuts ripen about October, soon thereafter falling from the widely spreading branches. Underneath this husk is the familiar globular nut, varying up to some two inches across. Sculptured bony shells, as everyone knows, surround the furrowed, deeply corrugated, sweet, four-celled nuts.

The hardest part about gathering and using wild walnuts is getting off the husks with their indelible, brownish dye. When we were youngsters we didn't mind this and, just stamping on the husks and breaking them off with bare fingers, we collected stained hands that defied parental scrubbings for weeks. Among adults, gloves are a more usual precaution. A knife will remove the green hides. Some pioneers also early discovered that if they spread the freshly gathered nuts in the sun until they partially dried, the husks were easily shucked off. The wetly stained nuts were then spread out to dry and lose bitterness until they were ready to be cracked open.

To locate the trees in the winter, look for light-brown to orange-brown twigs with small breathing pores. The pith is large, chambered, and light-brown in color. The alternate, heart-shaped leaf scars are three-lobed, with a notch along the top rim which has a tiny lateral bud in it. Ordinarily another bud is located directly above this, being about ¼ inch long, broadly egg-shaped, and blunt. The lateral buds are far smaller and are roundish, all the buds being covered with silky, grey, short hairs. The trunk bark is dark brown or almost black, with deeply cut, roughly diamond-shaped furrows and rounded ridges.

DISTRIBUTION - Six of the world's dozen species of *Juglans* are native to the U.S. In addition to the common black walnut *(Juglans nigra)* whose range extends throughout much of the East and partially into the Prairie States, there are two species of black walnuts in the Southwest and two more in California. Too, there is the Northeast's closely related white walnut, or butternut, to be considered elsewhere.

EDIBILITY - The red-bellied woodpecker and several species of squirrels eat the nuts, while some beaver gnaw on the wood when they get the chance.

Those of the sweet and somewhat oily kernels that are not eaten on the spot are much in demand for cakes, candies, and salads because of their strong and distinctive taste. A 100 grams of black walnut kernels have a hearty 628 calories, 20.5 grams of protein, and 59.3 of fat, while boasting nearly 15 grams of carbohydrates. The same edible portion contains phosphorus, 460 mg. of potassium, and 300 international units of Vitamin A, plus 22 mg. of thiamine, .11 of riboflavin, and .7 of niacin.

© AJA

BLUEBERRY *(Vaccinium) (Gaylussacia)*

FAMILY - Heath *(Ericaceae)*

OTHER NAMES - Whortleberry, Bilberry, Huckleberry, Oval-Leaf Whortleberry, Dwarf Bilberry, Sierra Bilberry, Great Bilberry, Bog Bilberry, Mountain Bilberry, Twin-Leaved Huckleberry, Blue Huckleberry, Mountain Huckleberry, Evergreen Huckleberry, Lowbush Blueberry, Swamp Blueberry, Farkleberry, Blueridge Blueberry, Box Blueberry, Big Whortleberry, Sour-Top Blueberry, Velvet-Leaf Blueberry, High Blueberry, Early Blueberry, Low Sweet Blueberry, Deerberry, Squaw Huckleberry, California Black Buckleberry, Tangleberry, Blue Tangle, Dangleberry, Late Low Blueberry, Early Sweet Blueberry, Sugar Blueberry, Dwarf Blueberry, Western Blueberry, Thin-Leaf Blueberry, Alaska Blueberry, Bog Blueberry, Dwarf Huckleberry, Whorts, Hurts.

DESCRIPTION - None of the blueberry-huckleberry tribe is inedible. As for the differences between these two very similar berries, the former *Vaccinium* is filled with numerous soft seeds, while the latter *Gaylussacia* contains precisely ten stony, seedlike nutlets. Too, if you bother to notice, huckleberries have waxy little spots on their foliage and fresh shoots. Blueberries and huckleberries are so much alike, however, that they are often picked and eaten together.

The berries, sometimes bright red when mature, are more often blue to black. A few ripen to a greenish or yellowish hue. They frequently have a bloom to them that can be rubbed off. Making the fruit unmistakable is a puckery edged indentation at each summit.

These members of the heath family many times grow by the acre on bushes so heavily laden that you can spread a sheet on the ground and gather mostly the ripe fruit by the bushel merely by shaking the limbs. A pioneer method of later cleaning them is to let them fall, a few at a time, from a tipped pail onto a slanted, preferably new and fuzzy woolen blanket, stretched tightly a few feet below. The ripe blueberries will roll into a large, wide container placed just below the lower edge of the blanket. Most of the harder green berries will bounce free. The leaves and other debris will remain on the blanket which can be brushed clean from time to time. Finally, stirred about in water to float away the remaining clutter, the booty will be ready to eat.

As may be judged from the difference in names, blueberries as a whole grow on a variety of shrubs from small low plants to thickets of tall bushes, all free of brambles. They like acid soil and sunlight, frequently springing up on freshly cleared land and on vast fire-blackened wilderness expanses. In fact, the woodlands and forests of this continent are frequently set afire to encourage blueberry crops which, aside from direct human use, bring in abundant game.

DISTRIBUTION - About 35 different members of this genus grow throughout Canada and the United States, some in swamps but most in open woodlands and clearings. They are among the most important berries of the Arctic and sub-Arctic.

EDIBILITY - Because the digestive system of the bear is better adapted to handling meat than fruit, anyone who has followed many bear trails in blueberry country can attest to the fact that this fruit forms a major part of the grizzly's and black bear's diet in late summer and fall.

The berries are also a prime portion of the diet of a number of the grouses, who also feast on the leaves and the pretty, bell-shaped, little blossoms. Gulls, cranes, pigeons, turkeys, and dozens of songbirds seek the fruit, especially as some of it clings, dry but still nourishing, to the shrubs well into winter. Living, too, in part on the fruit, twigs, and foliage is a large host of wildlife from foxes, opossums, raccoons, and squirrels to deer, moose, caribou, and elk.

Indians preceded the settlers and their present-day descendants in enjoying the fruit both raw and cooked in all sorts of ways, even to thickening stews and soups. In addition to its wide use as preserves, the plain fruit also keeps well frozen, as well as dried at room temperatures, both without additives of any sort.

© AJA

41

BUFFALO BERRY *(Shepherdia)*

FAMILY - Oleaster *(Elaeagnaceae)*

OTHER NAMES - Soapberry, Bull Berry, Rabbit Berry, Silverleaf, Canadian Buffalo Berry, Russet Buffalo Berry, Silver Buffalo Berry, Soopalallie.

DESCRIPTION - The three varieties of buffalo berries native to the United States and Canada are the only ones in the world. Indians used to enjoy them both fresh and dried, often with their buffalo roasts.

The Canada buffalo berry *(Shepherdia canadensis)* is the only plant with opposite leaves whose underneaths are covered with silvery or brownish scales. These also appear on the twigs. The leaves themselves are oval, up to about 2½ inches long, smooth-edged, green above, and many times a bit hairy. Small leaves are often to be found at the bottoms of the leafstems.

For a group of distinguishing negatives, the twigs and young branches are not angled, the leaves not leathery, the bark not papery, and the twig bases not scaly. Two scales, however, are to be found on nearly every one of the narrow-based buds. This shrub is from two to about seven feet tall.

Small yellow flowers appear at the same time as the leaves, growing near the angle between leaf and branch. They appear in bell-shaped clusters in April, May, and June, depending on the altitude and latitude. The edible berrylike fruit is small, round, translucent, and either a striking yellow or scarlet. It contains a bitterish substance that foams in water. Incidentally, nitrogen-fixing bacterial root lumps or tubercles are evident, unusual for plants that are not legumes; that is, members of the pea genus.

The silver buffalo berry, *S. argentea,* is similar to the above except that it has silvery scales only, none that are rusty. The leaves, somewhat wedge-shaped, are silvery on both sides. The shrubs are often thorny. The edible fruit is vivid red.

DISTRIBUTION - One or more of these three buffalo berries grows in nearly every part of the U.S. and Canada, including Alaska and the Arctic, except our Southeast.

EDIBILITY - Quail, catbirds, brown thrashers, chipmunks, ground squirrels, and the lumbering black bear eat the fruit.

Some of the Indians in Alaska still use the Canada buffalo berry, or soopalallie, mixing the fruit with sugar and water, then beating it with the hands to form a foam that is used on desserts as we utilize whipped cream. Otherwise, the raw berry is bitter because of the presence of saponin, utilized commercially as a foam producer.

The sourish but pectin-rich silver buffalo berry or bull berry is used in our Northwest, while it is still a bit on the immature side, for a most delicious jelly. Frosts sweeten this fruit, widely eaten both raw and cooked in cold weather.

© AJA

BUNCHBERRY (Cornus)

FAMILY - Dogwood (*Cornaceae*)

OTHER NAMES — Crackerberry, Dwarf Cornel, Dwarf Carnel.

DESCRIPTION - Bunchberries are attractively noticeable from the time their distinctive blossoms appear from May to July until their clusters of bright red berries form when, around our log cabin at Hudson Hope in northern British Columbia, the first moose hunters are invading the woods.

What seems to be single white flowers with four definite petals are, instead, each four modified leaves, spore cases, beneath and about an easily overlooked group of minute purplish-white or tawnily white blossoms. It is this bunch of tiny individual blossoms that develop into bright, vividly red clusters of small fruits. To complete the identification, beneath the summits of apparent petals and later the berries, on short single stems usually no more than two to six inches high but sometimes a foot tall, is a wheel of generally six broad, green leaves with smooth edges. Pairs of smaller but otherwise similar leaves often grow below these.

Typically, the fruits of this member of the dogwood family each contain a large, stony pit holding two seeds.

DISTRIBUTION - These easily recognized edibles grow in damp woodlands, meadows, and swamps from Alaska to Greenland, south to California in the West and to a few hundred miles below New England in the East.

EDIBILITY - Deer on both sides of the continent browse on the plants. Grouse, sparrows, thrushes, and vireos are among the birds seeking the buds and berries in their cool, moist habitats.

Indians used bunchberries more than they are utilized today, both eating them raw and cooking, then generally straining them, for sauces and puddings. The reason for this is that the scarlet bunchberries, although sustaining, are rather dry and tasteless unless mixed colorfully with other fruit.

BURDOCK *(Arctium)*

FAMILY - Composite *(Compositae)*

OTHER NAMES - Great Burdock, Common Burdock, Gobo, Wild Gobo, Clotbur, Bur Weed, Burs, Beggar's Buttons, Woolly Burdock.

DESCRIPTION - Burdocks, regarded by many as one of the peskier cousins of the thistle, belong to the composite family whose some 15,000 members make it one of the largest of our plant groups. Other associates include the familiar dandelions, sunflowers, and the many lettuces. Among the unlikely foods common throughout this continent, burdock is perhaps the most versatile and delicious, all this in addition to being familiar and not easily mistaken.

The adhesiveness of the prickly stickers, which are the seed pods, took this world-wide traveler across Europe with the Roman legions, brought it to the Americas with the earlier settlers, and has since distributed it throughout most of the United States and southern Canada; an important state of affairs, as it is such a top-notch edible that I've seen it being especially cultivated in Japan and elsewhere in the Eastern Hemisphere.

Although it is a rather coarse weed, burdocks have rather velvety smooth young leaves, although slightly woolly, that hint at the immigrant's tenderer traits. It is the thistlelike burs, actually the flower heads, that are most familiar, however. The hooked spore cases bristle formidably in short-stemmed or stemless round burs, ½ to about ¾ inch broad, this in the common burdock *(Arctium minus),* below the lavender to creamy florets. The lower leaves are large, with hollow and unfurrowed stems.

In the so-called great burdock, *Arctium lappa,* the burs are twice as large and grow on long stalks. The stems of the lower leaves are different, too, being solid and having grooves along their upper sides.

The woolly burdock, *Arctium tomentosum,* differs from the above great burdock in that there is an interlacing of fine bristles on the prickly spore cases or bracts. Another variance is that the leafstalks are hollow. Differences aside, parts of all three are very much edible.

Flowers of the burdock family vary from purple to white, but about the rounded, some-inch-wide heads of them all are slender, hooked tendrils that attach themselves to clothing and to animal coats. The mature biennials are alive with roundish burs which fall apart once they are ripe. In fact, one of the difficulties in removing the burs from one's apparel or pet is that they tend to break up, making the dispersal of each part a separate chore.

The big, alternate, egg-shaped, vein-webbed, somewhat roughly woolly, dark green leaves of the burdock, some of them two feet long by half that wide, grow from darkly green, multi-veined stems that often have a purple pattern. Plump flower stalks, an inch or more thick, grow with perhaps astonishing rapidity from the tops of the weeds, not infrequently reaching heights of a yard or more.

DISTRIBUTION - Growing almost everywhere in southern Canada and in the United States where it can be near people and their animals, except for a southern stretch from California eastward, burdock is common along paths, roadsides, stone walls, fences, and yards, wastelands, and particularly around old barns, stables, and deserted farm buildings, sawmills, and logging camps.

EDIBILITY - Peeled, sliced, simmered for twenty minutes in water to which ¼ teaspoon of baking soda has been added, drained, then barely covered with boiling water and simmered until tender, the first-year roots are deliciously nutritious. Slender and deep-growing, these appear before the biennials have flower or bur stalks.

The leaf stems are edible early in the spring, most of the bitterness coming off when they are peeled. Good raw, particularly with a little salt, they are generally preferred boiled.

When harvested early enough, the young leaves prove tender enough to be boiled in two waters and served as greens.

Tastiest to most palates is the long, plump flower stalk, diligently gathered before the leaves open entirely and well before the first blossom buds swell. Every shred of the strong, bitter, green skin must be peeled away. Then slice into convenient discs and cook until tender any way you might potatoes.

When the aspiring medicine men of some of the Indian tribes fasted for up to a week, they sometimes drank the bitter brew of burdock, which was supposed both to help them learn better and to keep the acquired lore sticking in their minds.

©AJA

BUTTERNUT *(Juglans)*

FAMILY - Walnut *(Juglandaceae)*

OTHER NAMES - White Walnut, Oilnut.

DESCRIPTION - Confederate soldiers and partisans were known as Butternuts during the War Between the States because of the brown homespun clothes of the military, often dyed with the green nut husks and the inner bark of these familiar trees. Some of the earliest North American colonists made the same use of them. As far back as the American Revolution, a common laxative was made of the same inner bark, a spoonful of finely cut pieces to a cup of boiling water, drunk cold.

The butternut prospers in chillier climates than the black walnut, ranging higher in the mountains and further north. Otherwise, this tree, also known as the white walnut, closely resembles its cousin except for being smaller and lighter hued. Its wood is comparatively soft, weak, and lightweight, although still close-grained. The larger trees, moreover, are nearly always unsound.

Butternuts are medium-sized trees, ordinarily from about thirty to fifty feet tall, with a diameter of up to three feet. Some trees, however, tower up to ninety feet or more. The furrowed and broadly ridged bark is grey, the wider ridges being smooth-topped and making a characteristically shiny network superimposed on the black fissures.

The alternate, compound leaves are from 15 to 30 inches long. Each is made up of 11 to 17 lancehead-shaped, nearly stemless leaflets, 2 to 6 inches long and about half as broad, with abruptly pointed tips, sawtoothed edges, and unequally rounded bases. Yellowish green on top, these are paler and softly downy beneath. The twigs and leafstalks are also somewhat hairy. The catkins and short flower spikes appear in the springtime when the leaves are about half grown.

The nuts are oblong rather than round, blunt, rather pear-shaped, and about 2 to 2½ inches in length. Thin, one-pieced husks, notably sticky and coated with mats of rusty hairs, enclose the nuts whose bony shells are roughly ridged, deeply furrowed, and hard. The crushed fruits of this tree, too, will illegally and unsportingly poison fish for human food purposes when surivival is at stake. Frequently growing in small clusters of from two to five, these ripen in October and November and soon fall from the branches.

To find butternut trees in winter, look for stout, smooth or somewhat downy, greenish-grey to reddish-yellow twigs, dotted with tiny pores. The pith is large, obviously chambered, and the color of dark unsweetened chocolate. There is a raised downy pad above the convex upper margins of the inversely triangular, three-lobed, alternate leaf scars. All buds are coated with a pale grey fuzz. The bark on the younger branches and trunks is smooth and light grey, on the older trunks becoming blackly furrowed, although the plateau-topped ridges stay light grey.

DISTRIBUTION - Butternuts grow from the Maritimes to Ontario, south to the northern mountainous areas of Georgia and Alabama and west to Arkansas, Kansas, and the Dakotas.

EDIBILITY - Wildlife has the same regard for the butternut as for its close cousin, the black walnut.

The young nuts, when they have nearly attained their full size, can be picked green and used for pickles. If you can still easily shove a needle through the nuts, it will not be too late to pickle them, husks and all, after they have been scalded and the outer fuzz rubbed off.

Then immerse them in a strong brine for a week, changing the salt water every other day and keeping them tightly covered. Afterward, drain and wipe them. Pierce each nut all the way through several times with a large needle. Finally, place them in a glass jar with a sprinkling of powdered ginger, mace, nutmeg, and cloves between each layer. Bring some cider vinegar to a boil, immediately fill each jar to the brim, seal, and allow to season for at least two weeks.

The nuts are also good as a nibble, in salads, and cooked in pies, cookies, and the like. The Indians used to boil the nuts to release the oil that, skimmed off the top, they used like butter, afterwards collecting and drying the kernels. A 100 grams of the raw meat contains 628 calories, 23.7 grams of protein, 61.2 grams of fat, 8.4 grams of carbohydrates, plus a big 6.8 milligrams of healthful iron.

In the springtimes, the sap of both the butternut and the black walnut was boiled down to make a delectably sweet syrup.

© AJA

CATTAIL *(Typha)*

FAMILY - Cattail *(Typhaceae)*

OTHER NAMES - Flags, Rushes, Bulrushes, Cossack Asparagus, Cattail Flag, Broadleaf Cattail, Narrow-Leaved Cattail, Cat-o'Nine Tails, Reed Mace.

DESCRIPTION - Everyone knows these tall strap-leaved plants with their sausagelike heads which, growing in groups from about two to ten feet tall, enliven wet places throughout North America except in the Arctic.

The slender, flat, 3- to 6-feet long, ½-1 inch wide, tapering, pointed basal leaves, dried and then soaked to make them pliable, afford rush seats and backs for chairs, as well as rugged material for mats and rugs. The longest of them are nearly always at least a couple of feet shorter than the round, smooth stems and spring up in the very early spring among the dried leaves of the year before.

Atop each unbranched stalk is a thickly flowered spike of tiny brown blossoms, each on its separate stem and maturing from the base upward. The lower several inches of these massed flowers, at first green, are a crowded, sausagelike compactness of female blossoms. Just above these, enabling them later to produce their cottony seeds, are the male flowers which, without benefit of the usual insects, drop their golden pollen as the summer proceeds, eventually leaving the naked upper part of the stem spiking and withering above the feminine inflorescence.

Red-winged blackbirds and many other kinds of birds find cattails fine protective nesting and roosting cover.

DISTRIBUTION - Cattails grow throughout the United States and Canada except in the Far Northern regions.

EDIBILITY - Although cattail seeds are too minute and hairy to attract most birds, some like the teal feed on them. The starchy underground roots and the bright green shoots are relished by geese and muskrats. The shoots, too, are sought by moose and elk when they first appear each new spring.

The roots, as well as the lower portions of the stem, are sweetish with more than half weight-sustaining carbohydrates. These are fairly easy to pull up or to dig out, even in deep snow, with no more help than a pointed stick. They are delicious and nutritious raw, baked, roasted ash-sheathed in the glowing embers of a campfire, or briefly boiled. First scrub, then peel while still wet.

The cores can also be dried and ground into a substantial white flour, which you may want to sift to get out any fibers.

The tender young shoots, which somewhat resemble cucumbers in taste, are very much edible. If they are starting to get tough, drop them into boiling salted water to simmer to tenderness. These young shoots also make tasty pickles.

Peeled of their outer rind, the tender white insides of the first 1 or 1½ feet of the young stems gives this worldwide delicacy its provocative name of Cossack asparagus. Again, these are edible both raw and cooked.

The greenish-yellow flower spikes, before they become tawny with pollen, can be gathered, husked as you would corn, and dropped into rapidly boiling salted water to simmer until tender. Or steam them to retain even more of the goodness. Eat like corn, dripping with butter or oleomargarine. Or scrape these boiled flower buds from the wiry cobs and use them like cooked corn kernels.

These flower spikes later are gilded with thick pollen which, easily and quickly rubbed or shaken into a container, is a flour substitute for breadstuffs. It can be cleaned if necessary by passing through a sieve. For delectable golden hot cakes in camp, mix half and half with the regular flour in any pancake recipe.

Finally, there is a pithy little tidbit where the new green stem sprouts out of the rootstocks which can be roasted or boiled like young potatoes.

© AJA

CHOKECHERRY *(Prunus)*

FAMILY - Rose *(Roseceae)*

OTHER NAMES - Western Chokecherry, Black Chokecherry, Common Chokecherry, Eastern Chokecherry, Wild Cherry.

DESCRIPTION - Frequently seen and enjoyed as a large shrub, the chokecherry also grows into a small tree up to some two-dozen feet high with a trunk about eight inches in diameter, ripe with thirst-quenching fruit that can be either red or black. Such trees are the exception, however, and the wood, although strong and richly dark like that of the rum cherry, lacks similar commercial value because of its smallness.

Chokecherry leaves are either inversely egg-shaped or oval with rounded or widely wedgelike bases. Abruptly pointed, they vary from about 1 to 4 inches in length and from ½ to 2 inches in width. Narrowly pointed teeth make the edges finely and sharply jagged. Smooth on both sides, these blades are dully dark green on top and paler below. Their stems are short, seldom being more than ¾ inch long, and boast twin glands at their tops.

The long clusters of blossoms flower when the leaves are nearly grown, later developing into red or black fruits, the dimensions of garden peas, that often become so plentiful that the branches sag with their juice-laden weight. Each berry has one big, hard stone.

Chokecherry shrubs and trees can also be recognized when the woods and fence rows thin out in winter, and marked at that time for warm-weather pilgrimages. The somewhat plump, light brown twigs often are dulled with a greyish film. They have an odor that most find unpleasant, in contrast to that of some of the other wild cherries.

The thinly oval buds are pointed. Each is distinguished with a half-dozen or more tannish scales with lighter, greenish margins.

Reddish yellow pores are conspicuous over the dully grey-brown bark. Darker but slightly grooved on the more mature trunks, this bark frequently peels from young trunks and branches in papery layers to expose the brightly green inner bark.

DISTRIBUTION - Possibly the most widely distributed tree on this continent and certainly the most common wild cherry in North America, the chokecherry thrives from Mexico to the Arctic Ocean and from one ocean shore to the other.

Preferring ground that is rich and moist, it also adapts itself to poorer and drier areas. Occurring in open woodlands, it frequently follows civilization to roadsides, fence rows, and to those otherwise waste thickets seen in many a farm corner. It is also cultivated as an ornamental and as a bird feedery.

EDIBILITY - Both a lot of the common songbirds and many of the more toothsome game birds feast on chokecherries. The fruit is also relished by numerous fur and game animals and by a multitude of smaller forest folk, a number of whom feast on the harvest that has fallen to the ground after the birds have eaten their fill. Moose, elk, mountain sheep, deer, and even the lowly but more numerous rabbit feed extensively on the buds, leaves, twigs, foliage, and sometimes the bark of this wild cherry.

Especially tart before it ripens, the chokecherry is both refreshing and sustaining when one is thirsty, hungry, or both. The fruit is frequently sought for wine and for jelly, the latter requiring the addition of either pectin or a pectin-rich supplement such as apples.

The pits, like that of the domestic peach, should be avoided because of their poisonous cyanogenetic content, although Indians used to cook and crush the whole berry, leach out the poison, and both eat the resulting cakes as is and use it to flavor pemmican. The leaves are also poisonous, especially springs and early summers.

CHIA *(Salvia)*

FAMILY - Mint *(Labiatae)*

OTHER NAMES - Sage, Salvia.

DESCRIPTION - This sage, an aromatic member of the huge mint family which includes the lavender, rosemary, basil, thyme, hyssop, and pennyroyal, is one of the most famous and nutritious of all the wild foods on which the Indians thrived. Just to give you an idea, a mere teaspoonful of the tiny little brown, grey, and white seeds were looked upon as enough to sustain an Indian for one day on a forced march.

Today, although largely unregarded except by some of the Spanish-speaking population in the southwestern United States where it grows, it is still used in Old Mexico, and you can sit down in some of the best restaurants in the interior and sip a chia drink, either non-alcoholic or stronger. This is because when this same teaspoon of chia seeds is added to a cup of cold water and soaked for several minutes, it provides an almost tasteless but extremely refreshing beverage, particularly valuable in desert country not only because of the way it assuages the thirst, but because it offsets to some degree the harshness of alkaline springs.

When larger amounts of this chia drink are prepared in advance, the usual proportion is ¼ pound of seeds to 1½ quarts of water. The procedure is to mix these in a large jug or jar and allow the whole to stand for at least five minutes, long enough for the seeds to swell and to become cloudily surrounded by a gelatinous cloaking. One can then add lime or lemon juice, plus sugar, to taste. This beverage is ordinarily chilled before serving.

The annual springs up on the prairies, hills, and dales of California, especially on dry slopes and sandy wastes, mostly below 3,500 feet, with the coming of the winter rains. It is a rough-leaved sage with coarse, deeply indented, often hairy, dark green leaves, most of them near the ground. There are usually one or two pairs of these leaves on each of the one or several stalks that rise up to some 16 inches high from the same root.

The two or three wheels of tiny blue flowers that grow, mint-fashion, in dense whorls in interrupted spikes around the tops of the plants have, below them, leafy bracts of a brightly contrasting maroon color. The projections of their outer parts are prickly. Once these blossoms have shriveled, the dried stems and seed-rich heads remain standing like skeletons.

The Indians harvested this abundance of seeds by bending and shaking the stalks over quickly filling baskets. Others bundled the whole plants into camp and threshed them with rods. The women then winnowed out the seeds, which were cleaned and dried.

The fact that there are not enough leaves on these seed-heavy edibles to give the wind much purchase makes it a profitable matter today, where they grow, to go among them with a paper bag and a stick and to beat the seeds into the sack by striking the dessicated flower heads.

DISTRIBUTION - Chia grows in Arizona, Nevada, Utah, and California.

EDIBILITY - The seeds can be ground into meal, then mixed in equal proportions with enough wheat flour or cornmeal to give a pleasantly nutty flavor to the foods prepared from them in the usual fashion.

But all you have to do to get all the vitamins, minerals, and other nutriments is to eat a pinch of chia seeds dry, dilute them to a drink in which each will become separately suspended in its own white mucilaginous coat, or mix them with water to form a particularly digestible gruel.

©AJA

CHICORY *(Chichorium)*

FAMILY - Composite *(Compositae)*

OTHER NAMES - Blue Sailors, Wild Succory, Succory, *Barbe de Capuchin,* Witloof, Ragged Sailors, Wild Bachelor Buttons, Blue Dandelion, Blue Daisy.

DESCRIPTION - Fields, roadsides, and old pastures are sometimes blue with the big showy flower of the chicory, also often white and very occasionally pink. However, what seems at first glance to be a single large blossom is actually a head of extremely small flowers, each with a broad, usually blue strap which has five square-edged straps to its outer rim. Minute lines extend from the outer edge of the strap to the base where this forms a brief tube. Emanating from the tube is a small stalk, composed of all the stamens joined together.

Although these June to October blossoms generally close in the noonday sun, in overcast weather they may remain open all day. Before they are all unfurled, those in the middle of the head resemble tiny blue stalks.

Sometimes occurring singly, these flower heads which have short stalks occasionally appear in clusters and at other times in pairs, scattered toward the top of the common wild edible. Outside each flower head are arrayed two rows of narrow leaves, each row pressing erectly against the blossoms, the other row spreading backward toward the stalk. The blooms are a beautiful 1 to 1½ inches in diameter.

A rather rigidly branching perennial with a deep and succulent taproot, chicory zigzags awkwardly upward one to four feet, sparsely festooned with raggedy leaves of no special shape or else that clasp the stalk and branches at their joints which, when broken anywhere, exude a milky and bitter dandelionish juice.

The leaves at the base of the stem are larger and longer, forming a rosette on the ground like that of the dandelion although not in such a numerous or firmly settled fashion. These are large, coarsely toothed leaves with a single big vein on the underside of each, plus numerous tiny veins branching from it to twist and join other small veins. The higher, stem-clasping leaves on the stalk are far smaller than those next to the ground.

DISTRIBUTION - Chicory, an alien from Europe and Asia, has escaped from the Maritimes to Florida, west to the prairies, then along the Pacific Coast from British Columbia to California and locally elsewhere.

EDIBILITY - Chicory, millions of pounds of whose roots have been roasted, ground, and used as an adulterant and as a substitute for coffee, also provides greens for salads and for cooking. As these leaves grow older they, like those of the dandelion, become more and more bitter, encouraging some cooks to drain off the first boiling water and then to simmer to tenderness in the second.

Raw chicory greens, although over 92% water, have for each 100 grams of the edible portion 86 milligrams of calcium, 40 mg. of phosphorus, .9 mg. of iron, 420 mg. of potassium, plus no less than 4,000 international units of Vitamin A, 22 mg. of Vitamin C, and goodly traces of thiamine, riboflavin, and niacin.

Much of the chicory root used on this continent as a coffee substitute, stretcher, and flavorer is imported from Europe, but exactly the same roots grow wild right here at home. If you'd like to proceed on your own, just dig some of the long roots, scrub them with a brush, and then roast them slowly in a partly open oven until they will break crisply between the fingers, exposing a dark brown interior. Then grind and store in a closed container for brewing perhaps as a coffee substitute, in lesser amounts like the similar product of the dandelion, as it's stronger, or for blending with your regular supply of the bean.

©AJA

CHUFA *(Cyperus)*

FAMILY - Sedge *(Cyperaceae)*

OTHER NAMES - Earth Almond, Nut Grass, Zula Nuts, Edible Galingale.

DESCRIPTION - Except for several smaller leaves at the top of the stalk supporting the flower clusters, all the light green, grasslike leaves of the chufa, which are about the same length as the central flower stalk, grow from the roots. These latter are composed of long horizontal runners, terminating in little nutlike tubers.

The numerous flowers grow in little, flat, yellowish-brown spikes. These widely spreading flower clusters, resembling an upside-down umbrella all the more because of the likeness of the upper tape-flat leaves to long ribs, have a feathery appearance.

The stalks, plump and triangular, run about one to two feet high. The whorl of some three to eight leaves that cup loosely about the numerous, spreading blossom-spikelets account for about two-fifths of this edible sedge's total height. All these lightly hued, green leaves, which have a conspicuous vein along their centers, are up to about ½ inch wide.

The edible tubers of this cousin to the historic papyrus, which the ancients ate when they weren't writing on it, are sweet, nutty, and milky with juice. Looking like dark, puckered ¼-to-½-inch nuts, these are clustered about the base of the plant, especially when it grows in sandy or loose soil where a few tugs will give a hungry man his dinner. In hard dirt, the nuts are widely scattered as well as being difficult to excavate.

DISTRIBUTION - Abounding from Alaska to Mexico, and from one coast to the other, Chufa also grows in Africa, Europe, and Asia. It spreads so easily, especially in rich, moist soil that has been built up by running water, that it is regarded in some localities as a troublesome weed, particularly in our South where attempts were once made to grow it commercially.

EDIBILITY - Chufa was so esteemed as a nutriment during early centuries that as long as four thousand years ago the Egyptians were including it among the choice foods placed in their tombs. Wildlife was enjoying it even before that. Both the edible tubers of this plant, also known as earth almond and as nut grass, and the seeds are sought by waterfowl, upland game birds, and other wildlife. Often abundant in mud flats that glisten with water in the late fall and early winter, the nutritious tubers are readily accessible to ducks. Where chufa occurs as a robust weed in other places, especially in sandy soil and loam, upland game birds and rodents are seen vigorously digging for the tubers.

All you have to do is wash and eat chufas, but they can also be enjoyed as a cooked vegetable. Too, they can be well dried, as in a slow open-doored oven, then ground to a powder as in the blender. This powder can be mixed with other flour for all sorts of appetizing, vitamin-and-mineral-rich cakes, breads, and cookies.

The Spanish make a refreshing cold drink from the chufa, enjoyed both as it is and as a base for stronger concoctions. A popular alcoholic drink, for instance, is made by partially freezing the beverage in the refrigerator, then adding an equal volume of light rum to make a sort of wild frozen daiquiri. The Spanish recipe calls for soaking ½ pound of the well-washed tubers for two days. Then drain them and either mash them or put them through the blender, along with 4 cups of water and ⅓ cup sugar. Strain the white, milky results, and you're in business.

Another beverage, this one a coffee substitute, can be made after roasting and grinding the sweetish, nutlike tubers. This was once popular in central Europe.

Chufa also lends itself to excellent conserves.

CLOVER *(Trifolium)*

FAMILY - Pea *(Leguminosae)*

OTHER NAMES - Red Clover, White Clover, Ditch Clover, Hop Clover, Trefoil, Longstalk Clover, Strawberry Clover, Low Hop-Clover, Smaller Hop-Clover, Tomcat Clover, Foothill Clover, Pinpoint Clover, Clammy Clover, Rabbitfoot Clover, Sweet Clover, Yellow Sweet Clover, Yellow Clover, White Sweet Clover, Common Clover, Bighead Clover.

DESCRIPTION - The breezes of springtime and early summer are often cheered by the delicate fragrance of the clover, some 75 varieties of which extend their green beds throughout the United States alone. Nearly everyone knows this prolific wild edible, especially those who have searched the three-leaved beds for the so-called lucky four-leaf combinations.

Red clover is the colorful state flower of Vermont. White clover, especially because it does not have to be mowed, is appreciated by many a lawn-tender. The enriching roots of the clovers as a whole throng with bacteria which change nitrogen from the atmosphere into soil-improving organic compounds that can valuably fertilize other crops. Furthermore, a number of clovers, which frequently escape and become wild themselves, are cultivated for silage, hay, and green feed.

The tiny little flowers that collectively form the familiarly dense clover blossom have, individually, five petals, ten pollen-bearing stamens, and a minute seed vessel like the other flowerage of the pea family. The outer of the two series of floral leaves, the calyx, is a five-toothed green tube. Many a youngster learns early in life the pleasure of sucking honey from the tiny tubular florets of the white, yellow, pink, reddish, and purple blossoms.

Once the flowers commence to shrivel, they do not all fall off at once but, rather, dry up and darken along their outsides, often staying fresh and bright at their centers and still interesting the hungry bumblebee. When clover was first brought to the fields and gardens of Australia, it failed to reproduce until bumblebees were likewise imported.

The more common members of these low perennials have three leaflets, the middle of which extends from a slim stalk. The other two are generally stemless. All three leaflets have minutely toothed edges. Wherever a leaf stalk extends from the downy main stem there are a pair of small, green, pointed sheaths. If you want to have an easier time finding a four-leaf clover, hunt through a bed of a variety such as the big head clover which, growing in the western U.S. where it is sometimes cooked as a green, boasts from three to nine leaflets instead of just the usual trio.

DISTRIBUTION - Wild clovers thrive in often broad beds from an inch or two to two feet high in the valleys and foothills of the temperate parts of this continent, in meadows, pastures, fields, open woodlands, and along many a path, road, lane, and highway. Some varieties prefer damp grassy expanses, stream and lake shores, and up to nearly two miles high in the mountains. Others seek drier, frequently rocky areas. All in all, clover grows everywhere in North America where an open garden can be raised.

EDIBILITY - Clover is the preferred forage of everything from moose and elk, mountain sheep, and deer, and from the largest brown bear to the smallest black bear. It is important to game birds from Canada geese to grouse, pheasants, prairie chicken, and the warily sagacious turkey. Woodchuck, beaver, muskrat, rabbit, and raccoons are among the smaller mammals dining on the foliage. Larks, nuthatches, and pipits are among songbirds seeking the seeds.

Indians ate the clovers both raw and cooked, the Diggers, for example, steaming large quantities of well dampened plants between hot stones. Other tribes partially dried and smoked the sweetish roots, or rolled and dipped them in oil or meat drippings. Still others enjoyed the tender young leaves both raw and briefly cooked. The fresh raw stems, flowers, and leaves were sometimes first dipped in salty water.

The sweet-scented blossoms have been used for everything from flavoring cheeses and tobaccos to stowing with furs to keep away moths. They are also frequently eaten raw. Bread made from the seed-filled dried blossoms has nourished entire groups of people during famines.

A wholesome and reputed medicinally valuable tea can be made by picking the mature blossoms on a dry sunny day, drying them at room or sun temperature, rubbing them into tiny particles, and sealing them in jars or bottles to retain the aroma. Add a level teaspoon of these to each cup of boiling water in a warmed cup or teapot, steep for five minutes, and drink as you would regular tea.

Red Clover

COMMON CHICKWEED *(Stellaria) (Alsine)*

FAMILY - Pink *(Caryophylleae)*

OTHER NAMES - Chickweed, Stitchwort, Starwort.

DESCRIPTION - This deceivingly meek little member of the pink family is a seemingly feeble but really vigorous weed that thrives in green, ground-covering masses. Its usually branching stems, up to about a foot long, appear weak and brittle, for example, but on a side of each there is a single line of minute hairs that form a surprisingly tenacious green thread. In lawns and in gardens except when these latter are in stony, dry soil, it is regarded as troublesome by those who have not relished its edibility.

The leaves, which are smoothly oval and somewhat sharply pointed, grow in opposite pairs on numerous slim branches. Attached directly to the upper portions of the branches, they lift from flat, hairy stems along their lower parts. The single line of green threads that connects each pair of leaves alternates the side of the stalk along which it courses upon reaching each twin.

Each of the small white flowers has five minute petals which are deeply cleft, almost into two parts. Arranged like a verdant star behind the petals are five sharply pointed sepals which look like rays. Golden stamens are clustered within the petals, in whose very middle is the tiny seed vessel. Each blossom grows singly on the end of a stem which extends from the angle between a leaf and the main stalk. Closed nights and overcast days, they open to bright sunshine.

Common chickweed is unique in that it starts growing in the autumn, robustly survives the severity of frost and snow and ice even in the North, commences blossoming in late winter, and often concludes its life cycle and valuable seed production in the spring. However, it is so prolific in reseeding that in most States it can be seen blossoming twelve months of the year.

DISTRIBUTION - Growing in fields, gardens, lawns, waste lands, cultivated grounds, woods, dooryards, meadows, and in moist spots throughout the United States and much of the world, common chickweed is generally green and blossoming, even under light snowfall, somewhere in nearly every State at any given time. With such an early start, it often takes over in gardens in the early springtime before anything else has come to life. In the North it grows from Alaska to Greenland.

EDIBILITY - Chickweed, which gets its name from the avidity with which small birds snap up its juicy leaves and papery seed-filled capsules, is a favorite food among our game fowl. Mountain sheep, the most succulent of our big game, also share its mild tastiness.

Good in salads when young, it makes a particularly wholesome and nutritious potherb, especially when its blandness is touched up with some stronger-charactered wild edible such as dandelions or water cress. Because of its year-round availability, common chickweed is a valuable antiscorbutic. Tenderer than most wild greens, it can be enjoyed either raw or cooked very slightly.

©AJA

COWSLIP *(Caltha)*

FAMILY - Buttercup *(Ranunculaceae)*

OTHER NAMES - Marsh Marigold, Meadowbright, *Ahklingquahk.*

DESCRIPTION - Our North American Cowslip, not to be confused with a different wild edible of the same name in England although a similar *Caltha palustris* grows and is eaten there, is a member of the buttercup family and, raw, contains the poisonous *helleborin* which is dispelled with delectable results upon cooking.

The five or more petal-like divisions of the bright yellow flowers of this continent's marsh marigold, as it is also called, are bright, smooth, and glossy. Tiny greenish veins, more prominent on the sepals' backs, twine up from their bases. The golden blossoms somewhat resemble big buttercups, although these latter are two divisioned flowers with frontal petals backed up by sepals.

Numerous tawny stamens bristle up from inside this cowslip's blossoms, evening in length with age. Centered among these is a tiny mass of seed vessels which, gaining in length, spread apart there after the rest of the flowers have dropped off.

Slippery, hollow, thick stems support the bright blossoms, both single and grouped, where they lift stiffly among the leaves. The stalks, ridged along their sides, lose their easily snapped erectness when picked from the damp stream banks and the marshy coolnesses where they grow.

The leaves, smoothly and shiningly dark green above, have much lighter underneaths. From some three to seven inches across, they, too, are distinguished with a delicate network of veins. Either nearly round or kidney-shaped, they have crinkly or wavy edges. The lower leaves grow on fleshy, elongated stems. The higher leaves, on the other hand, protrude almost directly from the smooth stalks themselves.

Because cowslips always must be cooked before eating, it is sound procedure to gather them by themselves. Too, ordinary diligence should be exercised not to include any of the easily differentiated poisonous water hemlocks or hellebore that frequently are to be found in the same habitats. Entirely different in appearance from the distinctive cowslip, the water hemlock superficially resembles the domestic carrot plant but has coarser leaves and a taller, thicker stalk. The white hellebore, which can be mistaken for a loose-leaved cabbage, is a leafy plant that somewhat resembles skunk cabbage, one reason why that not always agreeable edible has been omitted from this guide.

DISTRIBUTION - These bright little harbingers of spring grow abundantly from the Aleutians, eastward through the coastal areas of the Gulf of Alaska, northward along the Arctic Coast, to Labrador and Greenland, and as far south as the Carolinas and Tennessee.

One reason why this cousin of the crowfoot family got its name of cowslip is that its brightness often gleams in wet meadows and barnyards and in the hoof-muddied sogginesses where cattle drink.

EDIBILITY - Few such familiar wild greens boil up so delectably so soon after the long, white winters, but for human consumption boiled they must be to rid them of the poisonous glucoside.

The safest and least vitamin-destructive procedure is to drop the otherwise pungent and acrid leaves into boiling water, discard this as soon as it has returned to a bubble, pour more boiling water over the thick leaves, and again drain it away once it has started simmering again. Then simmer or steam in a slight amount of water until barely tender. Cut into bite-size segments, salt lightly, and drench with butter or margarine and perhaps a bit of vinegar if that's what you like.

CRANBERRY *(Vaccinium)*

FAMILY - Heath *(Ericaceae)*

OTHER NAMES - Mountain Cranberry, Large Cranberry, Small Cranberry, Rock Cranberry, Bog Cranberry, Swamp Cranberry, *Pomme de Terre*, Partridgeberry, Cowberry, Lingonberry, Lengon, Northern Mountain Cranberry, American Cranberry, Lowbush Cranberry, Foxberry.

DESCRIPTION - The most important berry of the North Country, the wild cranberry although smaller and at the same time tastier, is known to most because of its similarity to the domesticated Thanksgiving staple.

Three wild species of these bright members of the heath family enliven the northern portions of this continent. Essentially all are low evergreen shrubs or vines, lifting some six inches above the wilderness floor, often so thickly that they form lush acre-wide mats.

The leathery green leaves are small, usually somewhat glossy on top, lighter and hairy or spotted underneath. The tiny reddish or whitish blossoms, which have four deep petal-like divisions, are affixed to the ends of slender stalks in such a fashion that the early colonists here in the New World knew the plant as craneberry because the flowers, which nod when ground drafts are blowing, are formed like the necks and heads of these tall wading birds. The cognomen was subsequently shortened to cranberry.

The so-called bog or swamp cranberry *(Vaccinium oxycoccus)*, native to northern Europe and Asia as well as Alaska, has extremely slender, 4- to 16-inch vines which creep through the moss, rooting at the points where subsidiary parts center. The leaves differ from other species in that they are pointed, white underneath, and have rolled edges. Otherwise, they grow alternately in leathery, small, thick fashion. The flower stalks are different in that they emerge from the tips of the stems. Narrow and recurved, their four pink or red petals nod on elongated, threadlike stalks. The berries, growing on boggy or peaty soil, look translucent against their bedding of sphagnum moss.

The so-called wild large or American cranberry *(V. macrocarpon)*, the common species of the southeastern United States north to Newfoundland and Wisconsin, is another creeping shrub with small, oval to oblong leaves that grow alternately. Recurving, pale pinkish petals form a cuplike flower, the eight or ten stamens of which grow together like a beak. The difference between this and other species is that the juicy red berries, the stalks of which are separated from one another by blunt leaves, do not stem from the tips of the plants.

The mountain cranberry *(V. vitis-idaea)* has leathery, dark-green, persisting, oval leaves that characteristically in this particular species have black dots beneath. The white or pink, bell-shaped flowers that grow in small, nodding, terminal clusters lack the recurving lobes of the other two. Although this low, creeping shrub occurs north to the Arctic seacoast, it does not customarily produce fruit north of the tree line. Preferring an acid soil, either moist or dry, it is most prolific in open birch or willow thickets where it often reddens the ground as far south as Minnesota and New England where, unfortunately, the berries, most mellow after the first frost, are frequently picked too soon.

DISTRIBUTION - Wild cranberries, which have more flavor and color than the familiar domesticated species, the majority of which are cultivated in Massachusetts, grow along the northern borders of the contiguous forty-eight States and from Alaska to Newfoundland, south to Virginia, North Carolina, and Oregon.

EDIBILITY - Bear devour these by the thousands of bushels.

Wild cranberries cling to the stems all winter and when kept fresh by snow are available until the following spring. Most advantageously harvested after the first frost of autumn, they can be easily stored without preserving if the fully ripened fruit is gathered on dry days and kept in porous cloth sacks in a cold place. Tighter containers are inadvisable as in them the berries tend to mold unless kept frozen.

They can also be easily and successfully dried, perhaps spread shallowly on newspapers in a warm attic, until they become so shell-like they'll easily crush to a powder. For using, just soak in water, then simmer briefly, adding sugar to taste. Incidentally, try cutting the sugar in half in any recipe and substituting a level teaspoon of salt for every other ½ cup of the sweetener.

Although unappetizing if edible raw, a few thinly sliced wild cranberries will add a holiday touch to a green salad. Wild cranberries can be advantageously substituted for store varieties in any favorite recipe.

©AJA

CURRANTS and GOOSEBERRIES *(Ribes)*

FAMILY - Gooseberry *(Grossulariaceae)*

OTHER NAMES - Buffalo Currant, Wax Currant, Whitestem Gooseberry, Sticky Currant, Western Black Currant, Golden Currant, Red Garden Currant, Swamp Red Currant, American Red Currant, Fetid Currant, Skunk Currant, Wild Black Currant, Missouri Currant, Clove Bush, Black Currant, Wild Gooseberry, Prickly Gooseberry, Smooth-Fruited Gooseberry, Slender Gooseberry, Missouri Gooseberry, Northern Gooseberry, Bristly Gooseberry, European Gooseberry, Eastern Wild Gooseberry, Garden Gooseberry, Swamp Gooseberry, Trailing Black Currant, Northern Black Currant, Blue Currant, Feverberry, Groser, California Black Currant, Dog Bramble, Hudson Bay Currant, Round-Leaved Gooseberry, Smooth Wild Gooseberry, Rock Gooseberry, Sierra Gooseberry.

DESCRIPTION - Some 75 species of currants and gooseberries, both of the *Ribes* genus, grow in this country where they are easily reachable, being similar to domesticated species. In fact, some of the more popular wild varieties are refugees from gardens. Generally speaking, the members of the *Ribes* family without spines are known as currants, while the better protected, thorny varieties are called gooseberries. The fruit of these latter shrubs may be either smooth or bristling. A maplelike leaf is common to both.

For example, there is the golden currant *(Ribes aureum)* also known as the buffalo currant and as the Missouri currant, which was first made known to civilization by Captain Meriwether Lewis who found it on the headwaters of the Missouri and Columbia Rivers during the Lewis and Clark Expedition in 1805. Here, feasting on the berries themselves, they found the Indians using them in the making of pemmican, concocted by a mixture of dried buffalo meat and rendered fat, flavored by dried berries of one kind or another.

Found now from coast to coast because of the way it has repeatedly escaped from Eastern gardens, the golden currant is a native shrub whose slenderly curving branches reach sometimes ten feet high. The maplelike leaves, each with three to five sawtoothed lobes, taper to a broadish base that is sometimes wider than the leaf is long.

Spicily fragrant golden blossoms, up to about an inch long and growing in short elongated clusters along single stalks with small modified leaves near their bottoms, give the edible its additional and descriptive name of clove bush. The lower parts of these yellowish flowers are shaped like little tubes.

The berries, about ¼ inch across on the wild shrubs but larger and frequently more agreeable on the varieties cultivated from this native, are yellow, reddish, or dark black.

DISTRIBUTION - The currants and gooseberries, partly because they are so prone to escape from gardens, grow from the Gulf of Alaska to the Gulf of Mexico and from the Pacific to the Atlantic.

Found in cool woods, swamps, ravines, near streams, foothills, and along many a thus more interesting fence, they generally prefer moist soil, and their presence at the base of an elevation in the desert often indicates the presence of water close underground.

EDIBILITY - The use of gooseberries and currants by the wildlife of North America was greater before so many of the shrubs were destroyed when it became known that the fungus known as blister rust, which kills the white and other five-needle pines, lives in one of its stages first on *Ribes* before spreading to the evergreens. Thus by eradicating the currants and gooseberries in or near our conifer forests has the life cycle of the blister rust been interrupted and its spread restrained.

Blue and sharp-tailed grouse vie for the fruit and foliage, while a number of songbirds including the robin and the cedar waxwing peck away at the berries. Coyotes, foxes, raccoons, and squirrels eat both fruit and foliage, while such small mammals as the chipmunk confine their appetites to the former. Deer, elk, and mountain sheep browse on the twigs and leaves. Black bear feast on the fruit.

Currants and gooseberries differ wonderfully in taste, especially raw, but even the seemingly less appetizing fruit can be appealing and refreshing when one is hungry and thirsty. Most, however, are generally more palatable cooked. All supply good fruit, and since colonial days, when they were introduced to the first settlers and frontiersmen by the Indians, they have been famous in the United States and Canada for pies, tarts, sauces, jams, jellies, and wine.

Top—Gooseberries; Below—Currants

DANDELION *(Taraxacum)*

FAMILY - Composite *(Compositae)*

OTHER NAMES - Common Dandelion, Red-Seeded Dandelion, Arctic Dandelion, Blowball, Alpine Dandelion.

DESCRIPTION - There's hardly a month in the year except when snow's on the ground, and sometimes even then, when you can't see the golden smile of the dandelion, probably the best known flower in the world if often the least appreciated.

The big yellow blossoms, often the first wild flowers that foretell the spring and one of the last in the fall, are composed of numerous, individual, tiny flower tubes, each broadening into a slim long strap. The golden tubes are arranged on a round disk with the straps extending in a circle, those at the edges unfurling first.

Because these yellow petals are like the golden teeth of the lion of heraldry, there is some dispute as to whether they or the toothed leaves are responsible for the French cognomen, *dent de lion,* from which the English name has been slurred. In any event, it is interesting that in almost every European country the local name is of similar significance.

Each of the flowers nods by itself at the end of a long hollow stalk which, when broken, emits a bitter milky juice similar to that which oozes from the cut or abraded roots. Directly beneath the golden head is a verdant cup composed of slender, pointed, green leaves, a few of which twist backward toward the cylindrical stem. Nights and on rainy days, the leaves of the cup lift and cover the gilded petals with their greenery.

Once the blossoms wither, the round disks that bear them become white with the unbranched, short, white hairs that radiate in tiny tufts from the tips of each of the multitudinous seeds. When winds blow on them, these whiten the landscape, spreading all the further this wild edible that still follows man throughout the civilized world. In the meantime, children blow the more fragilely mature of them and count everything from the time of day to the numbers of their future offspring by the seeds remaining.

The leaves of the dandelion are smooth and appetizingly green, unless you are looking at them from the eye of a gardener who is seeking to expel them from his lawn. They grow in rosettes directly from the roots, either upright or close to the ground, depending to some extent on both the environment and to which of the some twenty-five species in the world, three or more in the U.S., they belong. Their edges are indented into large teeth which, many say, resemble those of the king of beasts.

DISTRIBUTION - The humble and beautiful dandelion has followed man abundantly to almost every inhabited corner of Canada and the United States.

EDIBILITY - The dandelion's flowers and seed heads are a favorite spring and summer food of Canada geese, grouse, partridge, pheasant, prairie chicken, and quail. Blackbirds, siskins, and sparrows are among the songbirds relishing the seeds. Deer, moose, elk, both the black bears and the grizzlies, the little prairie dogs, and the even sprier and smaller chipmunks eat the plants.

The dandelion, which has saved peoples from starvation, is a three-tiered food; the succulent roots, the tender and tasty crowns, and the tops from young leaves to flower buds all being exceptionally tasty and sustaining. Even the older leaves are good, although ordinarily you can find enough young ones for a meal, always starting them in boiling water and when someone objects too strenuously to the clean tang of the bitterness changing the water at least once. Interestingly, the first few frosts in the fall revive the sweetness of the leaves.

Scraped and sliced, then boiled in salted water, the roots are of pleasant taste and texture and when you haven't tried them before surprisingly sweet. Incidentally, these roots can be roasted in an oven until nut-brown all the way through, grated, and used as a coffee stretcher or substitute, dandelions being close cousins of the similarly used chicory.

The white crowns, the parts of the perennial between the roots and the surface of the ground, are even finer flavored than the young leaves in many's estimations.

Raw dandelion greens, 85% water, have an abundant 14,000 international units of Vitamin A per 100 grams, plus .19 milligrams of thiamine, .26 mg. riboflavin, and 35 mg. of the vital ascorbic acid, all of which helps to explain why the lowly dandelion was so highly regarded as a tonic and general remedy by frontiersmen and early settlers long before the days of vitamin pills.

This same portion of edible greens is further enriched with 198 milligrams of calcium, 76 mg. of sodium, and 397 mg. of potassium. To get all this goodness undiluted, let the tender young greens enhance your fresh salads.

DOCK *(Rumex)*

FAMILY *(Portulacaceae)*

OTHER NAMES - Curled Dock, Curly Dock, Narrow-Leafed Dock, Narrow Dock, Patience Dock, Yellow Dock, Spur Dock, Bitter Dock, Blunt-Leaved Dock, Red-Veined Dock, Arctic Dock, Sour Dock, Wild Spinach, Wild Pie Plant.

DESCRIPTION - Docks are stylishly stout plants, bulky with mainly basal leaves. These dark-green leaves, usually a few inches to a foot in length but occasionally twice that long, are commonly tapering but sometimes heart-shaped. They are often characterized by wavy or curly edges. The lower portions and the underneaths are smooth.

Where the fleshy leafstalks are attached to the stem, papery membranous sheaths wrap themselves around the joints.

They flower in tall, batonlike, whorled clusters of tiny green blossoms that sometimes take on a regally purplish cast. The three inner series of the petals of these form tiny, thin-winged, reddish-brown seeds that are more noticeable than the parent blossoms. The erect dry stalks, up to about five feet tall, become conspicuous in the autumn, rusty as they are with hordes of minute seeds whose ribbed wings await the scattering wind.

DISTRIBUTION - Found and eaten the world over, the docks on this continent are scattered throughout Alaska and the Arctic, south across Canada and the United States, deep into Mexico. They have become what are regarded as often troublesome weeds, abounding as they do even in lawns. Yet dock greens are richer in Vitamin C than oranges and more abundant in Vitamin A than even carrots.

Although raw dock is 90.9% water, an edible portion of 100 grams contains 66 milligrams of calcium, 41 of phosphorous, 1.6 of iron, and a whopping 338 of the so-necessary potassium, plus worthwhile fractions of thiamine, riboflavin, and niacin, all free for the eating.

EDIBILITY - Although in many parts of the U.S. and Canada it is the foreign-born, remembering from Europe and Asia the bitterish lemon-like delectability of dock, who seek out this wild spinach for their tables, it was relished by some of the Indian tribes and is still sought by our Eskimos, being prized for cooking, chopping, mixing perhaps with blander greens, and then storing in kegs and barrels in cold places for enjoying during the long winters.

With a delicately bitter, lemonish flavor that makes a lot of seasoning unnecessary, in salads for instance very young dock, perhaps mixed with such other greens as water cress, dandelions, or mustard, is good with just oil, salt, and a scattering of pepper.

When boiled, steamed, or just wilted in a frypan with a couple of tablespoons apiece of water and butter or margarine, dock loses practically none of its bulk, unlike most greens with which you need a lot to get a little.

A delicious puree can be made from the young leaves, although it all depends on your particular palate. To some, all dock is too bitter for enjoying without cooking. In any event, some species of dock are more bitter than others, especially when older, and with these many cooks prefer to drain away the first boiling water, finishing with only a small amount of fluid to prevent the vegetable from becoming too watery. However, in many areas dock continues to put up new leaves despite frosts and can often be gathered, young and tender, throughout warm spells during the winter.

Being closely related to domestic buckwheat, the winged brown seeds were used, particularly by some of the western Indians, in preparing flour and meal. To duplicate this today at home, rub off the thin leaves between the palms, clean the remains by pouring from one pan to another in the wind, grind in a hand-operated gristmill or even between two stones, and then sift.

The dock *Rumex hymenosepalus,* known in Utah and California as the wild pie plant, not only has highly edible greens, but the leaf stems provide a fine rhubarb substitute for sauces and pies. The Indians used the tannin-rich roots for tanning their deerskins and for giving a mahogany-brown brightness to their painted bodies.

DULSE *(Rhodymenia)*

FAMILY - Red Algae *(Rhodophyceae)*

OTHER NAMES - Seaweed, Dillisk.

DESCRIPTION - Rich in vital minerals including iodine, the ingredient necessary for the proper functioning of the thyroid gland and for the prevention of goitre, this chewable is more popular in Europe than on this continent, although in places like New Brunswick and elsewhere in the Maritimes you find it for sale in grocery stores.

An edible portion of dulse weighing 100 grams contains 3.2 grams of fat in addition to 296 milligrams of calcium, a slightly lesser 267 mg. of phosphorus, a big 2,085 mg. of sodium, and a huge 8,060 mg. of potassium. And if you live along either seacoast of this continent, all you usually have to do is go down to a clean shore to gather all you want for free.

These sea plants have extremely brief stems that rapidly widen into thin, elastic fronds. Varying in color from purplish to reddish, the smooth flat expanses are frequently lobed and cleft. The whole seaweed grows from a few inches to about a foot in length.

DISTRIBUTION - Dulse is so prolific along our Atlantic and Pacific coasts that it grows from other seaweeds as well as from submerged rocks, ledges, and shells.

EDIBILITY - Chewed directly from the sea, dulse is tough and rubbery. The trick is to hang it or spread it out until it is partially dry. Or if you don't want to wait that long, just singe the fresh dulse on a hot stove, griddle, or campfire rock.

The Indians in southeast Alaska still gather this seaweed in quantity, usually during the low tides of May and early June. They then leave it in the sun and air as they do laver, eventually storing it for adding during the winter to soups and stews. People from the Mediterranean countries also use it as an ingredient in soup.

A premium you sometimes come by when harvesting dulse in Alaska during the midsummer herring runs is herring roe. All you have to do is drain this roe, season it with pepper and perhaps some extra salt, and saute it in butter or margarine in moderate heat until brown on both sides. About a dozen minutes will do the job. Then add lemon juice to the drippings that are now a delicate tan and pour this over the hot roe. Enjoy at once.

©AJA

ELDERBERRY *(Sambucus)*

FAMILY - Honeysuckle *(Caprifoliaceae)*

OTHER NAMES - Common Elderberry, American Elderberry, Elder, American Elder, Sweet Elder, Scarlet Elder, Common Elder, Red-Berried Elder, Blue-Berried Elder, Blue Elderberry, Red Elderberry, Pacific Red Elderberry, Florida Elderberry, Black Elderberry, Black Eider, Blackbead Elder, Canadian Elderberry, Mountain Blue Elderberry, Tree of Music.

DESCRIPTION - Too often neglected because their fruit is not usually appetizing raw, elderberries bearing thousands of bushels of easily and advantageously picked berry clusters are left to this continent's wildlife each fall. Yet the wild fruit is among Canada's and the United States' richest in Vitamin A, calcium, thiamine, and niacin, besides having nearly twice as many calories as the popular cranberry and three times more protein than blueberries.

Elderberries vary from shrubs five feet tall to treelike proportions of thirty feet or more, clustering upright from tangles of roots in often damp ground along shores, roads, fences, and in open woods, glades, and plains, around buildings, and in the mountains to around nine thousand feet. Clusters of minute, creamy blossoms become lacelike against their greennesses June and July, turning to such full myriads of mature berries around the last of August and the first of September that they fairly beg to be harvested.

In ancient times these members of the honeysuckle family were often planted around houses to keep away the evil spirits, as well as lightning.

The easily broken branches are filled with pith especially when they are young, the woody part becoming more predominant with age. The Indians used to press this incidentally poisonous pith out of straight stems with hot sticks to make flutes, using either portions of the tree or shrub that had died *in situ* or which have been especially removed in the spring and dried with the leaves on. This is a way to make sprouts for gathering the suger-rich sap of the maples, birches, and some other trees. Whistles for bugling in bull elk in the fall can also be fashioned the same way.

Young elderberry stems, then, have greenish bark and a thin woody shell, being mostly cylinders of whitish pith. Some of the larger of these became Indian arrows. Not only does the woodiness of these shoots increase with age, but the bark also changes, becoming more and more a greyish-brown.

The leaves, which grow opposite to one another, are made up of an uneven number of leaflets, usually from five to eleven, growing on short stalks from a single stem that is enlarged at the base. The lower of these leaflets are frequently lobed.

The clusters of pleasantly scented, star-shaped flowers vary from globular to flat-topped depending on the species. The colors of the branch-sagging, three-seeded berries developing from them differ, too, being blue, red, and amber to black.

DISTRIBUTION - Preferring rich and moist soil, elderberries grow from Alaska to Newfoundland, south throughout most of the United States to Georgia, Alabama, Florida, and California.

EDIBILITY - Bear are among the wild folk appreciating elderberries. Deer, elk, and moose browse on the twigs and foliage. Grouse, pheasants, and pigeons relish the berries, as do dozens of songbirds including cardinals, bluebirds, grosbeaks, mockingbirds, orioles, robins, tanagers, thrushes, vireos, cedar waxwings, and wrens.

There is some question about the elderberries that are red when ripe. Those I have tried have been bitterly unpleasant raw, while in Alaska digestive upsets have followed the eating of them in quantity. Although birds gobble them, they are even said by some researchers to be inedible for human beings.

The hordes of blue and blackish elderberries, some of them with an attractive bloom, are something else again even though the large majority of them are not appetizing straight off the shrubs and trees. Dried and cooked, they're very acceptable, particularly when mixed with more acid, tastier fruit. Elderberry jellies, made incidentally with added pectin, sauces, and wines are famous.

The flowers add flavor and lightness to flapjacks, muffins, and fritters.

©AJA

EVENING PRIMROSE *(Oenothera)*

FAMILY - Evening Primrose *(Onagraceae)*

OTHER NAMES - King's Cure-All, Sand Lily, Common Evening Primrose, Morning Primrose, Gumbo Primrose, German Rampion, Rock Rose.

DESCRIPTION - Keats speaks of a turf of evening primroses—one of the first American wild edibles to be introduced to Europe—disturbing all but a pleasantly sound sleep by the audible bursting of their buds into ripe flowers.

These fragrant blossoms are known to many because of their habit of opening after dusk, carrying on their reproductive functions in the dimness when their scent and light-colored hues lure the night-hovering moths upon whom they rely for fertilization. Although some of these showy but brief-lived blooms remain open in daylight, many of them shut their four broad petals toward dawn, wilt more and more for a day or two, and then drop off. Thickish, horn-like, upright capsules replace them.

Sometimes seen as a rather big white flower, becoming pink and then red with maturity, evening primroses are also yellow, with each of their four petals varying from ½ to 2 inches in length. Many of the blossoms spread close to the protecting ground, but other of the perennials become one to five feet high.

Several, showily large, pale yellow flowers group together near the top of the *Oenothera biennis,* to describe an evening primrose whose growth is wide-spread across this continent and which has long been cultivated in Europe. Where each flower meets the stalk, a leaf also grows.

Each of the quartet of wide petals is broadly notched at its outside center. Just inside each bloom is a limber ring of golden stamens, usually numbering eight. The top of the seed vessel, in the form of a green thread with four hairy divisions at its apex, runs up through the center of the blossom through what seems to be a hollow stalk. Underneath the petals are four narrow, long sepals, the modified leaves of the calyx at the outside of the flower. These usually appear in pairs, often joined lightly together at their tops, when the evening primrose blooms in late spring or early summer.

The leaves of this evening primrose, which are coarse in contrast to the delicate flower, are frailly toothed and up to about 2 inches long. Growing from the roots, they are football-to-oblong spoon-shaped.

The entire plant often bristles with fuzzy hairs that, frequently sticky, catch the dust when the distinctive edible grows beside freshly ploughed fields and along roadsides.

DISTRIBUTION - Seeking the dryness of stony slopes, well-drained steepnesses, sandy and gravelly areas, and often arid ridges up to those 1½ miles high, our native evening primroses grow from British Columbia to Newfoundland, southward throughout most of the United States.

EDIBILITY - Mule and white-tailed deer browse cheerfully on the evening primrose from one side of the continent to the other. Pronghorn antelopes also relish the plants. In addition to devouring aphids and caterpillars, goldfinches eat the seeds. So do other birds and small rodents.

It is mainly its nutritious, tasty, somewhat nutlike roots that are eaten by Americans, Canadians, and some Europeans. These are generally boiled by themselves or in stews. They are really good only the first year, before the plant blossoms. Their growth varies with the climate, as do the times in spring, summer, and fall when they are at their mildest best. Some local experimenting, for this reason, is generally necessary.

It's well worth the while, however, for peeled and then simmered in two changes of salted water, these stoutly branching roots when at their best quickly explain why the evening primrose, first exported to Europe about the start of the seventeenth century, was one of the initial wild North American edibles to be sailed back to the Old World for cultivation there.

©AJA

FIREWEED *(Epilobium) (Chamaenerion)*

FAMILY - Evening Primrose *(Onagrarieae)*

OTHER NAMES - Deerhorn, *Asperge,* Wild Asparagus, Great Willow Herb, *L'herbe Fret,* Blooming Sally, Willowweed.

DESCRIPTION - Spikes of four-petalled flowers, each up to about an inch across, are showy and conspicuous. These are bright pink, magenta, rose, reddish, lilac-purple, and occasionally white, growing on an unbranched stalk. The loosely developing blossoms begin blooming at the bottom of the single stem and climb slowly upward, so that the lower part of the spike may be covered with long seed pods, while the middle is bright with flowers, and the top is still budding.

The profusion of pods later become shaggy and bulging with numerous tiny seeds, each of which grows a white, fluffy parachute of long silken hairs that, caught up by the wind, fill air and streams in the autumn.

The lancehead-shaped, green leaves that cover these ordinarily undivided stems, from one to about eight feet in height and taller in moist and sunny locales, resemble those of the willow.

A perennial, fireweed spreads rapidly and profusely. It flowers from June through September.

DISTRIBUTION - Thousands of square miles of burned lands from the Aleutians and Greenland to Mexico brighten to amethyst from spring to fall, so attractively do these elongated perennials flame into spikelike clusters of color. Although not present in much of the eastern part of North America, fireweed is scattered throughout much of Asia and Europe except in the tropics, especially in regions disrupted by man.

EDIBILITY - The great willow herbs, as they are also known, are valuable honey flowers, and beekeepers sometimes move their hives to the vicinity of recent logging operations, woodland fires, and new wilderness roads to capitalize on them. About our log cabin in northern British Columbia, I have many times seen moose browsing on the plants. Deer, elk, roaming livestock, and even grizzly forage on fireweed, too.

Sectioned and dropped into boiling salted water to cook until easily pierced by a fork, very young fireweed stems somewhat resemble asparagus. Older stalks can be peeled and their whitish pith either eaten raw or simmered into thick soup.

The tender young leaves can be steamed or boiled into satisfactory greens. Green or dried, the leaves are also used to stretch dwindling supplies of tea and also by some to flavor this regular beverage. A wild tea can also be brewed from them alone.

© AJA

FRITILLARY *(Fritillaria)*

FAMILY - Lily *(Liliaceae)*

OTHER NAMES - Yellow Fritillary, Black Lily, Chocolate Lily, Indian Rice, Kamchatka Lily, Purple-Spot Fritillaria, Purple Fritillaria, Tiger Lily, Yellowbell, Koch, Rice Root, Mission Bells, Leopard Lily.

DESCRIPTION - It is the bulbs of these plants that are edible. While these are more or less similar, the tops differ markedly, especially in color.

For instance, there is the Black or Chocolate Lily of the North, *Fritillaria camchatcensis,* with single stems, one to two feet tall, lifting from bulbs with thick scales and numerous ricelike swellings. There are usually two or three whorls of long narrow leaves, plus a few scattered at the top. One to a half-dozen flowers nod like large bells at the tops of the plants. The colors of these vary from a dark winelike hue to a near-black tinged with yellowish-green on the outside.

Then there is the Yellow Fritillary or Yellowbell, *Fritillaria pudica,* also with a tall unbranched stem growing from a starchy bulb, whose single golden blossom, with three sepals and petals apiece, likewise has a bell-like shape. This species has up to a half-dozen narrow leaves, two to six inches tall, among and below which the blossom droops.

There are few or solitary, nodding flowers that are deep purple in *F. kamtschatcensis,* mottled with greenish-yellow in *F. lanceolata,* black or chocolate in *F. biflora* (which, despite the "two" in its name often has as many as ten blossoms), and dark purplish-brown with yellow-green spots in the pretty *F. atropurpurea* or Tiger Lily.

DISTRIBUTION - These important members of the lily family grow from Alaska, the Yukon, and British Columbia to Montana, south to New Mexico and California. They are found in open fields, ditch and creek banks, in woods that generally are well-drained in some instances and rich and damp in others, in sagebrush areas, and up to the timberline in the western mountains.

EDIBILITY - Black bears and grizzlies, including the great brown bears of the Northwest, vie with pocket gophers and ground squirrels for these starchy roots. Deer and other wild animals eat the leaves and the developing seed pods.

Tasting something like potatoes raw, more like rice when cooked, the starch-rich bulbs are nourishing and delicious, as are the tender, young, green seed pods. Where the foods of civilization have not become too prevalent, they are still enjoyed by the Eskimos for one.

Fritillary *(Fritillaria pudica)*

GLASSWORT *(Salicornia)*

FAMILY - Goosefoot *(Chenopodiaceae)*

OTHER NAMES - Bench Asparagus, Chicken Claws, Pickle Plant, Samphire, Dwarf Glasswort, Slender Glasswort, Woody Glasswort, Red Glasswort, Saltwort, Bigelow Glasswort, California Glasswort.

DESCRIPTION - Although one of the popular names of Glasswort on this continent is samphire because of its use for pickles like the samphire of Europe, it is different from this foreign coastal plant.

Many in North America are familiar with glasswort, although usually not as an edible, because of the oriental-carpetlike effect its scarlets, purples, bronzes, and tawny tans give great stretches of our salt marshes and other tidelands whether blazing bright with water-reflected sunlight or subtly subdued with fog. Other expanses enhance salty lands and alkaline mud flats rimming lakes in the western interior of the continent.

The plant is easily recognized, especially along the Pacific and Atlantic coasts, by its apparently leafless stems, usually branching from near the base, that are succulently green in summer and which are not found outside the salt lands. The generic name is descriptive in itself, *sal* being Latin for salt and *cornu* being translated as horn, giving the picture of a saline plant with horn-like stems which, indeed, the saltwort is.

Differences between the several species flourishing in North America are minor, *Salicornia europaea* or slender glasswort having joints that are longer than they are wide, for instance. On the other hand, *S. bigelovii* or dwarf glasswort boasts joints that are wider than they are long. For all practical purposes, however, the family can be described together.

Glasswort in the spring and the first part of the summer may be no more than an assemblage of green spikes, only two or three inches high, as translucent as fine green jadeite. Predominant joints appear as it continues to shoot upward, branching like a small, thin, leafless plastic Christmas fir.

Tiny opposite scales, though, are appearing at the joints as the edible's leaves. The flowers and seeds are even more difficult to find, concealed as they are beneath the nearly invisible scalelike leaves. What you see instead, most likely, are a series of succulent, jointed, cylindrical stems, around ¼ inch in diameter, lifting a few inches above shore lands that are inundated by high tides. Autumns give them their red and other brilliances, commencing where they first appear above the ground.

DISTRIBUTION - At least four species of glasswort grow in saline areas from Alaska and Labrador southward down the Pacific and Atlantic seaboards and around the Gulf of Mexico, as well as on alkaline mud flats bordering western lakes. Typical of seashores, brackish marshes, and gleaming tidal flats, these members of the beet and spinach families thrive in salty surroundings, taste salty, and appropriately are also called saltworts.

EDIBILITY - Snow and Canada geese feast on the somewhat fleshy branches of the glassworts. In the autumn the ducks, especially the pintails, eat the reddening stem tips with their nutritious seeds.

Glasswort has an especially delicate saltiness when it pokes up early in warm weather in a bed of bright green shoots, but the characteristically briny tips will still do a lot for a salad until frost-withering fall. It is also cooked as a potherb, but when so treated it loses much of its sprightliness.

Cut into tender lengths, packed in a jar or bottle, covered with boiling spiced vinegar, sealed, and let stand for at least a month, it makes conversation-provoking pickles for use as hors d'oeuvres.

GRAPE *(Vitis)*

FAMILY - Vine *(Vitaceae)*

OTHER NAMES - Fox Grape, Muscadine, Scuppernong, Plum Grape, Northern Fox Grape, Summer Grape, Small Grape, Wild Grape, Pigeon Grape, Southern Fox Grape, Bullace Grape, Blue Grape, Winter Grape, Downy Grape, Sweet Winter Grape, Chicken Grape, Sugar Grape, Mustang Grape, Arizona Grape, California Grape, Canyon Grape, Bunch Grape, Skunk Grape, Pinewood Grape, Post-Oak Grape, Turkey Grape, Frost Grape, Mountain Grape, Riverbank Grape, Bush Grape, Rock Grape, Cat Grape, Dune Grape, New England Grape, Possum Grape, Silverleaf Grape.

DESCRIPTION - At least half the world's numerous wild grapes are native to this continent, some two dozen or so species, depending on the particular botanist who's doing the classifying, being widely distributed over the U.S. and southern Canada. Favoring moist, fertile ground, they frequently twine towards sunlight along stream banks, beaches, fences, stone walls, and near the edges of woods. Birds find their dense foliage excellent sanctuary and even use the bark for some of their nests.

The various species of broad-leaved, tendril-clinging, high-climbing or trailing wild grapes, one of the survival foods of the Lewis and Clark Expedition and long an Indian mainstay throughout much of North America, include the large fox grape, the aromatic muscadine, the pleasant pigeon grape, and the notable scuppernong. Luckily, they were not disturbed by the most destructive plant louse known, the grape phylloxera which has long lived harmlessly among the wild grape vines of this continent but when accidentally transported to France nearly destroyed all the orchards there and has cost the nation tens of millions.

Our wild grapes are strong and vigorous edibles with few grave pests except for the Japanese beetle which has a serious partiality for their foliage. The various wild grape species vary in the minute characteristics of their wide leaves, the quality and quantity of their various-sized fruit, and in other details, but they all have value for both man and wildlife.

Broadly speaking, they are dark-stalked, thornless, verdant-blossoming, generally fragmented-and-shreddy barked, high-rising vines that lift themselves toward the sun on tendrils. The leaves are green, sawtoothed, heart-shaped especially those times when they draw back in deep indentations to meet the stems, and many times lobed. The color of the fruit is often white, red, amber, greenish, and black, as well as blue and dark purple. Large, frequently pear-shaped seeds are usually found inside. The buds are stubby, having a pair of scales.

DISTRIBUTION - The various species of wild grapes are widely scattered throughout southern Canada and the United States, and others have escaped from orchards. Some of the Indians used to cultivate them, and these have long ago gone wild.

EDIBILITY - Fruit, leaves, and young shoots are all edible. The roots, however, are poisonous. In the spring particularly, the sap tapped from a vine will provide a coolly refreshing drink, but this will kill that particular stem.

Although a 100-gram edible portion of North American grapes is over 81% water, it contains 69 calories, as well as 16 milligrams of calcium, 12 mg. of phosphorous, .4 mg. of iron, 3 mg. of sodium, and a rousing 158 mg. of potassium. One hundred international units of Vitamin A are present, too, along with measurable amounts of the Vitamin B complexes and 4 mg. of Vitamin C.

The fruit is a favored food of many a game bird, numerous songbirds, and some fur bearers as well, while hoofed browsers such as the deer relish the stems and foliage. Even the old, dehydrated clusters of wild grapes are sought in cold weather.

There are two satisfactory methods of securing wild grape juice for home use. For the first, wash, pick over, and stem your grapes. Have hot, sterilized jars waiting, arranged on toweling away from drafts, and have water boiling. Tip two cupfuls of wild grapes into each jar. Add a cup of sugar to each, planning to sweeten the final results more if necessary. Fill with boiling water. Seal immediately, allow to cool, label, and then store in a dark, cool place for about ten weeks before straining and using.

For the second, again wash, pick over, and stem your wild fruit. Mash the grapes in a kettle, not crushing the seeds. Cover with a minimum of water and bring to a simmer only. Heat that way for ½ hour, with only the occasional bubble plopping to the surface. Press through a sieve and then strain through a jelly bag. Season to taste with white sugar. Bring once more to a simmer, not a boil, for 15 minutes. Pour into hot, sterilized jars set on a towel, seal, cool away from drafts that might break the glass, label, and store in a dark, cool, dry area.

Wild grape jelly is luscious, being better if the majority of the fruit is on the underripe side. Then there are the conserves and the desserts like pies.

If you, too, enjoy dining occasionally at Middle East restaurants, you are likely already acquainted with the delicate acid savor that grape leaves lend to food. To use them for cooking, these should be gathered in the springtime when they have achieved their growth but are still tender. They can then be bottled in a saturated salt solution for use as you need them. Stuffed wild grape leaves, far simpler to prepare than one might imagine, are as exciting as they are exotic. For details, see *Feasting Free on Wild Edibles*.

©AJA

GREEN AMARANTH *(Amaranthus)*

FAMILY - Amaranth *(Amaranthaceae)*

OTHER NAMES - Wild Beet, Pigweed, Redroot, Amaranth.

DESCRIPTION - Every wild edible manufactures its own vitamins, and the nutritious and delicious green amaranth is rich in minerals as well. An edible 100-gram portion, as picked, contains a healthful 6,100 international units of Vitamin A. It also has 80 milligrams of Vitamin C and a multitude of B vitamins, including .08 milligrams of thiamine, .16 mg. of riboflavin, and 1.4 niacin.

Added to all these, the tender tops, stalks, and leaves of this wild spinach, which has none of the strong taste of market varieties and which is delightfully esculent from early spring to frost-blighting fall, boasts 267 mg. of calcium, 67 mg. of phosphorus, 3.9 of blood-reddening iron, and a big 411 mg. of potassium. And they're all free for the eating.

It is easy to mistake green amaranth for lamb's quarter, discussed elsewhere, although this does not make too much difference as both are almost equally delectable. But for the record, the stems and leaves of the amaranths are usually softly hairy, whereas those of the lamb's quarter or *Chenopodium* are smooth and whitely powdered. Too, the amaranths have strong, noticeable veins.

Growing as a weed over much of the continent including the tropics, the green amaranth, as well as the other edible amaranths, is familiar to most individuals although not usually as a food. The stout, rough stalks, generally unbranched, sometimes reach the height of a man, but small, tender plants can usually be found growing in the same patch. As has been suggested, even these are slightly fuzzy.

The alternately growing, dull green leaves are long-pointed ovals with wavy edges. Their stems, also edible, are nearly as long as are they themselves. The roots, the reason for the occasional name of redroot and wild beet, are attractively red. Another name is pigweed, applied because the green amaranth prefers rich, manured soil such as that found around pigpens, barns, and farm yards.

The flowers are small and greenish and, being such, are generally not recognized as blossoms. They grow, in the top angles between leafstems and stalks, in long, sometimes loosely branched, densely filled clusters. Exuding the faint, evocative scent of spring, they have a pleasant taste raw.

The resulting shiny black seeds were threshed by some of the Indians, roasted, and then used for cakes and porridge. In fact, Arizona tribes cultivated the amaranth for its seeds, over one hundred thousand of which are sometimes to be found on a single plant. Some outdoorsmen, including myself, still like to scatter a handful atop a bannock before consigning this frypan bread to the heat.

DISTRIBUTION - The amaranths grow all over the North American continent except where it is too cold.

EDIBILITY - Some of the thousands of seeds persist on their thickly clustered spikes into the winter and spring, when other foods are scarce, and are a boon to birds. The teal, dove, pheasant, and quail are among the game birds eating them. These are joined by a wide group of songbirds which include the bunting, finch, goldfinch, junco, lark, longspur, pipit, towhee, and well over a dozen different species of sparrows. Cottontails enjoy the plants.

The extremely delicate flavor of green amaranth is something many prefer to that of almost any other green. This fragility of taste lends itself to a wide range of cooking procedures. You can also influence the final results by including some less bland vegetable such as dandelions or mustard. Young green amaranth is also notable raw.

The plants do toughen and become overly bitter to many palates after they blossom.

The seeds can easily be rubbed free of their husks, then cleaned by being poured back and forth between two receptacles in a wind. The dark flour resulting from the grinding of these seeds is good for mush or for breads, waffles, hotcakes, and the like, especially if the somewhat mustily unfamiliar flavor is brought into line with the addition of store flour or cornmeal. The seeds, like the rest of the plant, are also nourishing raw.

GROUND CHERRY *(Physalis)*

FAMILY - Potato *(Solanaceae)*

OTHER NAMES - Strawberry Tomato, Tomatillo, Mexican Ground Cherry, Husk Tomato, Bladder Cherry, Poppers.

DESCRIPTION - The most outstanding individual characteristic of the ground cherry is the manner in which the small tomatolike fruit is encased, as by a lantern, in a papery husk. This balloon-resembling covering is actually the enlarged calyx, the outer series of floral leaves of the blossom which enlarge and completely cover each of the round golden berries almost like a visible stratosphere enwrapping a miniaturized world.

The yellow vegetable bladders so protect the edible fruit that even when these members of the potato family drop to the ground, they continue to sweeten and ripen safely inside. In fact, if they are picked too soon to be at their most delicious, they can be left encased to lose their unpleasantly strong green flavor and to mature properly.

The striking flowers, which have helped make one hardy perennial of the genus, the Chinese lantern plant or winter cherry, popular in many a flower garden, resemble tiny, dark-centered, golden bells soon after they form prolifically in the axils. Each has five closely grouped stamens, like a multiheaded clapper.

The branching or sometimes unbranched perennials grow close to the ground over which they rapidly sprawl, seldom rising much more than a foot high but usually spreading several times that distance. The rather sharply tipped, dark green, sometimes toothed, often unevenly fissured leaves are generally egg-shaped and one to three inches long. Several species of ground cherry are softly and delicately hairy.

DISTRIBUTION - Ground cherries, closely related to the tomato but not even distant cousins of the cherry family, grow in southern Canada and in all parts of the U.S. except Alaska. Escaping from a number of localities where some species are raised commercially, they spring up and mature speedily in fields, open country, deserted farmyards, waste areas, and especially in newly cleared and cultivated ground, where they ripen from July through September.

EDIBILITY - The fruit of the ground cherry is enjoyed by pheasants, quail, turkey, opossums, and even by tiny wood mice.

What you don't eat raw make excellent pies, sauces, preserves, and jams.

©AJA

GROUNDNUT *(Apios)*

FAMILY - Pea *(Leguminosae)*

OTHER NAMES - Indian Potato, Wild Bean, Bog Potato, Potato Bean, Hopniss.

DESCRIPTION - Asa Gray, the noted botanist, once opined that if civilization had started in the New World rather than the Old, the little groundnut would have been the first tuber to have been cultivated as a food. Many trying it for the first time do like it better than the modern potato. Although it is edible raw, the secret is that when it is cooked to eat, it should be eaten hot, as it loses both tenderness and taste when cold. It can be successfully rewarmed, however, as when buttered and roasted.

Known in some regions as the wild bean, this edible is a climbing and twining perennial with alternate compound leaves, made up of three to seven or nine broadly oval, sharply pointed, roundly based, leaflets, each one to three inches long, arranged on either side of a common leafstalk.

If the wind is right, you can smell the lushy, heady fragrance of the maroon to chocolate blossoms long before you discover the vine, where it is perhaps climbing a bush. The numerous velvety, pealike, often brownish-purple flowers are grouped in short, thick clusters in the angles between the leaves and soft stems which have a milky sap. Each individual bloom is some ½ inch in diameter and formed like that of a pea or bean. One of the ten stamens stands apart prominently.

As with other members of the pea family, the fruit is a beanlike pod, in this instance slim, almost straight, pointed, and some two or three inches long. When you can gather sufficient of them, the seeds inside can be cooked in salted water like peas.

The rootstocks have tuberous enlargements, some as big as eggs and others no more than an inch long, connected by fibrous strands a great deal like beads strung on a necklace. These take more than one season to develop fully, one of the characteristics that balked Europeans trying to make the groundnut a garden vegetable.

Lying in strings just beneath the surface, these can be easily uncovered, perhaps with the help of a sharp stick, unless the ground under the then dryly white vines is frozen.

DISTRIBUTION - Requiring damp but not wet soil, the groundnuts are selective in the moist woods and bottomlands where they grow from the Maritime Provinces to North Dakota, south to Florida, and west to Colorado and New Mexico, often as smooth slender vines, four to eleven feet long, along the rims of ponds, swamps, and marshes.

EDIBILITY - The Pilgrims, introduced to the groundnut by friendly Massachusetts Indians, depended on them to a large extent their first rugged winter in Plymouth. Other Indians along the Eastern Seaboard in particular regularly ate these potatolike vegetables. They thus became familiar to early European settlers, many of whom found the tubers very acceptable substitutes for bread. The beanlike seeds when you can find enough of them, are also edible.

HACKBERRY *(Celtis)*

FAMILY - Elm *(Ulmus)*

OTHER NAMES - Sugarberry, Nettle Tree, Honeyberry, Western Hackberry, Thick-Leaved Hackberry, Southern Hackberry, Rough-Leaved Hackberry, Bastard Elm, Hoop Ash, Upland Huckberry, Hacktree, Georgia Hackberry, Mississippi Hackberry, Desert Hackberry.

DESCRIPTION - Homer asserted that the thin, sugary pulp of the hackberry proved so delectable to the ancients that those who ate it forgot their native countries. The additional names of sugarberry and honeyberry tend somewhat to support this assertion.

The hackberries, shrubs or small trees from twenty to occasionally one hundred feet high, have one characteristic found in only a few of the trees native to this continent, such as the black walnut and the butternut which we have considered elsewhere. Its pith is chambered. That is, if you split a twig lengthwise, you'll see the pith as a series of white partitions that separate empty compartments.

Distinctive, too, is the fact that the smoothish light-grey bark becomes rough with dark, warty, corklike bumps and ridges. Typical, also, is the fact that the foliage is generally roughly hairy on top, although it is smooth in two widespread varieties, *Celtis canina* and *C. pumila*.

The leaves are unsymmetrical, being lopsided at their bases. Three prominent veins run from the top of the short stem. The leaves are long-pointed, alternate, single, and either smooth or coarsely toothed along their edges. Although the twigs are hairless, the bud scales are hirsute, the end buds being false. There are seldom more than a trio of bundle scars, the spots where the bundles of nerves to the leaves left the twigs.

The April and May flowers are greenly inconspicuous, followed by oval or rounded fruits that are actually orange-brown or purplish drupes, each consisting of sweet and thin pulp surrounding a large, round seed.

Two other characteristics distinguish the hackberry. It is subject to witch broom and abnormally swollen buds, caused by the sting of tiny mites called *Eriophyes*. The first of these disfigurements, dense clusters of twigs that may be scattered through the crowns in large numbers, make it frequently possible to recognize this tree at a great distance. Too, in the Southwest it is common to find hackberries filled with the common mistletoe, the parasitic plant so widely used for Christmas decorations.

DISTRIBUTION - These trees and shrubs range over a large proportion of the continent in habitats varying from swampy, wet areas and stream banks to rich, rocky hillsides and hardwood forests. Too, they are frequently planted for shade and decoration.

EDIBILITY - Cedar waxwings flit among the branches of the hackberries so long as the last frost-sweetened drupe remains. Such upland game birds as quail, wild turkeys, pigeons, and doves become more toothsome on a similar diet. So do beaver, raccoon, opossum, and squirrel. Both mule and white-tailed deer browse on the twigs and foliage.

Ripening in September and October but often persisting on the branches until well into the winter and becoming even more sweet with cold weather, hackberries although dry will pleasantly take the edge off hunger. The drupes were Indian favorites.

Some of these redmen pounded the dried pits into fine bits and used them to flavor their venison and other meat. The white kernels, exposed by cracking their chalky outer shells, are sweet and somewhat datelike in flavor.

© AJA

HAWTHORN (Crataegus)

FAMILY - Rose *(Rosaceae)*

OTHER NAMES - Haw, Thorn Plum, Thorn Apple, Red Haw, River Hawthorn, Thornbush, Western Black Hawthorn, Mayhaw, Thorn, Hagthorn, White Thorn, Scarlet Haws, Cockspur Thorn.

DESCRIPTION - The 1- to 5-inch long, undivided, straight or moderately curved thorns of the hawthorn are not shared by any of our other native shrubs or trees. Although readily distinguished as a genus, the numerous species are difficult in the extreme to differentiate among, although this is not too important to the individual seeking wild food. The fruit of all is edible, although it does differ greatly in quality when eaten raw.

Hawthorns apparently got their start in the underneaths of North America's virgin forests. With fires and with the clearing of dominant trees by advancing civilization, they were freed and ran wild, being abundant today in many clearings, along woodland rims, in deserted fields, in moist ground along ponds and streams, pampered in gardens, and wild and free as high as a mile-and-a-half in the mountains. As can be seen, they like the sun. Thriving in thickets as they often do, their autumnal rednesses often color large portions of countryside.

Depending on whether the botanist is a lumper or a splitter, these able professionals recognize from about one hundred to as many as twelve hundred separate species in the United States alone, hybrids being numerous.

The thorns, though, distinctively characterize these members of the apple family even in winter. Then the somewhat curving twigs are slender, round, set apart by a series of short sharp angles, and frequently lustrous. The scars left by the leaves look like narrow crescents, each with three marks on it. The buds, located on the twigs, are very important in making winter identification. Small and roundish or somewhat ovoid with the broad end toward the top, they are mainly smooth and reddish or bright chestnut in hue. Each has some six exposed scales.

This showy cousin of the rose grows alternate, singular, lobed or toothed leaves. Characteristically, it always has stiff, sharp thorns on stems and branches. These, incidentally, are actually modified plant stems instead of being related to the leaf growth as in much other vegetation. They often so protect the crown of the shrub or small tree that it becomes a favorite nest nook for small birds.

The spectacular white and occasionally pinkish flowers, each with a sweet-smelling perfection of five sepals and petals and numerous stamens, generally burst into flattish, terminal clusters with the central blossoms blooming.

The fruit, ordinarily reddish but sometimes yellow and very occasionally black or bluish, looks like tiny apples, especially as each is conspicuously tipped with the remains of the outer floral leaves. Each of the actually closely related pomes contains from one to five hard, bony, single-seeded nutlets. Dryish or pulpy flesh, often with a high sugar but low fat and protein content, surrounds these.

DISTRIBUTION - Hawthorns grow from coast to coast across southern Canada and the contiguous states, from low sunny lands to about 8,500 feet in the mountains.

EDIBILITY - Robins, grosbeaks, sparrows, woodpeckers, and cedar waxwings are among the smaller birds feasting on the haws which are valuable to wildlife not only in season, but when, dried or frozen, they continue to cling to the branches during the hungry wintertime. Grouse, pheasants, pigeons, and the smart wild turkeys eat the fruit and buds. Cottontails hop into hard-to-penetrate hawthorn thickets for both cover and food. Bears, with their thick protective fur, devour the fruit by the mouthful. Mule and white-tailed deer consume foliage, twigs, and fruit, and the rodents of the woodlands seek the seeds.

The Indians gathered vast quantities of the fruit, eating some fresh when it was particularly platable and drying the rest for mixing with pemmican as a flavoring agent and eating this either winters or for trail rations.

The early Europeans settling on these shores and ever spreading into the interior picked it for jams, marmalades, and jellies as is still done today. Unless the haws are too ripe, they contain sufficient natural pectin for this latter purpose.

Taste differs greatly, however, and the only way to determine the palatableness of the particular fruit you've come across is by sampling it. The better of these thorn apples are sugary raw and when transformed into jelly, if any are left for this purpose, require very little artificial sweetening.

©AJA

HAZELNUT *(Corylus)*

FAMILY - Birch *(Betulaceae)*

OTHER NAMES - Filbert, American Hazelnut, Beaked Hazelnut.

DESCRIPTION - The three native varieties of this multibranched shrub are much alike, although the nuts vary some. Those of the *Corylus Americana,* growing in open husks, have brown shells that are generally thick and hard. The beaked hazelnut, also of the East, has an exceedingly bristly husk that, instead of likewise flaring at the top, is contracted into a long neck about 1½ inches in length. The shell of this nut is more whitish-brown and is comparatively thin. The nuts of the California species are larger but similar.

The so-called American hazelnut, the first of the above-mentioned species and also called the filbert, is a shrub with wide, alternate, short-stemmed, 2- to 5-inch-long, sort of heart-shaped leaves with double teeth. The widely spreading branches reach a height of six or seven to ten feet. Both the twigs and the leafstalks are hairy.

The buds, each of which has several scales, are blunt, the end buds being false. Slender catkins, which sway in the breezes, make their appearance in the early spring before the new leaves burst forth, appearing singly in the angles between the branches and the previous year's leaves. The inconspicuous fertile flowers show up in the scaly buds near the tips of the branches. The brown nuts, which are ½ to ¾ of an inch long and enwrapped in a downy whorl of two leaflike bracts whose edges are fringed, are usually sweet and ripe in August and if not bothered, which is unlikely, cling to the shrubs until late in the autumn.

The beaked hazelnuts have ordinarily hairless twigs and not as many bud scales, the lower of these being large and paired. Bristly husks, lengthened to form a beak, enclose the delicious nuts.

DISTRIBUTION - Three species of hazelnuts are natives of the United States and Canada. Two grow in the East, making these wild edibles available from Newfoundland all the way across the Dominion of Canada to British Columbia, south to Georgia, Tennessee, and Florida. Another grows in the mountains of California. The low-spreading thickness of hazelnut bushes provides useful cover and nesting sites whenever these thickets occur along streams, woodland edges, pasture slopes, fences, and roadsides.

EDIBILITY - Squirrels, chipmunks, and other rodents feast on the nuts. Grouse pick off the catkins, while deer, moose, and rabbits browse on the plants themselves.

Hazelnuts, treats by themselves, go well with cookies, candies, and other delicately flavored delights. If you should wish to remove the inner skin from the nuts, this can be done without softening them. Just spread the hazelnuts in a pan and heat in a moderately warm oven twenty to thirty minutes. Do not brown. Let them cool. Then rub off the loosened hides with a towel.

©AJA

Hazelnut (*Corylus Americana*) above; Beaked Hazelnut (below)

HICKORY *(Carya)*

FAMILY - Walnut *(Juglandaceae)*

OTHER NAMES - Shagbark Hickory, Pecan, Water Hickory, Pignut Hickory, Black Hickory, Mannock Hickory, Sweet Pignut Hickory, Brown Hickory, Pale Hickory, White Heart Hickory, Mockernut Hickory, Nutmeg Hickory, Sand Hickory, Bitternut Hickory, Shellbark Hickory, Bottom Shellbark, Coast Pignut Hickory, Kingnut Hickory, Bullnut.

DESCRIPTION - Hickories are likely our most important native nuts. The Indians used them in great quantities. The colonists soon followed suit, even to tapping the sweet sap in the springtime for syrup. The crushed green nutshells of these, too, can be used in an emergency, as when survival is at stake, for the otherwise illegal and unsporting poisoning of fish for food.

Hickories can be distinguished from their close cousins, the walnut, by the following characteristics. The pith of the twigs is continuous in hickories, chambered in walnuts. Hickory nuts are smooth or ridged, whereas walnuts are rough and sculptured. The husk of the nuts splits into parts, whereas walnut meats remain intact. The tassels of the pollen-carrying blossoms of the hickories are stalked, flexible, slender, and occur in threes. In walnuts, they are unstemmed, compact, thin, and grow singly. The wood of the hickories is white to reddish-brown, with big pores arranged in rings with a common center. Walnut wood is light to dark brown, and the pores are divided somewhat evenly throughout the growth ring.

The shellbark hickory, also known as the shagbark, is the leader of the group. All hickories produce edible nuts, however, although the taste of some is not appealing. There are the sweet hickories, including the above, in which the husks split into four parts when the nuts are ripe. There are the pignuts, often bitter but sometimes delicious, in which the thin husk splits only above the middle or sometimes, late in season, all the way to the base. There are also the familiar pecans.

The stout twigs and the grey bark which loosens in shaggy narrow strips, attached at the middle, distinguish the shellbark and the shagbark, actually two different trees. The leaves, from seven to fourteen inches long, are composed of usually five but sometimes seven leaflets, the one on the end being the biggest. The shellbark usually has more leaflets than the shagbark, twigs that are lighter in color, and a thicker nutshell. Dark yellowish-green above, the leaves of both are lighter and often downy underneath, with fine sharp teeth marking the edges.

Hickories grow slowly, sometimes reaching an age of 250 years, and the shellbark does not produce nuts until about eighty years old. It becomes a large stately tree, attaining a height of up to 180 or more feet and a trunk diameter from one to three feet. Its wood is used for such outdoor implements as bows, skiis, and axe handles, while hickory-smoked hams and bacon are famous.

The shellbark, which leafs out later than most other trees and sheds its brown foliage earlier, has egg-shaped nuts ranging from an inch to nearly 2½ inches long, thick-husked, and angled but not ridged. The whitish nutshell is over ⅛ inch thick.

Hickory leaves are fragrant when crushed. The flowers come out with the leaves in the spring. Both the male and female blossoms grow on the same tree. The pollen is borne by the breezes.

The shellbark may be picked out from the other hickories in winter by its extremely stout, yellowish-red to orange-brown twigs which are rather downy and covered with tiny, orange-hued pores. The big leaf scars are somewhat three-lobed or heart-shaped. The terminal bud, covered with several dark, triangular, persistent outer scales, is about an inch long.

DISTRIBUTION - The hickories are typically North American trees. The pecan, for example, is a native of the south-central U.S., north as far as Illinois and Indiana but now widely escaped from cultivation in our southern States. The shagbark hickory extends its range from Quebec and Maine, south to Texas and Florida. The shellbark hickory grows from New York and Nebraska, south to North Carolina, Alabama, Mississippi, and Oklahoma.

EDIBILITY - Wood ducks, ring-necked pheasants, bobwhites, and the wary wild turkeys compete with man for the nuts. Black bears, raccoons, squirrels, and rabbits eat both the nuts and the bark, while the white-tailed deer relishes both these and the younger twigs it can reach.

The name hickory comes from the Indian name for a liquor that was concocted by pounding the shells and kernels of the sweet nuts in a mortar until they were powdered, at which time water was poured in and the action continued until a milky, oily meal remained.

You can have a happy time with a pocketful of hickory nuts and just a stone or hammer. But the pleasant, slightly aromatic kernels also excel in the kitchen, both with vegetables and in desserts.

Hickory nuts are very nutritious, 100 grams of the kernels yielding 673 calories, over 13 grams of protein and more than 68 grams of fat, plus a whopping 360 milligrams of phosphorous.

Shellbark (shagbark) Hickory

HIGHBUSH CRANBERRY *(Viburnum)*

FAMILY - Honeysuckle *(Caprifoliaceae)*

OTHER NAMES - Squashberry, Cranberry Bush, Cranberry Tree, Mooseberry, Pimbina.

DESCRIPTION - Despite the name a cousin of the elderberry rather than the familiar cranberry, this member of the honeysuckle family is easy for anyone to identify even blindfolded by its distinctive, not unpleasant musky odor. The flavor, too, is characteristically sweetish-sour and usually requires a conditioned palate. But come to like it and nothing satisfies the thirst quite so well.

The usually rather straggly but attractive shrubs grow up to about 8 feet tall. The branches are slim and grey. The leaves, which come out opposite one another, are mostly maple-shaped, with three short and often uneven lobes. Like those of the maple, they become brilliant in the autumn. Although they all have irregular, coarse teeth and some three to five main veins meeting near the base, some are not lobed at all. Most of them are some two to four inches across.

The berries, red or orangish, grow from white flowers in juicy, easily gathered flat clusters at the ends of the branches, whose raw flavor becomes mellower as they age. Actually drupes, each contains a single large, smooth, flat seed.

DISTRIBUTION - Highbush cranberries grow from Alaska to Labrador and Newfoundland, south through Canada and the northern States.

EDIBILITY - Moose and deer browse on these shrubs. Bear gorge themselves on the fruit, also eaten by fox, squirrels, and chipmunks. Grouse, pheasants, and turkeys are among the upland game birds seeking the fruit, also enjoyed by such songbirds as cardinals, robins, starlings, thrashers, thrushes, and the voracious cedar waxwings.

Shriveling but remaining on the branches all winter, the unmistakable fruit can be an important survival fruit in numerous Northern regions. Too, once one has acquired a taste for these distinctively flavored berries, a frozen cluster melting on the tongue like sherbet is an unforgettable taste treat.

Highbush cranberries are most famous for the sparklingly beautiful, salmon-red, perfectly textured, uniquely flavored jelly they produce when gathered just before the first freeze, while still firm and about half-ripe. The only other ingredients needed are water and sugar.

The fruit is rich in Vitamin C, containing about 30 milligrams of ascorbic acid per 100 grams, according to tests conducted by the Alaska Department of Health.

©AJA

HORSERADISH *(Armoracia)*

FAMILY - Mustard *(Cruciferae)*

OTHER NAMES - Red Cole, Wild Horseradish, Sting Nose.

DESCRIPTION - The tiny white blossoms of the horseradish, like those of the other members of the tasty mustard family, have just four petals in the form of a cross. They also boast four long and two short stamens. These flowers grow in loosely branched, short-stemmed clusters. Although seeds are not very often produced, there are the occasional roundly egg-shaped pods, each of which is divided into two cells with perhaps four to six seeds in each.

Numerous very large leaves grow from the white roots on strong, long stalks. These green leaves, often six inches wide and nearly twice as long, have wavy, scalloped edges. The much smaller, stemless leaves that grow directly from a smooth, round, erect, central spike, often several feet long, are oblong and serrated.

The fleshy roots, sometimes as long as a foot and as thick as one or two inches, are tapering, conical at the top, and many times abruptly branched near the end. They are white, both within and without. When scraped or bruised, they give off a strongly pungent odor. When a particle is transferred to the tongue, it is immediately hot and biting.

DISTRIBUTION - The perennial horseradish, regrowing in the same places for dozens of years and spreading where there is sufficient moisture, came to the New World from England. Originally planted about the cabins of the northeastern United States and southern Canada, it has thrived and dispersed until it now grows wild throughout much of the same general area.

EDIBILITY - The leaves when tender in the spring make greens that are tastier than most when dropped into a small amount of boiling salted water, cooked uncovered only until tender, and then served immediately with a crowning pat of butter or margarine. Caught young enough, they are also good raw.

But it is for its heartily peppery, raw roots that horseradish has been famous for thousands of years. There is little comparison between the freshly grated horseradish you can prepare yourself, using the wild roots and lemon juice instead of the commonly employed wine vinegar, and that from a store. Mouth-tickling horseradish, popular the world over, has been used for food seasoning for centuries.

There are innumerable refinements to the preparation of this masterful condiment, the easiest of which is to add by taste a small amount of sugar to the original mixture. In any event, for the most pleasing results make only small amounts of the sauce at one time, an easy thing to do as horseradish roots can be freshly gathered much of the year, except when the ground is frozen too hard.

Keep the sauce covered when not in use, preferably in a tightly closed jar or bottle. You may well want to keep this in the refrigerator. For best results, however, it should be allowed to return to room temperature before being used. Otherwise, some of its taste-tingling piquancy will be trapped by cold, and more will have to be used to achieve the same result.

Grated horseradish and sour cream make a combination that really brings out the flavor of meats. Freshly grated horseradish will also do much for sandwiches and for crisp small crackers—tidbits that will arouse the appetite even more if decorated with slices of pimento-stuffed olives.

Horseradish is also nutritious, there being 87 calories to 100 grams of the raw roots, plus 140 miligrams of calcium, 64 mg. of phosphorous, 1.4 mg. of iron, and a big 564 mg. of potassium. There are also 81 milligrams of the necessary ascorbic acid that the body can't store.

Besides enjoying horseradish roots and leaves, pioneers used to apply the freshly scraped roots externally as they would mustard plasters. Horseradish was also used as an internal medicine, a teaspoon of the grated root to a cup of boiling water. This was allowed to cool. One or two cupfuls were then drunk throughout the day, several sips at a time, as a stimulant to the stomach.

©AJA

ICELAND MOSS *(Cetraria)*

FAMILY - Iceland Moss *(Parmeliaceae)*

OTHER NAMES - Lichen, Caribou Moss.

DESCRIPTION - Icelanders say that by virtue of Iceland moss a munificent Heaven has provided them with bread from the very rocks. In Iceland, northern Europe, and across the treeless top of Alaska and Canada it has kept actual thousands of people from starving. It grows down into our contiguous States where it is equally nourishing.

Iceland moss, one of the edible lichens, consists of a fungus and an alga that form one of the most primitive and certainly one of the oldest plants on our earth. In the Arctic, Iceland moss and the other limited lichens there are a major part of the tundra flora on which the Far Northern browsers depend for most of their food. Too, bits of the lichens are commonly used in the nests of the wood pewee, the swift little hummingbird, and the blue-grey gnatcatcher. These perhaps most ancient of all plants are pioneers in soil manufacture. The organic acids they produce with the help of fog, rain, and snow and the minerals in stones help to decompose the rocks on which many of them grow. All in all, their importance cannot be overemphasized.

Iceland moss is a low, mosslike plant with a structure of branching stems in place of leaves. Forming tufts and tangled masses on the ground, it grows some two to four inches tall. Forking and branching freely, it is variously colored brown and greyish white to reddish.

From the odorless mats formed by this highly edible lichen arise numerous stalks, the majority of them being thin, flattened, and less than 1/10 inch wide. The upper surfaces of these are generally smooth, with wrinkles or channels toward the base. The stalks roll in at the edges, forming funnel-like tubes which terminate in flattened lobes with finely toothed edges. The spores, or fruits, when present grow mainly along the edges of the lobes.

Iceland moss has a marked rubbery texture during the summer. In winter, the cold and the wind dehydrate the plants to brittleness. Upon soaking, they regain their rubbery characteristic.

Another vital edible lichen is reindeer moss—*Cladonia rangiferina* of the reindeer lichen or *Cladoniaceae* family—which is also an important food of the caribou and reindeer and is similarly prepared and used for human consumption. This grows in carpetlike masses, sometimes a foot or more across. Sponge-shaped, reindeer moss has 2-to-4-inch high stalks that fork or branch in greyish-white or silvery pairs, with the majority of the tips drooping downward. The older stalks sometimes become suffused with tiny wartlike granules.

DISTRIBUTION - The invaluable Iceland moss grows across the roofs of Alaska and Canada, well above the tree line, throughout Canada, and across our northern States down into New Jersey, Pennsylvania, and the high country of North Carolina.

EDIBILITY - In the southern part of its range Iceland moss is eaten by moose, deer, elk, and grouse. In the Arctic realms it is one of the main foods of such widely ranging browsers as the reindeer and caribou, and to a lesser extent other herbivorous animals.

These lichens may play an important part in the opening of our Far North. In the northern European countries Iceland moss and several kinds of reindeer moss are harvested commercially and used extensively during the long winter months as fodder not only for reindeer but also for cattle, horses, sheep, pigs, and goats. When harvested commercially, the dry lichen is compressed and shipped in 100-pound bales. When it is to be used, hot water is poured over the lichen which, when sprinkled with salt, becomes a favorite fodder.

Like most others, this lichen must be soaked in water before it is edible by humans, this because of bitter organic acids that assist in decomposing the very rocks upon which many of them grow and which establish them as pioneers in soil manufacture. Otherwise, the unpleasantly acrid irritants are apt to cause severe intestinal discomfort.

These acids can be removed easily enough by soaking the Iceland moss in two changes of water, preferably with a teaspoon of baking soda added if you're where this is handy. Then drain it, dry it, and finally crush and pound it into a powder. The result is so digestible that it is sold in some drugstores as a nutritive for invalids and convalescents.

When simmered with milk or water, this powder forms a jelly-like gruel that becomes firm upon cooling. The soaked lichen is added, too, to soups and stews. You can also use it, either as is or mixed about half and half with wheat flour or cornmeal, to make breadstuffs.

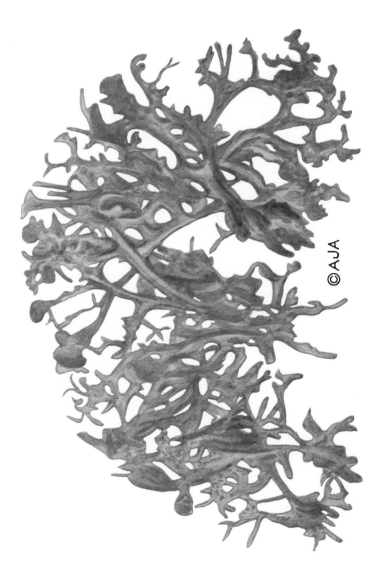

©AJA

IRISH MOSS (Chondrus)

FAMILY - Red Algae *(Rhodophyceae)*

OTHER NAMES - Sea Moss, Curly Moss, Jelly Moss, Pearl Moss, Carrageen Moss, Lichen.

DESCRIPTION - Irish moss is naturally on the red side, being also brownish, purplish, blackish, and greenish. Attached to submerged rocks by small disks, it consists of flat, cartilaginous, forked stems or fronds up to about a foot across but more usually about half that length and in such freely dividing quantities that, not looking anything like a moss individually, a mass of the plants in a tidal pool does resemble a bed of moss superficially.

Also known as sea moss, pearl moss, curly moss, and jelly moss, this marine alga was widely gathered and sometimes kept for years by those of our forefathers who early settled along the Atlantic Coast. Clinging to underwater rocks and ledges, it is gathered during low tides. Irish moss that has been cast up along the shore by the waves can also be harvested, often already bleached by the sun. Commercial processors do bleach their products in the sunlight to a creamy white. However, the natural, dark Irish moss has even more vitamins.

Replete in such valuable elements as sodium, phosphorous, magnesium, copper, calcium, potassium, chlorine, and sulphur, this starchy seaweed is also an excellent source of iodine. Furthermore, it is so digestible that it is recommended for convalescents. As if all that weren't enough, it is good the year around.

DISTRIBUTION - Irish moss is familiar along the eastern shores of this continent from the Carolinas to Labrador as well as in Europe, where on both sides of the world it has been eaten for centuries.

EDIBILITY - Scientists are finding a rich and nearly inexhaustible store of foods in the oceans that cover almost three-fourths of the globe's surface. Not the least of these is Irish moss, familiar to the eastern shores of North America as well as in Europe, where it has been enjoyed since ancient times.

It is extremely nourishing, a 100-gram edible portion containing only 19.2% water. There are also 1.8 grams of fat, 2.1 of fiber, and 17.6 of ash. This same tidbit will give you 885 milligrams of calcium, 157 mg. of phosphorous, 8.9 mg. of iron, and ultra-rich quantities of both sodium and potassium, 2,892 mg. of the first and an almost equal 2,844 mg. of the second.

Although it has a rather pleasant mucilaginous, saline taste, it is too tough to eat raw. Drying this particular seaweed makes it almost bonelike.

But just a small amount of boiling, after it has been well washed in fresh water, will tenderize it. It can then be eaten in a number of ways. It is just the extract that is commonly used. However, a handful cut up and cooked with a soup or stew makes a tasty and thickening additive. Soup made from Irish moss and fresh water alone, or the jelly that this forms upon cooling, is a palatable and nourishing emergency food.

Irish moss, as well as being nutritious, is also soothing to the digestive tract, and it used to be considered useful in allaying diarrhea. The dose was one teaspoon of the dried plant in a cup of boiling water, drunk cold one or two cupfuls a day, several sips at a time.

Irish moss lemonade is still brewed in some parts of the country for anyone who is suffering from a cold or flu. To make a quart of this, start by soaking ½ cup of the seaweed until soft in enough water to cover. Then drain, add the moss and a quart of boiling water to the top of a double boiler, and simmer about ½ hour until the sea moss, as it is also called, has dissolved. Strain, add the juice of two fresh lemons, sweeten to taste, and share with your patient.

Blancmange can be a treat for both invalid and gourmet. Properly, you'll need the bleached variety for this. Wash the moss well to remove any sand, and in this instance pick out any discolored pieces. Add the remainder to a quart of milk in the top of a double boiler and cook ½ hour. Then strain. Flavor to taste with salt, sugar, and one of the extracts such as vanilla. Pour into molds that have been immersed in cold water. Set aside, perhaps in the refrigerator, to become firm. Many like this with cream and sliced, sweetened, Vitamin-C-replete oranges.

JACK-IN-THE PULPIT *(Arisaema)*

FAMILY - Arum *(Araceae)*

OTHER NAMES - Indian Turnip, Wake-Robin, Dragonroot, Starch Plant, Memory Root, Wild Turnip, American Arum, Woodland Jack-in-the-Pulpit, Swamp Jack-in-the-Pulpit, Small Jack-in-the-Pulpit, Northern Jack-in-the-Pulpit.

DESCRIPTION - In the moist, sequestered woodlands of April and May, the jack-in-the-pulpit preaches his silent sermon to a congregation of wild violets and other spring neighbors. Unmistakable, the brown, purplish, and green "pulpit" is a striped 2- to 4-inch spathe, terminating with a hood over the top. The "preacher" is a clublike spadix, two or three inches long, with small greenish flowers, occasionally varying greatly in hues and in brightness, near its base. Male and female blossoms are often on separate plants.

The plant becomes from one to three feet high. Its pair of leaves, growing on long individual stems, are each composed of three egg-shaped, sometimes lobed, pointed leaflets. Green clusters of berries become handsome scarlet masses that brighten the dark woods in late August.

There are differences, which some experts look upon as varieties of a single species. In any event, all parts of the plant, especially the round roots, will burn the mouth like liquid fire if eaten raw. Many country youngsters used to have a standard ceremony of initiating city boys to town, and perhaps still do. This consisted of offering the greenhorn the tiniest morsel of what they claimed was the finest delicacy the local woods had to offer. At the first contact, this innocent-looking tidbit was palatable enough. But then the taste became as bitingly hot as a teaspoon of red pepper. This burning sensation, which was followed by inflammation and tenderness, seemed to permeate every part of the tongue, mouth, and throat and to linger for hours, although cold milk did appear to allay it some.

DISTRIBUTION - This North and South American member of the great arum family grows in rich woods from the Maritime Provinces to Florida, west to Minnesota and Louisiana.

EDIBILITY - Both the bright red fruit and the leaves are eaten by the ring-necked pheasant and the wild turkey. The wood thrush devours the fruit.

Many Indians relied on the dried and powdered roots of the familiar jack-in-the-pulpit for flour. The wonder is that aborigines the world over have learned to rid arum roots of their corrosive acridness and thus capitalize upon their nutritious, delicate, white starchiness.

Boiling won't do it! Drying will. The fastest way to do this is by roasting. The simplest method is just to cut the fresh roots into very thin slices, then set these aside in a dry place for upwards of 3 months. They then provide pleasant snacks, either as is or with a potato-chip dip. Or you can crumble the crisp slices into flour and use it in regular recipes, most satisfactorily half and half with wheat flour, to make special delicacies.

©AJA

JERUSALEM ARTICHOKE *(Helianthus)*

FAMILY - Composite *(Compositae)*

OTHER NAMES - Sunflower Artichoke, Earth Apple, Sunflower Root, Canada Potato, Wild Sunflower.

DESCRIPTION - This native of North America is a large perennial sunflower, often growing in congested clusters. Slender and branched 6 to 10 feet tall, it has narrower and more sharply tipped leaves than most of the other wild Sunflowers. The lower of these often grow opposite one another, but the upper leaves are more frequently alternate, occasionally in whorls of three. Shaped like jagged lanceheads, they are thick, broadly based, rough, and hard. Their stems are apt to be coarsely hairy.

Characteristic are numerous flower heads, two to three inches in diameter, which are lighter yellow than most other wild sunflower blossoms and which lack the brownish and purplish centers of these latter where develop the edible, oil-rich seeds. The yellowish Jerusalem artichoke disks are very much smaller. What this wild edible looks like above ground is more than compensated for, however, by slender flattish, medium-size tubers that are potatolike in appearance and that bulge from a thickly creeping root system.

They lack any connection with the Holy City. Sent back to Europe by the early settlers who found the Indians using the tubers and soon followed suit, the edibles became popular along the Mediterranean where they were known as *girasol* in Spain and *girasole* in Italy. These names, referring to the sun, became changed in English to Jerusalem. The artichoke part of the title arose from the circumstances that even centuries ago the flower buds of some of the edible sunflowers were boiled and eaten with butter like that vegetable.

DISTRIBUTION - Liking damp but not wet ground, Jerusalem artichokes grow along roads, ditches, streams, paths, and fences and in abandoned fields and other wastelands from Saskatchewan to Ontario, south to Kansas and Georgia. Formerly cultivated in the East by the Indians and later the settlers, it has widely escaped and grows wild throughout much of this area, as well as in widely scattered parts of the U.S. for the same reason.

EDIBILITY - Root-eating animals such as the prairie dog and the groundhog seek these tubers.

They should not be dug until after the first frosts of fall. Sought here then by the Indians and later the colonists, they took the place for years in the New World of the later popularized potato. They are still regarded as a favored, sweetly flavored food for invalids to whom other vegetables are denied.

A simple method of preparation is scrubbed, simmered in their skins in enough water to cover until just tender, then peeled, and served either with salt and butter or with a cream sauce. Or peel, oil, and roast. They are also turned into pickles and pies and are edible raw.

©AJA

JUNIPER *(Juniperus)*

FAMILY - Pine *(Pinaceae)*

OTHER NAMES - California Juniper, Red Juniper, Ground Juniper, Common Juniper, Western Juniper, Mountain Juniper, Savin, Dwarf Juniper, Red Cedar, Mexican Juniper, Trailing Juniper.

DESCRIPTION - These evergreen trees and shrubs, members of the widespread pine family, are among the most widely ranging of all those on this continent. The fruit, whose flavor and aroma are familiar to anyone who has ever tasted or smelled gin, is often dark blue and has a bloom to it. Growing in large numbers on the shoots of the female plants, these berries are to be found the year around. The flesh surrounding the large seed is sweetish and resinously aromatic.

The dwarf juniper *(Juniperus communis)* for example, the only one of the species with needles in groups of three and with those which are robustly whitened, is infrequently a tree but more often a shrub with sharp, hollowed, three-edged needles or scalelike leaves appearing in whorls. The blue-black, round, hard berries are powdered with white.

The so-called red cedar, actually *Juniperus virginiana,* is a tree of medium size with both scalelike and longer, pointedly three-sided awl-like, green leaves that grow in pairs along twigs and branches that are four-sided, whereas those of the dwarf juniper have three definite sides. The generally round, greenish-black to dark blue berries, often floured with a whitish bloom, have one to two seeds and are about ¼ inch across. In addition to a flavoring being extracted from its berries, a volatile oil from its leaves is used in perfumery. The fragrance of the wood is esteemed for warding off moths and other destructive insects.

The Mexican juniper *(J. Mexicana),* growing from Missouri and Texas westward, is a trunkless, round-topped shrub. The seeds may be nearly ½ inch long, and there can be from one to three in a berry.

The trailing juniper *(J. horizontalis),* more northerly, is prostrate and trailing, often forming thick mats in which, if your clothing is not too thin, it is a pleasure to sprawl while glassing the countryside.

The western juniper, *J. occidentalis,* is a high-mountain tree of deep snows and heavy winds. Its environment makes its trunk short and thick, its open, round-topped crown extending to within a few feet of the ground. Stubby and chunky, it seldom has more than 3 to 8 feet of clear trunk, this being covered with a distinctive thin, scaly, reddish-brown bark. The scalelike leaves are characteristically marked on their backs with glandular, resin-filled pits. The fruit, again, is made up of dark blue berries, ¼ to nearly ½ inch long, which mature about September.

DISTRIBUTION - Junipers grow from Alaska to Labrador, south into Mexico.

EDIBILITY - Band-tailed pigeons, quail, and wild turkeys are among the game birds eating the fruit of the junipers. Bluebirds, crossbills, finches, jays, mockingbirds, certainly the cedar waxwings, and a host of other songbirds also eat this fruit, as does the black bear, coyote, fox, opossum, armadillo, and ring-tailed cat. Antelope, deer, elk, and mountain sheep browse on the twigs and foliage.

Indians used to dry and grind juniper berries and use them for cake and for mush. These berries, too, were sometimes roasted for a coffee substitute. The ripe fruit was also sometimes crushed and sieved and used like butter.

The principal individual, non-commercial use of juniper berries today is as a nibble and as a woodsy seasoning. A few will take the edge off hunger. Too many, though, are irritating to the kidneys. In fact, a diuretic is made from the fruit, a teaspoon to a cup of boiling water, drunk cold, a large mouthful at a time, one or two cups a day.

Juniper tea, quaffed in small amounts, is one of the decidedly pleasant and vitamin-rich evergreen beverages. Add about a dozen young berryless sprigs to a quart of cold water. Bring this to a boil, cover, reduce the heat, and allow to simmer for ten minutes. Then remove from the fire and steep another ten minutes. Strain and serve like regular tea. For really high Vitamin C content, though, steep overnight after covering with boiling water.

©AJA

Top—*Juniperus communis*; Bottom—*Juniperus occidentalis*

115

KELP *(Nereocystis)*

FAMILY - Brown Algae *(Phaeophyceae)*

OTHER NAMES - Giant Kelp, Bull Kelp, Ribbon Kelp, Edible Kelp.

DESCRIPTION - Kelp, glowingly recommended by dieticians, is found in powdered form in the health food stores, but why not eat it fresh and tasty from the ocean; that is, if you do not live so far inland that you never reach the seashore even for vacations. It thrives on both the Pacific and the Atlantic margins of our continent.

All varieties are edible, but it is the ribbon or giant kelp that is the most conspicuous seaweed in the ocean from Alaska to California. Anchored as much as 75 feet below the surface, this kelp has wavering blades that appear in large fields offshore, where you can often see whales during their migrations, sea lions, and sometimes sea otters swimming among them.

Air bladders filled with a quart or two of air and incidentally carbon monoxide as well, keep the kelp floating, the smooth undivided, up-to-some-dozen-feet-long, glossy blades being dark brown and thin, becoming leathery and thick with age. The growth of the edible is extremely rapid, being about an inch a day in the summer when the pace has slackened some.

The long, hollow stalks, used by the Indians of southeastern Alaska as fishing lines for deep-sea angling, may be collected during June, July, and August when they are at their prime. Although for food purposes it is preferable to use only the ones rooted to the bottom, fresh kelp is also common along the beaches, especially after storms.

The so-called edible kelp of the East Coast has a brief, cylindrical stem with a major, greenish or brownish, elongated frond with a characteristic midrib running its entire length. Slimly stalked, ribless, secondary fronds which bear the fruit grow like numerous tongues near its base. The only other nearby kelp having such a strong and noticeable midrib in its main frond can be easily distinguished from the edible kelp because of innumerable round holes that make a sieve or colander of sorts of this blade.

DISTRIBUTION - These abundant marine algae, which often thrive in beds acres wide, grow along both our Atlantic and Pacific coasts.

EDIBILITY - Kelp, whose dry weight contains from 27% to 35% of potassium chloride, is rich in nourishing potash salts. A 100-gram edible portion, containing 21.7% water, will give you 1,093 milligrams of calcium, 240 mg. of phosphorous, and no less than 3,007 mg. of sodium and 5,273 mg. of potassium.

The small, lateral fronds of the edible kelp are edible as gathered, their flavor improving with drying. With the predominantly olive-hued membrane of the main frond removed, the thick midrib proves to be sweet and tender, making a welcome and nutritious addition to salads.

A major food use of the giant or ribbon kelp utilizes the hollow stalks which are washed, peeled, and used the same as green cucumbers or tomatoes for relishes. These and the hollow bulbs can also be peeled, cut into one-inch cubes, soaked in cold fresh water, rinsed, simmered until tender, and then turned into delectable pickles with the help of sugar, vinegar, cinnamon, and cloves.

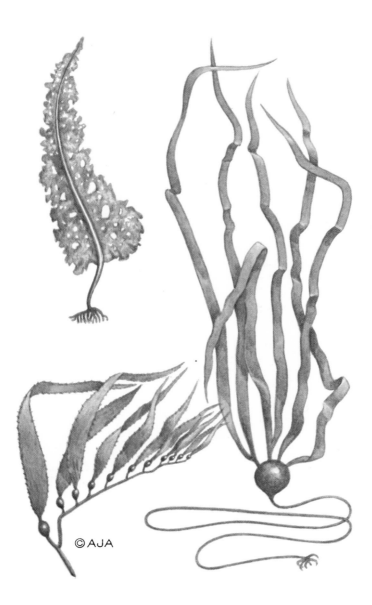

©AJA

KENTUCKY COFFEE TREE (Gymnocladus)

FAMILY - Pulse (*Leguminosae*)

OTHER NAMES - Coffee Nut, Mahogany, American Coffee Bean, Chicot.

DESCRIPTION - The Kentucky coffee tree is such an attention-getter that it is difficult to mistake it or its short, stout, stubby, flattened reddish-brown, woody, brief-stemmed, and persistent fruit pods for anything else.

It is ordinarily a medium-size tree, reaching a height of from forty to eighty and occasionally one hundred feet, with a trunk one or two feet in diameter. This trunk commonly divides within a few feet into three or four nearly vertically climbing limbs that form a narrow crown with its broad end uppermost.

The bark of the trunks is a dark greyish-brown. Irregular, shallow fissures, running up and down, divide low, narrow, hard, scaly ridges. On the twigs the bark is more a greenish brown, floured with a scaly whitish film. Small, downy buds, occurring one above the other, are embedded within a downy, incurving rim of this bark. There are large pores, especially conspicuous during the colder months. In fact, the tree's scientific name, *Gymnocladus,* means naked branch, and these are devoid of foliage almost half the year.

The doubly compound, alternate leaves, when they do appear, are very large, being from one to about three feet long and one to two feet wide. The sometimes forty leaflets are egg-shaped, with rounded or broadly wedge-formed bases, pointed tips, and smooth edges; measuring 2 to 2½ inches long and 1 to 1½ inches wide. Each is thinly but firmly structured, smoothly dark green above, and paler and often not quite so level underneath.

The leathery, 4- to 18-inch long and 1- to 2-inch wide seed pods, each containing from about a half-dozen to twenty large, flat chocolate-brown seeds, can scarcely be confused with the fruit of any other native or imported tree. Their thick stems hold them in place generally all winter.

DISTRIBUTION - The Kentucky coffee tree, often introduced as a shade or ornamental tree, is hardy as far north as New England. Its normal range extends from New York to Minnesota, south to Oklahoma and Tennessee.

EDIBILITY - Roasted and ground, the seeds of the Kentucky coffee tree were used by early settlers in the New World as a substitute coffee. Today you can still roast them slowly in the oven, grind them, and brew them like this drink. They have none of the caffeine of regular coffee, and the resulting beverage has always agreed with some people better.

Some of the Indians roasted them and ate them like nuts.

KINNIKINIC *(Arctostaphylos)*

FAMILY - Heath *(Ericaceae)*

OTHER NAMES - Bearberry, Mealberry, Manzanita, Upland Cranberry, Hog Cranberry, Arberry, Red Bearberry, Alpine Bearberry, Bear's Grape.

DESCRIPTION - When chinooks bare the Rocky Mountain foothills about our British Columbia log home winters and springtimes while white drifts are still deep in the woods, these slopes are encouragingly green with kinnikinic, early sought by the bears when they emerge from hibernation.

Edible red to orange berries, black in the *alpina* variety, are bright among the evergreen perennials all winter, too, making them prime emergency foods. Attractively bright and smooth, they are about the size of peas. Their dry, tough-skinned, mealy pulp is rather tasteless raw. Cooked, this pulp becomes more palatable, especially when as is frequently done, other berries are mixed in.

The ground-trailing shrub, with its loose reddish bark and long fibrous roots, forms yielding green mats where it grows. Innumerable, egg-shaped, briefly stemmed, finely toothed, veiny, thick, small, and tough leaves give it its verdancy. Having a hard shine on top, these are lighter beneath. Growing on prostrate branches up to several feet long, they seldom lift more than two or three inches off the ground they shield. These leaves persist on the vines for more than one season, browning and toughening with age. At all stages they are odorless.

The flowers, first appearing in May and June, form inconspicuous, single-stalked, pinkish to white, waxy clusters. Shaped like tiny, pedestaled vases, the blossoms each have five parts.

DISTRIBUTION - Kinnikinic is found in the Arctic and northern regions of North America, Asia, and Europe, extending south in this country to California and Virginia.

Common on limestone and other non-acid rock and in sandy, gravelly, and otherwise poor soil where it often checks erosion, kinnikinic is common in dry sunny woods and in mountains to up above the tree line.

EDIBILITY - Game birds, including grouse and wild turkey, seek the small plump berries of this member of the heath family. Bear eat them, too. Mountain sheep, deer, and moose browse on the foliage.

Edible and sustaining raw, the dry and rather tasteless berries are better cooked. They are best in the wilds after being simmered with some such other fruit as the blueberry.

An astringent tea, said to cleanse the kidneys, is made by steeping a teaspoonful of the younger leaves, dried at room temperature, with a cup of boiling water for five minutes. Or the leaves can first be soaked overnight in enough whiskey or such to cover, then the whole prepared the same way.

Interestingly, the dried and pulverized leaves of the kinnikinic have been used for centuries on this continent as a frontier tobacco substitute and stretcher.

KNOTWEED *(Polygonum)*

FAMILY - Buckwheat *(Polygonaceae)*

OTHER NAMES - Wild Rhubarb, Japanese Knotweed, American Bamboo Shoots, Bistort, Alpine Bistort, American Bistort, Giant Knotweed, *Amatokoro,* Smartweed, Snakeweed, Serpentgrass, Lady's Thumb, Heartweed, Water Pepper, Beach Knotweed, Shasta Knotweed, Yard Knotweed, Silver-Sheathed Knotweed, Leafy Dwarf Knotweed, Sawatch Knotweed, Spurry Knotweed, California Knotweed, Western Bistort.

DESCRIPTION - The delectable member of the family known as *Polygonum bistorta* thrives in the dry tundra of Alaska and northern Canada, even north of the limit of trees where *Polygonum viviparum* is also to be found.

The former is a low, slender, perennial herb with plumes of white or pink flowers in solitary, dense spikes that before you approach them too closely resemble clumps of cotton. Covered with a waxy bloom, unbranched stems arise sometimes alone but mainly in clusters from the thick, scaly, twisting roots. The basal leaves, up to about 8 inches long, are oblong and lanceheadlike, the upper ones being stemless and smaller.

The closely related *viviparum,* frequently known locally as serpentgrass, has a shorter root, and its slender flower stems are generally heavied by bulblets.

Extremely common in the Yukon and the Northwest Territories, on the long Mackenzie River and its tributaries as far north as the tree line, is the *P. alpinum* which is more usually known there as wild rhubarb, often growing in moist open soil such as that found on river banks and recent landslides in exclusive stands of several acres. This is a perennial, freely branching herb, 3 to 6 feet tall, with thickened, sheathed joints. The reddish stems are enlivened with numerous pointed leaves from several to some eight inches long. The individually insignificant and small flowers grow in large, branched plumes. When cooked, the juicy, bright red stems that appear soon after the snows melt resemble rhubarb.

The rapidly and thickly spreading Japanese knotweed, *P. cuspidatum,* has already invaded the countryside from the Carolinas to Missouri, north to southern Canada and Newfoundland. The enlarged joints of the stalks, growing in heavy, coarse stands from about three to eight feet tall, are encased with thin, papery sheaths. When these hollow stalks die, they loom up against the landscape in bamboolike thickets which clack and rattle in the wind and which serve to identify the edible young shoots when, resembling asparagus in shape although not in taste, these thrust up lustily in the springtime.

The stemmed green leaves of Japanese knotweed are roundly egg-shaped, broad at their bases but rather abruptly pointed at their tips. The numerous whitish-green flowers, whose outside series of floral leaves have five lobes, burst out in branching clusters from the angles between leaves and stalks. All in all, this immigrating member of the worldwide buckwheat family is easily recognizable.

DISTRIBUTION - Well over five dozen species of knotweed grow in almost every part of this country except in the Southeast, as well as in most of Canada; which is fortunate, as it is a vegetable, fruit, and nut — all in one. Knotweed grows over the entire globe, although it springs up only sparsely in the Tropics.

EDIBILITY - Mankind, including our Eskimos and Indians, has long both relished and relied upon the knotweeds. Partridges, quail, mourning doves, pheasants, grouse, prairie chickens, and woodcocks snap up the dark, often large seeds. Deer and antelope browse on the plants.

Especially in the North, south to mountainous Colorado and New England, the thick tuberlike rootstocks are welcome because of their nutritious starchiness, tastiest when roasted but also good boiled, and because of the almondlike nibbles afforded by the bulbs which if left alone root and become tubers themselves.

Japanese knotweed shoots, before the leaves start to unfurl, are delicately delicious when no more than about a dozen inches tall. Cut these fat, asparaguslike sprouts off close to the ground, remove any open leaves, and drop into salted boiling water to simmer briefly for about five minutes, only until a fork pierces them easily. Melting butter or margarine points up the toothsome acidity. Chill for salad, which you'll probably like to try first with mayonnaise, or for purees. A bit of sugar will enhance its soups.

If these hollow shoots are several feet high before you reach them, section, peel sparingly, slice, and cook like domestic rhubarb.

Knotweed *(Polygonum Bistorta)*

LABRADOR TEA (Ledum)

FAMILY - Heath *(Ericaceae)*

OTHER NAMES - Bog Tea, Muskeg Tea, Hudson's Bay Tea.

DESCRIPTION - The rustily dense woolliness which clothes the inwardly rolling undersides of the usually about 2-inches-long Labrador tea's leaves, the part used, easily identifies this wild edible. Otherwise, the thickish leaves of this erect if straggling shrub, some one to four feet high, are evergreen, dryly leathery, smooth-edged, bluntly oblong, and fragrant especially when crushed.

The flowers, when they appear in end clusters during May or June or later, are small, white, and bell-like. The tiny calyx has five separate sepals and a regular corella of five distinct petals, while there are ordinarily five stamens. Growing on slim individual stems, they form showy, unbrellalike clumps at the tops of their woolly stalks, followed by slimly oblong or more circular, five-celled seedpods.

The branches grow in small bunches from the same group of roots, reaching up to about four feet in height, and then die from the tips downward.

DISTRIBUTION - Labrador tea, also known as Hudson's Bay tea across much of northern Canada where the Hudson's Bay Company still maintains its red-roofed white trading posts, is a pretty evergreen shrub whose robustly aromatic leaves still make it one of the most famous teas of the North Country. It is found growing densely in woods, muskegs, bogs, swamps, damp mountain meadows, and across the tundra of Alaska and the Dominion south to New England, Pennsylvania, New Jersey, and the Great Lakes States, where it is seen mainly in mountain bogs and swamps.

EDIBILITY - This member of the heath family is eaten by moose and deer.

Available in winter as well as during the warm months, the spicy leaves of Labrador tea, which were among those gathered for tea during the American Revolution, make a palatable and refreshing, if somewhat invigoratingly bitter and astringent, beverage. Although I seldom bother to measure exactly, about one tablespoon a cup, heaping or otherwise depending on your palate, makes a pleasant brew. Drop them into bubbling water and immediately set this away from the heat to steep for five minutes.

Oldtime sourdoughs have warned me that drunk in too large quantities the tea may have a cathartic effect. But, using it sparingly over the years, I have never experienced any ill effects. As a matter of fact, I often find it both refreshing and thirst-quenching to chew on a few leaves while hiking or getting in wood.

LAMB'S QUARTER *(Chenopodium)*

FAMILY - Goosefoot *(Chenopodiaceae)*

OTHER NAMES - Wild Spinach, Goosefoot, Pigweed, White Goosefoot, Smooth Pigweed.

DESCRIPTION - This wild spinach, a branching annual growing from one to about six feet high, was widely used as a green, both raw and cooked, by the North American Indians, many of whom also gathered its abundant seeds, nearly seventy-five thousand of which have been counted on a single plant.

A characteristic is that the greyish-green or bluish-green leaves have a floury white, water-repellent mealiness, particularly on their underneath portions. Adding to the color, there is frequently a red-streaked appearance to the stalks of the older plants. The more or less diamond-shaped leaves are like egg-shaped parallelograms with oblique angles, those on top being formed more like lanceheads with broadly toothed edges. From one to four inches long, their general overall shape has given the wild edible its name *Chenopodium* which is Greek for goosefoot.

The flowers, all the more inconspicuous for being green, although this may turn reddish, grow in spiked clusters at the tips of the plants or in angles between the stalk and leaves, as well as in additional clusters on the topmost parts of the stems. They later evolve into tiny, black, often dullish, flattish but convex seeds.

DISTRIBUTION - A native of Asia and Europe, this relative of beets and spinach is now distributed throughout the United States and Canada from Alaska to Labrador southward. It is found mainly where the soil has been disturbed, as in old gardens and yards, once-ploughed meadows, ditches, and along fences and roadsides.

EDIBILITY - The lamb's quarters' seeds are devoured in quantity by mourning doves, grouse, partridge, pheasants, quail, buntings, finches, juncos, larks, and by more than a dozen different species of sparrows. Chipmunks, gophers, ground squirrels, and kangaroo rats also relish them. Deer and moose are among the animals browsing on the entire plants.

Because lamb's quarter has no harsh flavors, many deem it the best of the wild greens. The entire young plant is edible, whereas from the older ones quantities of tender small leaves can generally be stripped. The seeds, ground into a dark meal, were utilized by the Southwest Indians in particular for everything from cakes to gruel. Today they make a hearty flour when mixed half-and-half with the regular wheat product. Or for a nourishing breakfast cereal, just boil the whole seeds until they are soft.

Lamb's quarter has been found to contain 309 milligrams of calcium per 100 grams of the raw edible portions and 258 grams after this same amount has been boiled and drained, a percentage that is all the more remarkable when you consider that the green is roughly from 80% to 90% water. The same portion boasts 11,600 international units of Vitamin A when raw, 9,700 when cooked, plus significant amounts of thiamine, riboflavin, and niacin.

LAVER (Porphyra)

FAMILY - Red Algae *(Rhodophyceae)*

OTHER NAMES - Red Laver, Seaweed.

DESCRIPTION - Floating in the waves and eddies along both the Atlantic and the Pacific shores of North America, young laver has a beautiful red luminosity, the single flattish blade with its ruffled edges swaying in the restless tides. Out of the water, this seaweed becomes dull. It is only the young plants that are a vivid red. When older, the then broader and usually deeply slashed and torn blade becomes more of a filmy greyish, greenish, or brownish-purple.

Laver, then, is the thin frond spied at low tide growing from rock ledges, boulders, and pier supports. You can see it wavering beneath the surface in still high tides, while heavy seas tear considerable quantities of it loose and toss them up on the shore. The single unmarked blade, attached only by a small disk, is very fragile, having but one layer of cells when young. However, with maturity it becomes practically a pair of layers when the reproductive elements start to form along its edges. This thickening occurs with the swelling of the jelly that surrounds the sexual bodies at the time of ripening.

Thousands of spores are loosed upon maturity. When they land on suitable surfaces and when other conditions are favorable, germination takes place immediately, and a new red laver growth appears as early as the next season, having the satiny gloss and the elasticity of youth.

DISTRIBUTION - Laver is common along the Atlantic and Pacific shores of this continent. This abundant seaweed furnishes a regular food crop in the Orient, and some has long been exported to this country. But exactly the same delicacy can be harvested here for free.

EDIBILITY - Although laver is perfectly edible raw, it is better dried. In Alaska, for example, the natives gather it during the low tides of May and early June. It is separated from any foreign matter, then partially air-and-sun-dried by being spread outdoors on fair days on a large cloth laid on the ground or on a table. It is chopped or ground in a food chopper, then again put out on sunny days, being repeatedly turned over and over until, blackening, it is thoroughly dried. Stored in closed containers in a cool, dry place, this dried laver with its high salt content can be kept indefinitely.

Dried laver is widely used in fish stews and soups, a cup to every two cups of liquid, after first being soaked for about an hour until tender. Too, it is commonly enjoyed raw, its salty crispness being reminiscent of popcorn.

© AJA

LETTUCE SAXIFRAGE *(Saxifrage)*

FAMILY - Saxifrage *(Saxifragaceae)*

OTHER NAMES - Mountain Lettuce, Deer Tongue, Early Saxifrage, Saxifrage, Swamp Saxifrage, Red-Stemmed Saxifrage, Purple Saxifrage, Spotted Saxifrage, Tufted Saxifrage.

DESCRIPTION - The *Saxifrage* portion of the name comes from the Latin meaning rock-breaker, a redoubtable and amusing designation for such a fragile little edible. Because it sometimes grows in rock fissures, the supposition arose that it split the stones. It can thrive in such a cramped crevice because it is a small plant and can get along with little water.

The white little blossoms grow in clusters at the top of the edible. When they first start to develop they crowd very close together. In the center of each tidy little group are numerous minute, round, green buds. As these latter start to unfurl, the group widens, and you can see that the cluster is made up of several tiny stems, each with a few white, or perhaps greenish or purplish depending on the species, flowers at its tip. Some like to dry these blossoms and enjoy their enduring vanillalike fragrance.

Each blossom has five narrow petals whose tops curl back. Beneath is the green calyx, a little emerald cup with five points along its rim. Within the tube formed by the quintet of petals are several, tightly packed, little, yellow stamens. The seed vessels do not become evident until the petals fall later in the year. Then two tiny pods develop that many times redden further along in the spring.

Also known as deer tongue because of the shape of its leaves and as mountain lettuce because of their edibility, lettuce saxifrage concentrates its growth at first in a crisp green rosette of leaves. The members of this thick mat are up to about 11 inches long, somewhat thickly shaped like an animal's tongue, and serrated with keen, sharp teeth. They grow close to the ground and have fine hair scattered over them. Those closer to the center of the pack are shorter than those on the outside.

It is when these leaves begin to age and to lose their tenderness that the flower stalk rises one or two feet from their midst. In Alaska, with the *Saxifraga punctata*, this may be delayed until very late in the season within mountain and shoreline gulches where the snow often persists until midsummer.

DISTRIBUTION - The lettuce saxifrage abounds in rocky ground, in moist meadows, along the cool edges of brooks, in marshy places, and on damp slopes from Pennsylvania on through the Appalachians to Tennessee. Edible cousins prosper over much of the continent except for the west central portion, from Alaska and California to Georgia.

EDIBILITY - The highly discriminating gopher is one of the animals relishing the saxifrages.

The young and tender leaves, picked before the plant flowers, will supply considerable amounts of vitamins and flavor to salads. Both wilted saxifrage and saxifrage soup start a hungry man's nostrils quivering. Or just cook with bacon and a splash of sour cream. Any lettuce recipe can be advantageously followed with this particular wild green.

©AJA

LIVE-FOREVER *(Sedum)*

FAMILY - Orpine *(Crassulaceae)*

OTHER NAMES - Stonecrop, Wild Stonecrop, Orpine, Rosecrown, Frog Plant, Rosy-Flowered Stone-crop, Evergreen Orpine, Red Orpine, Aaron's Rod.

DESCRIPTION - This is the wild edible that youngsters sometimes call frog plant because of the way one of its fleshy green leaves, after being loosened as by holding it between the warm tongue and the roof of the mouth, can be blown up like an inflated frog's throat. Our pioneer predecessors went one step further and used the insides of these leaves, once they had been blown or cut apart, to apply to warts. The fresh leaves also have a cooling quality and have been long used to soothe burns, insect bites, bruises, and other such irritations.

The familiar live-forever, also called other names in different parts of the country, is a close cousin of roseroot whose succulencies we have considered elsewhere. As with the roseroot, both the plant tops and the roots are deliciously edible, making them both pleasant table companions as well as prime survival foods.

The oblong, thickish leaves of this member of the orpine family ascend, in crowded spirals, stems one or two feet tall. Because of the way they can be inflated by blowing into the loosened slit at the base, they are unmistakable. Broad round clusters of tiny blossoms, differing in hue from crimson and garnet to whitish, appear in midsummer.

The stout, rounded or fingerlike tuberous roots become stringy and tough when the plant blooms. Again in late autumn, however, large masses of new-grown, crisp, white tubers can again be found.

There are a number of species. *Sedum ternatum,* for example, has prostrate or spreading weak stems, with several pairs of fat, smooth-edged, flat leaves, usually in whorls of three, and a terminal rosette of crowded leaves. The clusters of tiny April to June flowers are frequently one-sided. Each blossom has four or five sharply pointed petals plus an equal number of leaflike sepals. This stonecrop grows in damp rocky ground, in mossy banks, and along the edges of streams from Georgia to New York, west to Illinois and Michigan, mainly in the hills.

About a dozen species occur in the Rocky Mountain area, one of the better tasting of which is *Sedum rhodanthum*. This is topped from June to August with small but dense-growing red flowers which appear in the angles of the upper leaves in tight, elongated blossom clusters along single stalks with each flower on a separate tiny stem, the younger of them at the top coming into blossom last. Clusters of unbranched stalks, up to about sixteen inches high, lift from fleshy rootstocks, densely covered with fat, oblongish leaves except on their lower parts. Ranging from Montana to New Mexico and Arizona, this is found in moist to wet ground from near timberline to well above it.

DISTRIBUTION - Live-forever frequently escapes from gardens, from Greenland southward, here and in Europe and Asia.

EDIBILITY - Except for *Sedum acre,* a multi-branched common little plant with small, deeply toothed leaves laid as closely upon some of the stems as shakes on a roof—first a large pair, then a small pair and so on—the members of this genus are widely used for salads and potherbs. This particular species, however, is overly peppery.

Both the stems and leaves of the others, when very young, are tender enough to enjoy raw. Later, until the plants flower, they may be briefly cooked until tender.

The sliced young tubers in the spring and again in late autumn will add to provocative salads.

Live-Forever (Sedum purpureum)

133

MAPLE *(Acer)*

FAMILY - Maple *(Aceraceae)*

OTHER NAMES - Sugar Maple, River Maple, Silver Maple, Ashleaf Maple, Box Elder, Florida Maple, Hedge Maple, Mountain Maple, Norway Maple, Siberian Maple, Striped Maple, Sycamore Maple, Moosewood, Black Maple, Soft Maple, Black Sugar Maple, White Maple, Chalk Maple, Carolina Red Maple, Drummond Red Maple, Japanese Maple, Rocky Mountain Maple, Bigleaf Maple, Vine Maple, Hard Maple, Rock Maple, White-Barked Sugar Maple.

DESCRIPTION - The first colonists to venture along the Atlantic seaboard of this New World were introduced to the sweetness of our native maples by the Indians, who trapped the swiftly dripping sap in birch bark containers and in tightly woven baskets and skin vessels. All the maples have sugar-rich sap. So do other native trees, for that matter, such as the birch and the hickory, but it is the sugar maple, *Acer saccharum,* that is by far the most famous for this characteristic. It is also a highly desirable shade and ornamental tree, so perhaps you have your own private source of maple sugar growing right by your home.

There are some dozen to a dozen-and-a-half native maples growing on this continent, depending on the botanist who's doing the counting, and others have been introduced from different parts of the world. Groves of maple trees, with rude sugar houses, are familiar landmarks in many parts of the country, inasmuch as the sugar maple, for one, grows from Newfoundland to Ontario and Minnesota, south as far as Georgia and Louisiana. The trees, reaching a height of sixty to almost one hundred feet, are tapped in late winter or early spring, before the buds begin to expand. Sharp frosty nights, followed by mild thawing during the daylight hours, make for the free flow of sap.

The sweetness of this varies, but it usually takes from thirty to forty gallons to boil down into a gallon of the consequently high-priced syrup. Additional boiling makes maple sugar. During early American years, this was about the consistency of present-day brown sugar. In fact, it was used in place of cane sugar by colonists who couldn't afford the then much more expensive sweetening even when it was available. Maple sugar is still more nourishing than the mass-manufactured product, containing the B vitamins, calcium, phosphorous, and enzymes refined from today's sugar beets and sugar cane.

The maple leaf, emblem of Canada and a major reason why such regions as northern New England are so magnificently colored in the fall, is known to everyone. The fruits, too, are very characteristic, being made up of a pair of brown wings with the edible seeds enclosed in their plump juncture.

Each one of the maples native to this continent, showing greater variations in their parts than any other group of native trees, has a number of outstanding characteristics. Their opposite leaves may be simple or palmately compound, big or little, and smooth or hairy. The leaf scars are crescent or V-shaped. The flowers are variable, although ordinarily the staminate and the pistillate blossoms occur on separate trees, being pollinated in the main by insects. But they grow in drooping bunches, small lateral clusters, and in long terminal spikes. Their twigs, ranging from slim to stout, may be green, red, grey, or brown in hue. All the fruits take the form of the so-called maple key, but that of each separate species has some distinctive points. Maples also show a great range of site preferences.

The leaves of the sugar maple, to pick one major species, generally have five lobes, each sparsely and irregularly toothed, both the teeth and the tips of the lobes being pointed. The connecting tissues between the lobes are rounded or U-shaped at the bases. These leaves are from three to five inches long and about the same width. Thin but firm, they are dark green on top, paler and smooth beneath, with slender, long stems. In the fall, especially when frost-hazed nights are succeeded by brisk, smoky days, the leaves become golden yellow, often tinged regally with scarlets and crimsons.

The sugar maple may be distinguished in the wintertime by its sharply pointed, multi-scaled, narrowly conical buds which are a pale brown. The bud on the end is about ¼ inch long, the ones on the sides being tinier and more or less pressed into the twigs. These winter twigs are slim and smooth, differing in color from a brownish-red to a pale reddish-brown and characterized by numerous pale pores. The bark on the more mature trunks, dark grey, is deeply furrowed into thick long plates which are often loose along one edge. Some of the typically winged seeds commonly persist in cold weather.

The sugar or rock maple, ranking very high as a timber tree, is handsome, often reaching sixty to almost one hundred feet in height, with a trunk diameter of three to four feet. Trees growing by themselves in the open have broadly rounded crowns.

DISTRIBUTION - The maples, including many both domestic and imported escapees from cultivation, grow throughout southern Canada and the United States with exceptions in the plains states and the lower Rocky Mountains. Preferring moist situations in deference to their usually enormous sap yield, they are also frequently seen on hills and slopes.

The sugar maple, for instance, prefers well-drained rich soil in the valleys and mountains. The mountain maple thrives in rocky, moist, shady, and cool mountain forests. The silver maple is a tree of stream rims and bottomlands periodically flooded by rising waters. The sycamore maple is common in parks and along streets.

134

Sugar Maple (*Acer saccharum*)

EDIBILITY - With maple seeds maturing in the springtime, summer, or fall depending on the species, they, as well as the buds and flowers, provide food for many kinds of birds and animals. Both chipmunks and squirrels store the seeds in caches, first removing the hulls and wings. Birds commonly utilize the leaves and seed stems in nest building. Both mule and white-tailed deer, elk, mountain sheep, and the giant moose browse on the sweetly tasting foliage and twigs.

Maple seeds are edible for humans, too, some Indians formerly hulling the larger of them and then boiling them. So are the sugar-rich young leaves. The inner bark of the maple is one of the more appetizing sap layers and is eaten in times of need, either raw or cooked. But it is for the sap that the tree has been famous since redskin days.

You can purchase the necessary spiles and pails for sap gathering. Unless you anticipate going in for sugaring in a big way, however, you can do very well on your own. The Indians used to cut a V-shaped gash in the tree, at the point of which they drove maybe an elderberry spout. The latter was made by cutting straight elderberry limbs, discussed elsewhere in this book, in the spring, drying them with the leaves on, and then poking out the incidentally poisonous soft pith of their interiors with hot sticks.

You may find it more conservative to drill about a 2-inch-deep hole with a little gimlet, or brace and bit, and to close this with a peg when you're finished. For the spout, just make a single bend in a can top cut off by one of the smooth-cutting openers. Don't try to suspend the can or pail from this, however. Instead, drive a small nail into the tree for the purpose. As a precaution, empty the containers, which may be large fruit cans with wire bail handles, often enough so that the sap doesn't hang too long in the sun and sour.

Then it's just a matter of boiling the sap, and spooning off the characteristic scum as it rises, until some 35 or so parts of water evaporate, leaving a clear amber syrup. This you'll want to strain carefully. Or, for sugar, you'll wish to continue boiling until a test portion of the syrup forms a very soft ball in cold water. Then remove from the heat, agitate with an egg beater if you're making only a small amount or with a regular sugar beater if you have a large quantity, and pour into dry molds. Delectable!

MAY APPLE *(Podophyllum)*

FAMILY - Barberry *(Berberidaceae)*

OTHER NAMES - Umbrella-Leaf, Mandrake, American Mandrake, Raccoon Berry, Wild Lemon, Hog Apple.

DESCRIPTION - Springtimes these little plants open like crowds of elfin umbrellas, in throngs in wet meadows and damp open woodlands, so dense that they shade the ground.

Growing eventually up to two feet high, the plant first generally unfurls a single big leaf from the horizontal rootstock. Shield-shaped, the leaf is affixed to its supporting handlelike stem in the center of the lower surface. The may apple leaves are roundish, their edges being deeply cut so that each leaf has from five to some nine lobes, each multi-veined and tooth-edged. When the plant is to be flowerless there is just the one leaf attached at its middle to a stout, hollow stem.

The flowering plants have a pair of semicircular leaves, a single blossom growing to nod in the parasoled shade in the angle between the two leafstalks. Growing on a long, slim, curved stalk, each waxy flower is a showy inch or two in diameter. It consists of an outer series of six briefly lived sepals and an inner group of six to nine flat petals, each of these latter being so hollowed that the hole resembles a deep saucer.

Centered in each blossom is the single, stout, egg-shaped, thickly skinned, tomatolike, multi-seeded, edible may apple. Their sweet scent often betrays their presence when one is ambling along outdoors in late summer.

DISTRIBUTION - This member of the small barberry family grows, often in large colonies, from New England, Quebec, Ontario, and Minnesota, southward to Florida and Texas.

EDIBILITY - The fruit is the only part of the may apple that is edible. The root, which Indians dug up soon after the fruit had matured and employed in small amounts as a cathartic, is poisonous. So are the stems and leaves.

Not everyone likes the flavor of the may apple, but among those who do, many prefer it raw, either in its natural state or as a juice or an uncooked jam. Others like stove-prepared may apple jams and marmalades. All are different enough to have gourmet qualities.

©AJA

MILKWEED *(Asclepias)*

FAMILY - Milkweed *(Asclepiadaceae)*

OTHER NAMES - Silkweed, Common Milkweed, Showy Milkweed, Pink Milkweed, Narrow-leaved Milkweed, Coast Milkweed, Pleurisyroot, Tuber Root, Butterfly Weed, Cotton Tree.

DESCRIPTION - Milkweeds, as might be expected, have a milky sap, but do not depend upon this for identification. This latex, which the Indians used to rub on warts and ringworm infections to eradicate them, was the subject of rubber-making experiments during World War II when this commodity became scarce in this part of the world. In fact, even the silken fluff which makes the seeds airborne in autumn winds, was the temporary subject of Department of Agriculture tests to determine if it could replace kapok in life-preserving gear.

There are something like a hundred, usually slightly differing species of milkweed whose botanical title comes from the name of the Grecian god of medicine, but it is the so-called common milkweed, *Asclepias syriaca,* with which many wild-food users are most familiar. This native perennial thrusts up its stout stems, two to five feet high, in gardens, old fields, meadows, pastures, marshes, and along roads and fences where, in the fall, its hundreds of thousands of seeds with their familiar flossy appendages are parachuted by the whitened winds.

Look, too, for the way the leaves of this non-branching edible appear in opposite pairs. Their brief stems, like the main stalks, are plump and robust. From four to nine inches long, and somewhat less than half as wide, these egg-shaped to oblong leaves are tapered at both ends. The smooth-edged leaves, which have neither divisions nor lobes, are sturdily marked with wide central ribs.

Round clusters of pleasantly fragrant flowers, whose stems all lift from the same spot, are borne directly from the central stalk in angles between the opposite leaves. The numerous minute blossoms differ in hue from a greenish amethyst to almost white. Each of the sections of the delicate-appearing blossoms, which are mortal traps to many of the insects hunting their honey, is made up of five parts. There are five petals, each with an erect cowl and an inwardly hooked horn, five outer leaflike sepals, and even five stamens, the organs which hold the pollen.

These alluringly sweet-smelling blossoms eventually develop into roughly long, green pods which grow about three to five inches long. Showy and warty, the sheaths of these eventually split of their own accord along one side, revealing an intricately packed filling of flat seeds, each with its soft tuft of long silky hairs.

Growing in like habitats on the other side of the continent is the *Asclepias speciosa,* known here in the West also as the common milkweed. Rising slightly taller than its Eastern cousin, this similarly eaten perennial also has opposite leaves, these being somewhat thickly coarse, characteristically ribbed, and lancehead-shaped, the larger of them being close to a foot long. The colors of the otherwise similar flowers vary from pink to white. The pods, seeds, and the milkiness of the plant as a whole are the same.

Although not a characteristic that can be depended upon for identification, the stalks yield tough fibers from which a strong fishline can be twisted in an emergency.

DISTRIBUTION - Milkweeds abound from coast to coast, from southern Canada to the Southern States.

The eastern *Asclepias syriaca* is found from the Maritime Provinces to windy Saskatchewan, south to the Carolinas and Kansas. The western *Asclepias speciosa,* the other common milkweed, grows throughout the driest parts of British Columbia east of the Coast Mountains to Minnesota, south throughout California to the Gulf of Mexico.

EDIBILITY - Perhaps the most interesting non-human food use of milkweeds is how the far-ranging monarch butterfly, which migrates from Canada throughout most of the United States, is also called the milkweed butterfly because of the way its larva feeds upon the milkweed. When fully grown this bitter-tasting butterfly, generally avoided by the birds, is a widely black-banded light yellow, many times with a greenish tinge. The chrysalis, if you want to look for it, is an inch-long, light-green entity that is dotted with gold. It stays in the pupa stage some two weeks, then comes out a complete insect. Ordinarily, three broods are brought forth in a summer.

Tender young milkweed sprouts, up to about 8 inches high, are cooked like asparagus. Afterwards, the young leaves can be boiled for greens. The flower buds are regarded by many as a dainty. The firm, young pods also boil up deliciously up to the time they begin to feel at all elastic, a sign that the silkiness of the seeds has become too developed to make for good eating.

However, all sections of the plant are bitter with the milky sap, and this must first be removed by boiling. Place the cleaned sprouts, leaves, flower buds, or seedpods into a pot. Cover with boiling water, bring once more to a bubble over high heat, and pour off. Do this at least once more, maybe oftener depending on your palate. The last time simmer until tender, which takes longer than with most other greens.

Milkweed *(Asclepias syriaca)*

139

MINER'S LETTUCE *(Montia)*

FAMILY - Purslane *(Portulacaceae)*

OTHER NAMES - Indian Lettuce, Spanish Lettuce, Winter Purslane.

DESCRIPTION - Several stems, each some 4 to 12 inches long, lift from a cluster of basal leaves which, themselves arising on long stems, vary in shape from slim and narrow to kidney-form or even roundish, whose greenness sometimes takes on a pale pinkish hue. The characteristic feature of the miner's lettuce, though, is that usually about 2/3 of the way up each stem a pair of round leaves grow together to form a sort of cup through whose middle the stalk continues.

Above these disks of leaves, the stalks develop an elongated flower cluster, each blossom having its own short stem and the whole maturing from the bottom upward. The flowers are small, white or pinkish, and nodding, each usually with five petals and two sepals. They develop into shiny black seeds.

DISTRIBUTION - The native miner's lettuce grows profusely in shaded, moist situations from British Columbia across to North Dakota, down to California and Arizona. It has spread to Europe and the Caribbean where it is also eaten.

EDIBILITY - Doves and quail seek the shiny dark seeds, as do buntings, finches, grosbeaks, juncos, large siskins, sparrows, and towhees. A number of mammals eat the leaves.

When the 49ers stampeded throughout California with their gold pans and rockers, the scarcity of fresh food brought scurvy and allied infections into some of what often are now ghost towns. The Indians and Spanish taught many of the argonauts how to beat these vitamin-deficiency troubles by showing them the antiscorbutic miner's lettuce. Those prospectors who didn't relish salads, or who gathered the plant so long after spring that it was tough, settled for boiling it, ideally in a very small amount of water until just tender.

© AJA

MINT *(Mentha)*

FAMILY - Mint *(Labiatae)*

OTHER NAMES - Spearmint, Oswego Tea, Beebalm, Lemon Mint, Wild Bergamot, Horsemint, Peppermint, Pennyroyal, American Pennyroyal, Mountain Pennyroyal, Western Pennyroyal, Lamb Mint, Fieldmint, Brandy Mint, Watermint, Wild Mint, Horehound, American Mint, Giant Hyssop.

DESCRIPTION - The various wild mints—important to us from ancient times to the present as foods, scents, flavorings, medicines, and the like—are numerous and widespread but, fortunately, easy as a whole to recognize because of their square stems, opposite leaves, and pleasantly familiar fragrance. This characteristic aroma may not be perceptibly in the air where just a few mints grow together, but you've only to rub a leaf between thumb and forefinger to smell it.

For instance, there is spearmint with its square stems, oblong or lancehead-shaped leaves growing opposite one another, and its odor that is so familiar to anyone who's chewed gum. Growing from about one to two feet tall, this is a smooth green perennial whose creeping roots spread it rapidly through wet areas. Blanched, it has odoriferous green leaves that are stemless or nearly so, a bright inch or two long, pointed narrow-based, and unevenly sawtoothed. Small, pinkly purple to white blossoms encircle a thronged spike at the top, which is usually set off at each lower side by a smaller flower cluster.

Peppermint grows similarly in the same sort of habitats but has leaves that are somewhat shaggy beneath rather than smooth like the spearmint's and which are different, too, in that their edges are uniformly indented. There is also the marked variance in scent.

Oswego tea, or beebalm as it is frequently called, blooms from June through August with distinctively large, showily beautiful lavender to scarlet flowers, usually bunched on unbranched stems, atop a one to three-foot, square, branching stalk. The opposite, bright green, sawtooth-edged leaves are oval or shaped like lanceheads. The plant as a whole is rather coarse, sharply pointed, and hairy.

DISTRIBUTION - The wild mints, many of which have escaped from cultivation, are widely distributed throughout the United States and the southern half of Canada, preferring damp ground.

Spearmint, to be more specific, is abundant in spots from British Columbia and the State of Washington to the Maritime Provinces, south to Florida and California.

Peppermint is common from the Maritimes to Manitoba, south to Florida and Louisiana, being scattered elsewhere. Oswego tea brightens the landscape particularly from British Columbia to Quebec, south to Tennessee and Arizona.

EDIBILITY - The mint family as a whole has glands filled with aromatic oil. This is so volatile, incidentally, that much of it will be wasted if you try to extract it by boiling unless your purpose is to perfume the surroundings. Instead, immerse a handful or so of fresh mint leaves in hot water, cover, and leave to steep overnight. Then strain and use. This not only conserves a large part of the aroma, but it is also saving of the abundant Vitamins A and C.

Another thrifty way to use fresh young mint leaves is finely chopped in green salads. You'll want to do a bit of experimenting first, though, as there are considerable taste differences among various species.

For off-season use, young mint leaves freshly picked during a dry morning can be dried at room temperatures, then put away in tightly capped jars to conserve the volatile aroma. Tea can be made from these in similar proportions to regular orange pekoe and formosa oolong.

© AJA

MOUNTAIN ASH *(Sorbus)*

FAMILY - Rose *(Rosaceae)*

OTHER NAMES - American Mountain Ash, European Mountain Ash, Quickbeam, Rowan Tree.

DESCRIPTION - The trees and shrubs of the mountain ash make such decorative ornamentals that they have been planted in the gardens and parks of this continent, so extensively that in addition to some dozen natives a number of imports, including the European mountain ash, have now escaped to our woodlands. The foliage and bright reddish berries of the group make them both prominently attractive and prizes that are eagerly sought by the birds, particularly as the fruit that is left by them and by human harvesters remains attached all winter.

The mountain ashes are both shrubs, 2 to 15 feet tall, and medium-sized trees with narrowish, round-crowned tops. The trees, sometimes twenty to thirty feet tall, occasionally reach up to fifty feet.

The compound leaves, growing alternately about 2 to 10 inches long, have 7 to 17 sawtoothed leaflets extending directly and stemlessly from the stalks. They burst forth in the springtime from reddish-purple, bristly, short buds that appear as sharply tipped cones and are generally roundish or oblong in shape. The scars they leave on the branches in winter are formed like somewhat large U's, each with three to five grouped indentations.

The bark, sometimes smooth and on other occasions scaly, is thin and grey.

Flat clusters of many tiny flowers, the whole about three to six inches across, appear from May until nearly August depending on the elevation and latitude. Multi-stamened, these are showily white.

However, these distinctive snowy masses develop into vividly reddish-orange clusters of berries, each with a characteristic rose-family pucker at its summit. These mature toward the end of September and can be advantageously gathered during autumns and winters. Anyone seeing these gleaming against hoar frost or snow is unlikely ever to forget the attractive mountain ash.

DISTRIBUTION - The mountain ash grows from Alaska to Newfoundland, south to North Carolina, New Mexico, and California. Preferring moist to wet soils, it is the predominant growth along many a northern slope and cold swamp where many times it forms dense thickets.

EDIBILITY - Grouse, cedar waxwings, and thrushes seek out the berries remaining after the pre-hibernation fall ravages of the bears, that continue to cling to the mountain ashes during winter.

Despite the fact that they are somewhat bitter in tannin, the flavoring ingredient in tea, Indians collected and ate the berries of the mountain ash, devouring some of them fresh and drying others, in lean years often grinding these latter into meal and flour. They are also cooked into jams, jellies, and marmalades, while a few find their ways into sweetly bitter wines.

©AJA

MOUNTAIN SORREL *(Oxyria)*

FAMILY - Buckwheat *(Polygonaceae)*

OTHER NAMES - Alpine Sorrel, Scurvy Grass, Sourgrass.

DESCRIPTION - This green, whose official name comes from the Greek noun meaning sour, grows from a few inches to usually a foot high from a deep, scaly, perennial root. It somewhat resembles a dwarfed rhubarb, its leaves even tasting like rhubarb stems, although it should be noted that the leaves of the domestic rhubarb are poisonous whether raw or cooked. Those of the mountain sorrel, on the other hand, are tartly and deliciously edible.

It has tufts of broadly smooth, kidney-shaped or roundish leaves arising on their own long, individual stems from the top of the root. Fleshy and succulent, these have an agreeable acid flavor.

Inconspicuous greenish or crimson flowers grow from late June to early September in rising clusters on long, full, branching stems. These bloom from the bottom of the spire upward, each blossom on its own tiny stalk. Reddish, more noticeable fruits, each with a flatly encircling wing, follow.

DISTRIBUTION - This valuable plant, rich in Vitamin C, circles the North Pole, being found in Europe and Asia as well as in North America. Here it is distributed from Alaska to Greenland, throughout the Barren Lands, and on the higher mountains south of the limit of trees, preferring somewhat shaded slopes and ravines where the snow accumulates during the winter and affords moisture that lasts throughout the growing season. In Alaska, where Eskimos often journey long distances to find it, it is common in the interior on moise alpine ground near small streams and rivulets and in sheltered gulches on the Arctic Coast. In British Columbia it is seen mostly on higher elevations throughout the Province where, toward the south, elk browse on it.

In the contiguous U.S., it thrives in New Hampshire's green-sloped White Mountains and on the higher Western eminences in New Mexico and Southern California.

EDIBILITY - Fresh and succulent throughout the summer, the leaves of the mountain sorrel are particularly refreshing raw and, besides enlivening a thirsty hike where they'll lengthen rations that may be restricted because of space and weight, are sourly flavorsome in salads and purees. The tender young leaves are also a tangy addition to sandwiches. Up in the Arctic, in Asia as well as America, Eskimos ferment some of it as a sauerkraut.

In the Far North especially, the reason for their auxiliary name of scurvy grass, they are an excellent source of the Vitamin C which the body cannot store and which is necessary to prevent scurvy.

Particularly when the leaves get mature enough to begin to be a bit tough, mountain sorrel can also be dropped into boiling salted water, briefly simmered only until tender, and enjoyed as a pot herb, a frequent use for it around mining camps of yore. They are also welcome for adding a pungent zip to the blander soups.

©AJA

MULBERRY *(Morus)*

FAMILY - Nettle *(Urticacaea)*

OTHER NAMES - Red Mulberry, White Mulberry, Black Mulberry, Texas Mulberry.

DESCRIPTION - Although up to some dozen different species of mulberries are distributed over our north temperate regions, the best of the fruit comes from our native red mulberry. This becomes so abundant that I have gathered it by the gallon merely by shaking a heavily laden branch over an outspread tarpaulin.

The red mulberry is a small tree, generally twenty to thirty feet high but sometimes reaching eighty feet into the sky, with a trunk diameter of from one to three or four feet, which prefers the moist richness of bottomlands and foothill forests. It is the only mulberry native to the eastern U.S., although its range has been extended by its introduction to many yards and streets.

Summers, the big, roundish, dark green, sharply tipped, sawtoothed leaves, with their upper-surface deeply sunken veins, are characteristic. Three to ten inches long and almost as wide, these are often irregular from their generally heart-shaped bases to their pointed ends, some of them being lobed and a few resembling a mitten in silhouette. The underneaths are paler than the rough tops and many times slightly downy. Perhaps the most positive characteristic of these leaves is the fact that the stems, when cut, emit a milky sap. This is also true of the twigs, which have a sweetish taste.

Winters, the silhouette of the entire tree is characteristic, the often crooked branches of the red mulberry commonly spreading into dense, broad, round domes. The twigs are clean, usually smooth, and a pale greenish-brown. They have hollow and oval leaf scars, in which there are many bundle scars that form closed ellipses, where fibers formerly ran to the leaves. The buds have some half-dozen scales, the end buds being false. The thinnish bark is reddish-brown to greyish-brown, flaky, and ridged.

In May and June the flowers appear in dense, dangling spikes, growing like catkins from the angles between leaves and branches, male and female blossoms thriving separately but generally on the same tree. The June and July berries are composed of many one-seeded drupes, growing rather like the blackberry in shape as well as color, becoming dark purple when mature. They average about a juicy inch long.

Although the wood of the red mulberry is soft, it is surprisingly tough and proves durable when in contact with the ground, making excellent fence posts for many a farmer. It is also used in making furniture.

The white mulberry, introduced here by the British prior to the American Revolution in an unsuccessful try to set up a silkworm industry, is a similar tree. However, the leaves are hairless, the buds reddish-brown without darker scale borders, and the bark a yellowish-brown. The fruit, which is whitish with sometimes a pinkish or purplish tinge, does not have the same keen flavor, being rather tasteless though very sweet.

DISTRIBUTION - A standby of Indians and of early European explorers and settlers, the red mulberry *(Morus rubra)* grows as a native from New England to the Dakotas and south to Texas and Florida, being especially prolific in the Mississippi and Ohio Valleys.

The white mulberry *(M. alba)* although seen most frequently east of the Appalachians from New England to Florida, has extended its range as far west as Texas and Minnesota.

The so-called Texas mulberry *(M. microphylla)* grows from Texas and Arizona to Old Mexico, being a shrub or small tree seldom much more than a dozen feet high. The fruit is pleasant but not as sweet as the previous two species.

EDIBILITY - When mulberries ripen in early summer, they become one of the fruits sought most avidly by songbirds. In fact, a lot of the birds eat them green, apparently partly influenced by the seeds which some experts hold to be about as nutritious as the fleshy portions. Birds not deterred by the disfigurement known as witch broom, caused mostly by the action of various fungi on some of the trees, include the band-tailed pigeon, cardinal, catbird, crested flycatcher, purple grackle, rosebreasted grosbeak, northern blue jay, scarlet and summer and western tanager, russet-backed and wood thrush, tufted titmouse, cedar waxwing, and red-headed woodpecker. The armadillo, fox, opossum, skunk, raccoon, and several of the squirrels also relish the fruit.

Mulberries, popular raw, are also widely favored for pies, jellies, and such, especially when their sweetness is modified by a dash of lemon. Hot mulberries and steaming dumplings are a happy combination. The juice makes an excellent and often easily obtained warm-weather drink.

Incidentally, the twigs are sweetish and, particularly when tender in the spring, are edible either raw or boiled.

Red Mulberries

MUSTARD *(Brassica)*

FAMILY - Mustard *(Cruciferae)*

OTHER NAMES - White Mustard, Black Mustard, Chinese Mustard, Field Mustard, Rape, Indian Mustard, Charlock, Common Black Mustard.

DESCRIPTION - In *Ramona,* the Helen Hunt Jackson classic, there is a description of mustard upon which it is difficult to improve: "The wild mustard in Southern California is like that spoken of in the New Testament, in the branches of which the birds of the air may rest. Coming up out of the earth, so slender a stem that dozens can find starting points in an inch, it darts up a slender, straight shoot, five, ten, twenty feet, with hundreds of fine, feathery branches locking and interlocking with all the other hundreds around it, till it is an inextricable network, like lace. Then it bursts into yellow bloom, still finer, more feathery, and lacelike. The stems are so infinitesimally small and of so dark a green, that at a short distance they do not show, and the cloud of blossoms seems floating in the air; at times it looks like a golden dust. With a clear, blue sky behind it, as it is often seen, it looks like a golden snowstorm."

The Biblical description is: "It groweth up, and becometh greater than all herbs, and shooteth out great branches; so that the fowls of the air may lodge under the shadow of it."

Each of the small mustard flowers has four petals in, as with the whole family, the typical shape of a cross. Prominent is the broader flat part in the upper end of the petal, which is greatly narrower toward its base. Too, there are always four green leaflike sepals, standing close against the lower parts of the quartet of petals. There are six small, thin stamens, the organs bearing the pollen grains, four of these stamens being longer than the remaining two.

Centered in the blossom is a single green seed vessel which remains concealed until the petals and stamens fall off. At that time it grows into a long, lean pod, crammed with minute, dark, peppery seeds. Numerous of these slim pods stand out from the stems.

The annual black mustard, to pick the most important domestic member of the *Brassica* genus, ordinarily grows from two to six feet tall, although in moist fertile ground in California I have seen it as tall as the shorter telephone poles. A cousin of the cabbage and cauliflower, this *Brassica nigra* shoots up erectly, with broadly spreading branches.

The leaves on the young plants, which are the ones to gather for greens, are usually covered rather roughly with hairs, while others are smooth, especially at the tops of the plants. Although the deeply indented and finely toothed bottom leaves have slim stems, the lobeless and extremely bitter upper ones come close to growing directly from the main stalks. The upright, four-sided pods hug the bitter stems, their pungently pleasant seeds maturing during the hot days of summer.

DISTRIBUTION - Five species of the genus *Brassica* are widely distributed over southern Canada and the United States, where they are especially abundant and important in the Pacific region, particularly in California.

EDIBILITY - The oily seeds of these edibles, often fed to caged birds, are also sought by doves, pheasants, woodcock, finches, larks, and nuthatches among others. Ground squirrels eat the seeds, too. The plants are relished by deer.

The easily gathered seeds, even after the greens have grown too bitter and tough to use, are difficult to equal for garnishing salads, seasoning pickles and such, lending authority to barbeque sauces, and adding zest to soups and stews. Mustard's name comes from these seeds, being a corruption of *must seeds* which goes back to Roman-occupied Britain where these were processed by soaking them in grape juice or *must.*

Homemade table mustard can be prepared by finely grinding wild mustard seeds, between two stones if you're camping or in the family food chopper at home, then adding enough water or vinegar to make a paste. If you choose to modify your raw mustard with up to an equal bulk of flour, first brown this latter slowly and lightly in an oven to eradicate the starchy flavor. The vinegar may be diluted, depending on its initial strength, up to half and half with water. On occasion the maker may like the added flavor of horseradish. This white-flowered member of the same mustard family, with its pungent white roots described elsewhere in this volume, likewise thrives wild.

The young greens are a favorite potherb in many homes. To be at its best, mustard requires more cooking than most greens, something like ½ hour, and you need a lot, too, as it shrinks considerably.

The young golden flowers, simmered for only several minutes so that they do not lose their character, make a broccolilike dish, particularly tasty with vinegar and butter or margarine and especially rich in proteins and Vitamin A.

Mustard greens are no slouches in the nutrition department, either, 100 grams of them boiled and drained containing 183 milligrams of calcium, 30 of phosphorous, 3 of iron, 32 of potassium, and no less than 7,000 international units of Vitamin A, plus sturdy amounts of thiamine, riboflavin, niacin, and 97 milligrams of Vitamin C.

Black Mustard

NETTLES *(Urtica)*

FAMILY - Nettle *(Urticaceae)*

OTHER NAMES - Stinging Nettle, Slender Nettle, Great Nettle, Dwarf Nettle.

DESCRIPTION - The protein-rich nettles are among the most versatile and potentially valuable of all plants. In some parts of the world you can sleep between nettle sheets, eat off a nettle tablecloth, dine on nettle-enriched steaks and eggs ordered from a nettle-paper menu, in an emergency fish with a nettle line, and in the springtime especially revel with delectable nettle dishes washed down with nettle beer. In fact, this is only a portion of this wild edible's capabilities.

These perennials are for the most part single-stemmed greens which grow from a few inches to some seven feet tall, depending mostly on the fertility and the moisture-content of the sun-warmed soil. The opposite pairs of leaves are coarsely veined, egg-shaped to oblong with heartlike bases and tapered tips, and are roughly and sharply toothed. Characteristically, the stalks, leafstems, and the underneaths of the leaves are fuzzy with fine stinging bristles whose pointed hollowness extends from swollen bases, filled with fluid in which formic acid is a principal ingredient.

For this reason it is best to gather the plants, which except in an emergency you'll most often want to do in the springtime, with a knife or scissors and leather or plastic gloves. If you still get stung, perhaps on the exposed wrists, rub the rash with alcohol or with the juice of the nettles themselves. Some Indians scoured the irritated skin with the dry, rusty, feltlike growth that sheathes young ferns or fiddleheads. Bruised green dock is also similarly used, although with a little trouble you can avoid the difficulty entirely. In fact, it is entirely practical to gather the young nettles with the bare hands by using scissors and a paper bag. Later in the year, the uppermost young, still tender leaves can also be so collected.

Long, slender, insignificant if multibranched clusters of tiny green flowers droop in late summer from the angles between leaves and stalk. Like those of the oak and walnut trees, these nettle blossoms often have both their male and female reproductive organs on the same plant.

DISTRIBUTION - Nettles grow from Alaska across Canada, south throughout much of the U.S. Their presence is usually a good sign that the ground is fertile.

EDIBILITY - Towhees are among the birds eating the seeds of the nettle. Although nettles when green are too formidable to be popular as a grazing plant, dried and ripened in hay they have been proved to be one of the most protein-rich foods available for farm stock, rivaling cottonseed meal.

It is as a boiled green that nettles are most frequently enjoyed on this continent, and they are among the best both in flavor and nutrition. Only the short, tender, young plants first appearing in the springtime should be used, along with the tender new leaves later in the year. Just dropping them into a very small amount of boiling water quells the bristles.

NEW JERSEY TEA (Ceanothus)

FAMILY - Buckthorn *(Rhamnaceae)*

OTHER NAMES - Redroot, Mountain Tea.

DESCRIPTION - The feathery, white, May to September blossom clusters of the New Jersey tea brighten many a shadowy nook in an otherwise flowerless neighborhood. One of the most historically famous of our native tea substitutes, this low shrub which is a member of the buckthorn family dies back to the woody base just above its red roots in the winter, putting up new green shoots every springtime. It is one of the few non-legumes, incidentally, to sprout nitrogen-fixing nodules on its large roots, these latter sometimes being used to make a cinnamon-red dye.

The alternate leaves of this low straggly shrub are oval to triangular, sharply tipped, finely and bluntly sawtoothed, and characteristically smooth above and rather velvety underneath. One of the species, on the other hand, *Ceanothus pitcheri*, has leaves with woolly tops and blunt tips. Dark green especially on their upper surfaces, the leaves have three strongly marked ribs running from the bottom almost to the apex. These leaves are from two to four inches long.

The occasionally branched twigs and the slim buds are a bit hairy.

The dense white flower heads, resembling in silhouette long-stalked clusters of grapes, grow in the upper angles between the leaves and the branches. The blossoms are fragrant, attracting a variety of insects. Individually, each flower is small, with a regular corolla of five hooded petals and a calyx of five leaflike sepals. There are five stamens and one pistil with three stigmas, the parts which receive the pollen grains and upon which these germinate.

They develop into three-lobed, dry pods with saucerlike bases, these latter often remaining after the fruits fall, from September to November.

DISTRIBUTION - New Jersey tea grows in rocky woodlands and on gravelly inclines from the Maritimes to Ontario, down to Florida and the Gulf of Mexico and westward to Kansas and Texas.

EDIBILITY - A number of birds, including quail and wild turkeys, eat the fruits.

The leaves of the New Jersey tea, both green and dried, were regularly brewed in and around the Thirteen Colonies when, about the time of the Boston Tea Party and later during the American Revolution, oriental blends were both in disfavor and scarce. More than one soldier under General George Washington's command kept up his spirits with such pleasantly flavored infusions which, even if they lacked the caffeine of the now more familiar tea, were at least hot and bracing.

Although the freshly picked leaves, best gathered while the edible is flowering, make a flavorful enough beverage, this is considerably improved if they are slowly dried first, particularly if cream and sugar are added. When we lived where they grow we used to gather several paper bagfuls of the leaves and hang them near the ceiling for a few months. Measure and use like oriental tea.

©AJA

ORACH *(Atriplex)*

FAMILY - Goosefoot *(Chenopodiaceae)*

OTHER NAMES - Saltbush, Shad Scale, Sea Purslane, Garden Orach, San Joaquin Saltbush, Saltweed, Spear Orach, Red Orach, Arrow Saltbush, Truncate Saltbush, Silver Saltbush, Silver Scale, Sea Scale, Quail Brush, Desert Holly, Ball Saltbush, Crown Saltbush, Australian Saltbush, Crown Scale.

DESCRIPTION - Some of the members of the orach family closely resemble both lamb's quarter and green amaranth, each discussed elsewhere in this book, but both their habitats and the way in which they flower are different. In fact, in a lot of households across the continent the acknowledged pick of the edible greens is orach. The tender tips and juicy young leaves of this wild food are saltily delectable from springtime to late autumn. Connoisseurs pronounce them equal to, if not better than, their two fine look-alikes.

This resemblance is only true with some species. Some of the orach genus, in fact, are only single stems that sprawl across the upper stones of the beaches reached only by the higher tides.

The leaves are distinctive, being triangularly shaped like ½-to-3-inch arrowheads except that the barb at each lower corner is turned outward rather than cuttingly downward. They are greyish to bright green, sometimes reddish, smooth-edged, and characteristically lighter and mealy-appearing underneath.

The small, green flowers grow in narrow, interrupted spikes in the angles between leaves and stalks. The fruits, when they develop, have a large pair of winglike sepals. Later there is an abundance of small, starchy seeds.

DISTRIBUTION - Orach provides top eating from British Columbia to Labrador, south to California and Virginia, growing luxuriantly on salt marshes, beaches, and wet flats along the coast and on moist alkaline lands in the interior.

EDIBILITY - Orach is a favorite food of the big Canada goose which feeds on its seeds, leaves, and stems. Quail are among the upland game birds dining on the seeds. Deer, rabbits, antelopes, mountain sheep, and some of the remaining herds of buffalo browse on the twigs and foliage.

You have to be careful not to add too much salt to orach, but outside of that it can be used in any of the recipes for wild greens. It is also excellent raw, being a particularly intriguing nibble when you're strolling along the seashore. The starchy seeds were eaten by some of the Indian tribes.

©AJA

PASTURE BRAKE *(Pteridium)*

FAMILY -Fern *(Polypodiaceae)*

OTHER NAMES — Brakes, Eagle Fern, Hog Brake, Brake Fern, Bracken Fern.

DESCRIPTION - Coarse and strong, the commonest of this continent's ferns, the pasture brake is one of the first to appear in the spring and until killed by the first frost continues to produce new leaves during the warm months. These leaves, so called, are held nearly straight upward.

The darkly green fronds, heavy and leathery, differ in height from one to about four feet, unlike most ferns often covering large sunny expanses in dry areas. Each one lifts singly from an often common root and, when they are dead, remain in brown masses to point up the presence of the emerging fiddleheads in the springtime.

The triangular-shaped fronds are divided into three major divisions, each of which is cleft pinnately once or twice with narrow lobes not reaching to the midrib. The distinguishing mark is the location of the fruit dots in an unbroken narrow line along the under edge of each leaflet, which is turned under to protect them. Silvery at first, these dots later become dark brown.

The leaflets are oblong, each with a blunted and distinctly narrowed tip. The lower leaflets are further divided into subleaflets; narrow, closely crowded, variably shaped, midveined, usually with characteristic blunted, narrow tips that are somewhat hairy. The tall stalks, about the same length as the leaf, are partially grooved in front. Smooth and rigid, they are green early in the summer, turning dark brown with maturity.

The rootstocks are about ½ inch thick, dark, scaleless although occasionally hairy, deep-growing and extensively creeping. Stout, black, widely spreading roots are sparsely scattered along this main rootstock.

The young fiddleheads, which are the edible parts above ground, are good when from about four to ten inches in height, depending on the locality. They are covered with silvery grey or brownish hair which can be removed by rubbing them between the hands. Called fiddleheads because of their resemblance in this emerging stage to the tuning ends of violins, they are also known in some places as croziers because of their likeness to the shepherds' crooklike staffs of abbots, bishops, and abbesses. The three sections of the leaf later uncoil like the opening of an eagle's claw, on their way to toughening and becoming poisonous to cattle as well as humans.

DISTRIBUTION - This genus with only one species, *Pteridium aquilinum,* is cosmopolitan and widely spread over North America, from Alaska and Labrador southward, as it is over the surface of the world.

At home in most places, although rarely in the rich and moist locales so typical for most ferns, it is found in the full sunlight, in woods, old pastures, new roadsides, burned-over-regions, sandy and partially shaded areas, and in thickets.

EDIBILITY - The mountain beaver is one of the animals eating the pasture brake which would be used more extensively if it did not develop a poisonous quality upon maturity.

The fiddleheads, while still in the uncurled stage, are edible both raw and cooked, in many widespread localities being regarded as pleasantly mucilaginous delicacies. Do not eat too many raw, however, because of the enzyme thiaminase which, destroyed by cooking, attacks the species of Vitamin B_1 in the body when sufficient quantities are devoured.

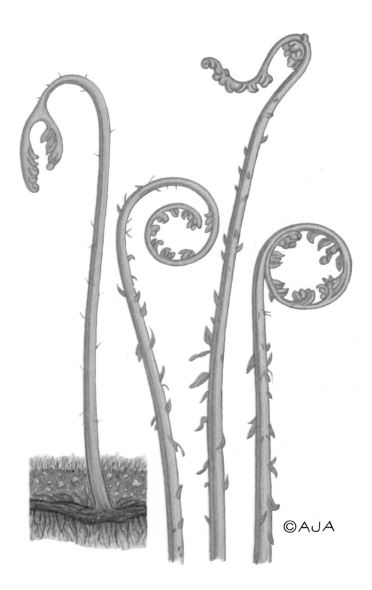

©AJA

PAPAW *(Asimina)*

FAMILY - Custard Apple *(Anonaceae)*

OTHER NAMES - False Banana, Poor Man's Banana, Custard Apple, Michigan Banana, Tall Papaw, Common Papaw.

DESCRIPTION - Our papaw is the only native custard apple growing in the north United States, although we do have the pond apple *(Annona glabra),* a member of the same family, in southern Florida where the fruit, rather similar to that of the papaw, was eaten by the Seminole Indians. Papaws, though, grow as far north as New York, Michigan, and even Ontario.

The only hardy member of the mostly tropical custard apple group, the papaw is a shrub or small tree, occasionally reaching a height of some 40 feet with a trunk up to a foot in diameter. In the North, however, it seldom grows higher than twenty feet, with trunks only a few inches through. Large and often drooping leaves give the plant a distinctively tropical aspect.

The single leaves of the papaw are alternate and narrowly egg-shaped in outline, narrowing gradually from the abruptly pointed upper third to the pointed base, where they are attached by short stems. Some four to twelve inches long, and from two to four inches wide, their conspicuous veins are emphasized by their rather thin texture. The smooth upper surfaces are dark green, the underneaths pale but also smooth, Young stems and unfurling leaves, though, are bedecked with a rusty down that falls off as they mature. The edges are smooth except for pointed tips and bottoms.

At the same time that fresh green leaves are starting to burst forth along the branches, the papaws begin putting forth their peculiar, solitary, three-part, greenish-purple to reddish or brownish-purple flowers. Measuring about 1½ inches across, each blossom has six petals in two sets of three, as well as three sepals. Numerous stamens make their presence evident, but there are only a few ovule-bearing pistils which later become the large pulpy fruits. Incidentally, these should not be confused with a different Florida fruit also known as papaw. Two varieties of this latter tree, actually the papaya, grow wild in Florida.

In the winter, if like a lot of us you like to stake out your food sources ahead of time, the papaw can be positively identified by its long, slim, somewhat flat, brown buds with their coats of rust-colored hairs. The bud at the end of the twig is about ½ inch long. The smooth bark is thin and brown, often with chalky blotches. U-shaped leaf scars are another distinctive feature.

The easiest time to identify the papaw is, of course, in the fall when its unique fruit, resembling stubby bananas, is growing. Some three to five inches long when mature, and sometimes nearly two inches thick, these start out with a firm green skin that becomes yellowish-brown with ripeness. The egg-custardlike pulp, almost as sweet as the fruit smells, is interspersed with several flat seeds.

Like the highbush cranberry, which is described elsewhere in this book, papaws are apt to require an acquired taste, although the hungry members of the Lewis and Clark Expedition returning through Missouri where game happened to be scarce and where their regular rations had been cut to one biscuit a day found the fruit to have few shortcomings. A lot, that is, depends on the hunger and the adaptability of the eater, but it might be added that those who come to esteem the papaw often regard it as their favorite wild fruit.

DISTRIBUTION - Papaws, which like shade, are found most often in moist and fertile situations, as in alluvial soil along streams or on the lower slopes of adjoining hillsides. Essentially a tropical plant, it grows wild from Michigan, southern Ontario, and New York, west to Nebraska and Texas and southward to Florida. Both decorative and delicious, it is a likely candidate for gardens from which it frequently escapes.

EDIBILITY - Fully ripened fruit is usually difficult to find in the woods, for you have to beat coons, possums, squirrels, foxes, and their fellows to it. Too, it has the habit of falling to the ground when mature. But you can gather the fruit green and let it ripen at home in a cool, dark place, preferably outside the house because of the perfumed fragrance that for many can become all too pervading.

Perhaps best raw, depending on who's doing the eating, it is also cooked into desserts.

PARTRIDGEBERRY *(Mitchella)*

FAMILY - Bedstraw *(Rubiaceae)*

OTHER NAMES - Twin Berries, Checkerberries, Squaw Vine, Partridge Vine.

DESCRIPTION - Creeping close to the ground and putting down new roots wherever its prostrate stem branches, the partridgeberry forms trailing evergreen mats that can be seen any time of the year in damp woods and on sandy knolls, in winter studded with edible red berries.

The distinctive thing about this wild edible is the way two flowers grow together in twinlike proximity at the end of the creeping stem, sometimes in the angles between leaves and stalk, to form a single red berry. These June blossoms burst forth in pairs, many times with the previous year's coral red fruit. Creamy white or pale pink, they emit a pleasant fragrance. The four petals of each come together to make a miniature tube, at the top of which the quartet spread apart conspicuously in four sometimes recurving lobes, hairy along their insides. On occasion there are only three petals.

Further distinguishing these edibles is that each of the twin flowers is different, one having a tall pistil and short stamens and the other boasting a short pistil but long stamens. This results in the blossom with the tall pistil being almost always fertilized by the other's tall stamens—the short pistil by the companion's short stamens—this being a built-in guard against too close fertilization and the reason the genus has remained robust over the centuries. The ovaries of the paired blossoms, which appear during June and July, are united so that only a single globular berry is formed.

The shiny, opposite, evergreen leaves grow on very short stems and are egg-shaped or heartlike and smooth along their trim edges. Ordinarily they run about ½ inch long, occasionally bigger, extending close to ¾ inch in some localities, but generally smaller. Some have whitish veins.

Pleasantly aromatic, the bright red berries, seldom very numerous, are about ¼ inch across. Most of those not devoured by the birds remain conspicuously on the plants all winter, well into the next spring when the twin flowers are forming once more.

DISTRIBUTION - Partridgeberries, which also grown in Japan, are found on this continent from the Maritime Provinces and Quebec to Florida, west to Alaska, Colorado, and Texas.

EDIBILITY -Grouse, quail, and wild turkey are among the birds eating the aromatic berries, especially when other fruit becomes scarce. Fox also seek them.

Especially common in pine forests, the easily distinguished partridgeberries, although seldom available in quantity, make a good emergency food as well as a pleasant woodland snack.

PIN CHERRY *(Prunus)*

FAMILY - Rose *(Rosaceae)*

OTHER NAMES - Bird Cherry, Fire Cherry, Wild Red Cherry.

DESCRIPTION - This is the one and only early and light-red wild cherry in Canada and the northern States.

Unlike the chokecherry and the rum cherry, the pin cherry bears its blossoms in small, lateral, roundly flat tufts. The fruits, ripening during midsummer, are light-red drupes about ¼ inch across, each with its single seed which is surrounded with thin, extremely sour pulp. As with the flowers, the stems grow from a common spot, forming a flattish and rounded fruit cluster.

The oblong leaves have a lancehead aspect, with rounded or wedge-shaped bases and with tips that taper to a point. Measuring some three to five inches in length, they are about one-fourth as wide. Fine, sharp teeth roughen the edges. Thin and shiny, they are brightly yellowish-green on both sides, being a bit paler beneath. The stems are seldom longer than a slim inch, and for further identification they have twin glands at their tops.

To identify this tree in the winter, look for twigs that are smooth, slim, frequently lustrous, and a reddish-brown with somewhat of a grey film. The buds are ⅛ inch or less long, egg-shaped, dully tipped, and dark reddish-brown in hue. Many of them are characteristically clustered at the end of the twigs. The buds on the sides ordinarily have auxiliary buds beside them.

The young trees and branches, and this is a short-lived tree, have a very bright and gleaming reddish-brown bark, strikingly marked with long, horizontal lenticels or pores. This bark frequently peels away in horizontal strips, exposing a green inner bark that is aromatic to the smell and bitter with poisonous hydrocyanic acid to the taste. Too, the outer bark has a tendency to crack horizontally. More mature trees assume a shaggier, curlier roughness.

The pin cherry is ordinarily a small tree, very occasionally reaching a height of 25 to 30 feet, with a trunk up to about a foot in width. It is commonly found in clearings and along fences and roads where the birds have regurgitated and thus distributed the seeds. Along with the poplars, it springs up on burned or cut-over forest areas, especially those formerly covered with hemlock, white pine, or some of the northern hardwoods. Because it cannot stand shade, it dies soon after it is topped by the crowns of other trees. The wood has no commercial value.

DISTRIBUTION - This wild cherry, common to many burned or forested areas, thickets, and young woods, grows from Newfoundland and Labrador to British Columbia, south to Colorado, South Dakota, and the mountains of Georgia and Tennessee.

EDIBILITY - Birds soon strip the trees, and small forest folk harvest what's left on the ground.

Sour raw but thirst-quenching and sustaining, the pin cherry is most famous when turned into jelly or syrup. Boiled down in a small amount of water, strained, simmered with sugar to taste, and then bottled, the latter goes well on steaming hot flapjacks on frosty winter mornings.

PINE *(Pinus)*

FAMILY - Pine *(Pinaceae)*

OTHER NAMES - White Pine, Scotch Pine, Fir, Piñon, Nut Pine, Norway Pine, Alaska Pine, Blister Pine, Shortleaf Pine, North Carolina Pine, Oregon Pine, Rosemary Pine, Eastern Yellow Pine, Digger Pine, Monterey Pine, Four-Leaved Pine, One-Leaved Nut Pine, Parry Pine, Sugar Pine, Scrub Pine, Giant Pine, Stone Pine, Jack Pine, Loblolly Pine, Longleaf Pine, Mountain Pine, Pitch Pine, Red Pine, Swamp Pine, Lodgepole Pine, Ponderosa, Western White Pine, Austrian Pine, Bank Pine, Black Pine, Bur Pine, Eastern White Pine, Gray Pine, Hard Pine, Jersey Pine, Marsh Pine, Northern Scrub Pine, Oldfield Pine, Pocosin Pine, Pond Pine, Poverty Pine, Prickly-Cone Pine, Sand Pine, Slash Pine, Table Mountain Pine, Virginia Pine, Walter Pine.

DESCRIPTION - The pines as a species have needlelike leaves in clusters of from two to five which remain in place for two, three or more years. The flowers appear in the springtime, producing a plentitude of sulphurlike pollen which dusts everything and everyone within reach. As soon as this fertilizes the stigmas of the pistillate blossoms, there develop the familiar woody-scaled cones which take two and occasionally three years to reach maturity and disperse their winged seeds on the wind.

However, the great pine family is made up of no less than 28 to 36 different units of shrubs and trees, the count depending on whether the botanist is a lumper or a splitter, with a complete roster of some three hundred distinct species. The main North American groups of trees belonging to the pine group, all collectively known as conifers, include the pines themselves, the larches and spruces, both the true and false firs, the great hemlocks, the arbor vitaes which were so-named because they saved an early troupe of explorers from scurvy, the sequoias, the bald cypresses and the various cedars.

If you mistake a spruce for a pine, for example, it makes no great difference. Both have an edible inner bark, and both are rich in life-maintaining Vitamin C. Thousands have starved to death in pine forests, or have suffered and died from scurvy, when a little of the knowledge we are considering would have saved them. This can be all the more important as this continent's rich flora includes a large share of the world's pines.

Incidentally, the poison hemlock from which the ancients brewed their lethal tea is a completely different plant, a member of the parsley or *Umbelliferae* family, and no relation of our wholesome evergreen hemlock, a somewhat pyramidal tree with slim horizontal or drooping branches. The long flattened leaves or needles are attached to these limbs with slight wooden stalks that remain in place when the needles fall after three or more years. The easily overlooked, small flowers, both pistillate and staminate, come out on the same tree in the springtime, developing cones that mature in a single season. Often hanging on throughout the winter, they have thin scales holding pairs of tiny winged seeds.

Although all these growths are generally evergreen, such native conifers as the bald cypress and the tamarack shed all their needles in the fall.

DISTRIBUTION - The pines as a whole grow abundantly throughout the United States and Canada, up to the timber line, except in the central plains, the tundras, and the deserts.

EDIBILITY - Pines occupy a position very close to the top in importance to wildlife. Just their seeds, for example, make up more than half the diet of the white-headed woodpecker, the red crossbill, and the Clarke nutcracker. Numerous other birds and mammals depend on these tasty, oily, and extremely nutritious seeds to a large extent. The needles are eaten by several types of grouse and by some of the browsers. In fact, when other food is scarce cattle seek them. There are also the buds. Porcupines and small rodents consume the bark and wood. Then there are the facts that the evergreen furnish cover, favorite roosting and nesting places, and home-building materials.

The entire pine family comprises one of the most vital groups of wild edibles in the world. The inner bark, eaten both raw and cooked, has saved hundreds of people from starvation. The Indians made great use of this. In fact, Adirondacks is the Indian name for tree-eaters.

The colonists early learned to gather this inner bark in the springtime, dry it throughout the summer, and then grind it or mix it with regular flour. Next to devouring it raw, though, the easiest way to eat this sweet cambium is to cut it into thin strips, then cook it like spaghetti either alone or with meat.

Some of the tribes went to more elaborate preparations, even to making a sort of bread. The squaws mashed the pine's inner bark to a pulp in water, then molded this into big cakes. While this was going on, a rousing fire was kindled in a rock-lined hole. The coals were then removed, the cakes laid in on green leaves, and the embers raked back over a thick topping of more leaves. Damp moss covered everything, which was left to cook for upwards of an hour. The cakes were then placed on pole frames and smoked for a week, after which they could be carried as trail rations. The results were so sturdy that before use, the cake was customarily broken into bits and boiled until soft.

Even pine needles, when they are new and starchy, are pleasantly nutritious to chew upon. Some Indians boiled the still firm, spikelike flower clusters, in which the petalless blossoms grow on slim stalks in circular rows, to flavor their game. As for the cones, the young ones can be ground and used to flavor

©AJA

Eastern White Pine

meat sauces. Some Indians used to roast the soft centers of green cones in the fringes of their campfires and feast on the syrupy results. Then, of course, there are the gums, the sugary sap of some of the conifers, and the bared young shoots of the white pine in particular which are sometimes candied.

Hemlock tea is famous in northern New England and Canada. Drunk hot and black, its taste is reminiscent of the way a Christmas tree smells. More important for prospectors, trappers, loggers, and other outdoorsmen, this tea contains the vital Vitamin C.

It doesn't really make too much difference if you mistake one of the other conifers for hemlock. All these members of the pine family provide aromatic and beneficial tea. The bright green young tips, when they appear in the springtime, are best. Older green needles will do, too. Just place a handful in a receptacle, cover them with boiling water, and let them steep until the tea tastes strong enough. For a much higher ascorbic acid content, cover and let stand overnight. If you prefer this black as I do, there's no need of any straining. Just narrow your lips on the rim and quaff it down.

Then there are the pinons. These soft little nuts from the pinecones of millions of low-spreading conifers in the western U.S. and Mexico are among the most delicious to be had anywhere especially when they have been roasted, after being shelled with the help of pliers or hammer, by spreading them in a single layer in a pan and placing this for five minutes in a moderate 360° oven, shaking the pan several times during the process.

A 100-gram portion of piñons has been found by U.S. Department of Agriculture experts to contain 635 calories, 13 grams of protein, 60.5 grams of fat, 20.5 grams of carbohydrates, plus a huge 604 milligrams of phosphorous, 5.2 of iron, 1.28 of thiamine, .23 of riboflavin, and no less than 4.5 mg. of niacin. And if there is any more delectable way to get these necessary ingredients than in the subtly piquant little nuts, I've never discovered it.

PLANTAIN *(Plantago)*

FAMILY - Plantain *(Plantaginaceae)*

OTHER NAMES - Seaside Plantain, Goosetongue, Cart-Track Plant, Pale Plantain, English Plantain, Seashore Plantain, Common Plantain, Plain Plantain, Indian Wheat, Snake Weed, Rippleseed Plantain, Cuckoo's Bread, Ribwort, Soldiers Herb.

DESCRIPTION - Although nearly everyone knows plantain, few realize it is edible. It is a sturdy, persistent, little plant, and I've seen it poking up through sidewalks in such busy cities as Boston, New York, and San Francisco.

It is the short, stemless perennial, instantly recognizable from its picture, where strongly ribbed, spadelike, green leaves lift directly from the root about one or more straight central spikes. What there is of a stem is troughlike.

Seaside plantain grows along the shores, cliffs, and a bit inland from both the Pacific and Atlantic Coasts, and the leaves of this are fleshier, longer, and less tough. Many are up to 10 inches in length and about an inch wide. The flowers are crowded into a spike at the end of a leafless stalk. It is the shape of these leaves, as well as those of the alien English plantain which has become common on this continent, that give the potherb its name of goosetongue.

The spikes of the plantain, although likely you've never noticed it, flower with tiny greenish or drab bronze blossoms that mature into equally inconspicuous seeds.

Plain plantain, another of the some 19 varieties of the wild edible that thrive in the Eastern Hemisphere, has thinner and brighter green leaves than the first-described common plantain. The stalks are reddish at their bottoms. The flower heads are not as dense and are even thinner and less crowded at their tips.

DISTRIBUTION - Plantain grows from Alaska to Labrador, southward throughout Canada and the United States.

EDIBILITY - Grouse eat the plants, while cardinals, sparrows, and a host of other songbirds feast on the seeds. Rabbits, squirrels, and deer are among the animals eating the plants.

Rich in Vitamins A and C and in many of the minerals, plantain is used raw when caught young enough and is later cooked like spinach. The narrow-leaved varieties are the tenderest. When older, it has a woodsy flavor and is best appreciated with a cream sauce, after the plant has been pureed and pressed through a fine sieve to exclude its fibers.

The leaves also make one of the backwoods teas, each ½ handful being covered by a cup of boiling water and steeped for ½ hour.

© AJA

POKEWEED *(Phytolacca)*

FAMILY - Pokeweed *(Phytolaccaceae)*

OTHER NAMES - Pigeonberry, Garget, Poke, Scoke, Caokum, Inkberry, Pocan, Virginia Poke.

DESCRIPTION - Many a soldier writing home during the Civil War cut his own quill pen from the wing feather of a turkey, then squeezed some of the red juice from the ripe, deeply purple berries of the pokeweed to use as his ink. A few of these letters, still legible, can be seen in museums today, recommending the enduring permanence of what are often still called inkberries.

The Indians found pokeweed delicious, and some of the first post-Columbus adventurers on these shores were in such agreement that they took the startings back to England and southern Europe, where the vegetable became popular. Today pokeweed, whose sprouts find their way into some of our stores, provide some of the first wild greens of the spring. Some devotees like it so much that they even grow it in their cellars.

Where it has room to spread, pokeweed becomes a surprisingly attractive plant whose dark green leaves are brightened at almost every angle between them and the branches with tassels of whitish-yellow flowers, succeeded by berry clusters that change from green to red and eventually in the autumn to a rich, royally lush purple. Each individual berry is packed with numerous seeds.

For some reason, few of the billions of the long, shiny, black seeds produced each year have been able to find conditions suitable for their germination and growth. A usual way to plant poke for the home has been to break or cut into six-inch lengths the preferably medium-size roots, those some three or four inches in diameter, and to sow these in garden soil, perhaps in a deep, flat box in a dark and warm cellar or outdoors along a protective fence. Regularly watered in the cellar, about a dozen such starts will do for a family of three, regularly sending up shoots for months.

University of Arkansas researchers have now found that mature seeds that have been soaked for precisely five minutes in concentrated sulphuric acid, then tipped into a fine-meshed sieve and quickly and thoroughly washed with running water, will germinate within two weeks with an 80% to 90% rate of success. Spring crops of pokeweed greens, therefore, are now produced in some places in the Southern States as soon as the soil warms.

So as not to harm the young plants, only one crop of greens is taken the first year. In the second growing season, however, three cuttings are made, about mid-May, early June, and late June. Home users continue to enjoy the sprouts until blossoming begins in July.

If you plan to plant a crop with your own seed, harvest the wild berries when they become dark purple and ripe about early August. Place in some non-metallic receptacle, crush, and allow to ferment for three or four days. Then wash out the seeds with water and dry them in a thin layer, perhaps on cheesecloth or outspread paper. Treat the clean, dry seed with the acid, then either plant at once for fall and early winter greens or hold for sowing the next spring.

The fat young sprouts, especially when they are some six to eight inches high, are the only part of pokeweed that is good to eat. The bitter roots—cathartic, emetic and somewhat narcotic—are poisonous. So are the mature stalks when they take on a purplish cast. You may have seen birds get tipsy on the berries.

You'll want to be able to recognize the fully grown plants, however, as in the spring it is near their dried remains that the tender young shoots will arrow upward. The leaves, which are shaped like lanceheads, have stems on one end and points on the other. Scattered, smooth on both sides, and wavy-edged, they are up to about ten inches long. The reddish juice from the ripe berries, as country boys sometimes still confirm when school classes reopen in the fall, will also serve as ink for steel pen points.

DISTRIBUTION - Pokeweed, a hardy perennial throughout the South, flourishes in the eastern half of the United States except along the Canadian border, west to Texas and south to the tropics.

EDIBILITY - An important source of food for the mourning dove, the berries are also loved by a host of other birds including the robin, bluejay, cardinal, yellow-breasted chat, rose-breasted grosbeak, yellow-bellied sapsucker, cedar waxwing, and the golden-fronted woodpecker. Fox, opossums, raccoons, and the white-footed mice also eat the fruit.

Gather your small, tender pokeweed shoots when they are no more than about 8 inches tall. Remove skin and leaves, saving the latter for greens. Simmer the whole stems in a small amount of lightly salted water only until tender. Serve like asparagus, perhaps with drawn butter and a dash of lemon juice or on toast with hollandaise or a light cheese sauce.

©AJA

POPLAR *(Populus)*

FAMILY - Willow *(Salicaceae)*

OTHER NAMES - Aspen, Quaking Aspen, Trembling Aspen, Large-Toothed Aspen, White Poplar, Lombardy Poplar, Silver-Leaf Poplar, Bolles Poplar, Small-Toothed Aspen, American Aspen, Big-Toothed Aspen, Balsam Poplar, Balm of Gilead, Hairy Balm of Gilead, Hackmatack, Tacamahac, Eastern Cottonwood, Whitewood, Swamp Cottonwood, Swamp Poplar, Downy Poplar, Black Cottonwood, River Cottonwood, Popple, Carolina Poplar, Silver Poplar.

DESCRIPTION - The poplars are in many ways the pioneers of the tree community, for it is they who often first seed vast open reaches of soil denuded by forest fires or bared by logging, leading the way for other trees.

These members of the willow family have alternate, entire, autumn-falling leaves with toothed and sometimes lobed edges. These leaves, mostly somewhat triangular, have three to five major veins that meet near the base. Their slim, unusually long stems are occasionally flat, a reason why the leaves flutter in even the slightest breeze. The branches are brittle, as anyone gathering firewood has found, breaking away easily from the trunks.

Poplar buds are unique in plants with a trio of bundle scars, the tiny and somewhat circular dots within the leaf scar that are made by the breakage of the bundles of ducts leading into the leaf stem, in that the lowest bud scale of side buds is always situated directly above the leaf scar in the outside position.

The bark of most poplars is distinctively smooth when young, with a greenish-white bloom that comes off on hands and clothing, and darkly furrowed when more mature.

The flowers appear before the leaves in early spring, the trees bearing either male of female blossoms that hang in drooping spikelike clusters, having no petals but growing in close circular rows on a slim stalk. Upon maturity they split open to reveal numerous tiny seeds, each with long silky hairs that bear them aloft in the wind. It is this cottony aspect of the amassed seeds that is responsible for some species being called cottonwoods.

DISTRIBUTION - Extending from Alaska down through the Hudson Bay area to Newfoundland, poplars grow south to Pennsylvania and along the mountains to Kentucky, west through the Rockies to New Mexico and California.

EDIBILITY - The resinous catkins and buds supply valuable winter and spring food for various species of grouse. The tender bark, twigs, and foliage are eaten abundantly by rabbits and hoofed browsers, especially moose. It is the favorite food of the beaver in many localities.

The poplar's sweetish, starchy sap layer is edible both raw and cooked. This lies between the wood of the trunks, branches, and twigs and outside bark, the latter being intensely bitter with salacin which is an ingredient in some tonics concocted for the benefit of mankind and as a factor in reducing fever.

It can be scraped off and eaten on the spot. It can also be cut into strips or chunks and cooked like noodles in soups and stews. Dried and powdered, it is a flour additive and substitute.

©AJA

PRAIRIE TURNIP *(Psoralea)*

FAMILY - Pulse *(Leguminosae)*

OTHER NAMES - Breadroot, Wild Potato, Prairie Apple, *Pomme Blanche, Pomme de Prairie,* Wild Turnip, Prairie Potato, Indian Breadroot.

DESCRIPTION - When John Colter, mountain man once with the Lewis and Clark Expedition, escaped from the Indians and came back safely to his friends with his incredible story of what now is Yellowstone National Park, he lived for a week largely on prairie turnips. This famous vegetable of the plains and the West was a mainstay of such Indians as the Sioux and in the northwest of the Cree. Early plainsmen, settlers, frontiersmen, trappers, explorers, and traders came to relish its starchy, sweetish, somewhat turniplike taste.

The prairie turnip, also widely known as breadroot, is a cousin of the garden pea, being a fellow legume. It is a perennial whose large root, or sometimes group of roots, resembling sweet potato roots and having an agreeable odor, lies entirely beneath the ground. The generally branched stalks, characterized by soft whitish bristles, are erect and from 6 to 18 inches tall.

Five inversely ovate leaflets, narrowest at their bases, comprise each compound leaf. These leaflets are from about ½ to an inch wide and twice as long. The plant blooms in May and June with dense spikes of small, purplish-blue, pealike flowers, less than ½ inch long, which eventually become tiny pods, enveloped in a remaining calyx tube whose original lobes were nearly as long as the blossoms.

The tops of the prairie turnip mature early. Breaking off in the sweeping winds and bounding over the plains like tumbleweed, which incidentally is edible when gathered very young and simmered until tender, they thus leave the roots unmarked. To find them, the Indians had to harvest them in the early summer. They were then peeled by some of the tribes and hung up in long strings within the teepees to dry for winter use. The Crees used to eat a lot of them raw.

DISTRIBUTION - The prairie turnip thrives on the prairies and high plains from Manitoba and Wisconsin to New Mexico and Texas, west to the soaring Rockies.

EDIBILITY - Prairie turnips, edible peeled and raw, were even better liked by the early frontiersmen when roasted in small campfires or pounded into meal and cooked with meat. The Indians also made a kind of pudding with the flour, flavored with buffalo berries which are considered elsewhere in this volume.

©AJA

PRICKLY LETTUCE *(Lactuca)*

FAMILY - Composite *(Compositae)*

OTHER NAMES - Wild Lettuce, Compass Plant.

DESCRIPTION - The ancient and delectable ancestor of a modern green, prickly lettuce is believed by many botanists to be the forerunner of the lettuce we now buy in stores, although these days there is little resemblance between the two except when the wild variety is very young. Characteristic of prickly lettuce are the short, quite sharp spines bristling from the stems and the underneaths of the leaves.

These leaves, which are divided into several lobes, have even more sharply pointed teeth, and on the under portion of each leaf there is a row of short, stiff spines. Stalkless, each leaf has two lower projections that wrap themselves around the main stem.

This wild edible gets its name of compass plant by the fact that when sufficiently in the open most of the leaves twist edgewise north and south at noon.

The neighborly, light yellow flowers of this wild lettuce group together, several to a head. Resembling dandelions, they are smaller and not so bright. Each minute blossom has a tawny strap with five teeth. At its bottom, where it briefly becomes a tube, it is fastened to the seed vessel. Surrounding, closely growing, tiny, green leaves press the blossoms into heads, one at each end of the multi-branching tops.

Still resembling in smaller fashion the dandelion when in seed, the heads of the prickly lettuce later become downy balls, the stem of each little brownish seed bearing a ringed tuft of hairy white down which is soon borne aloft by the winds.

As with its cousin dandelion, all parts of the prickly lettuce exude a bitter white sap when broken. But the prickly lettuce, sometimes reaching heights of the loftier basketball players, grows much taller.

DISTRIBUTION - An immigrant from Europe where it adorned many an ancient's table, the prickly lettuce began spreading over North America soon after Columbus' voyages. Both an annual and a biennial, it is now found throughout most of southern Canada and the United States. Inhabiting fields, slopes, gardens, yards, and roadsides, it is often regarded as a troublesome weed by those who don't eat it.

EDIBILITY - Deer, antelope, and other hoofed browsers seek out this wild lettuce, especially when it is young. Game birds and songsters like the seeds.

Gathered young enough, prickly lettuce is good in salads. As a cooked green, even the larger leaves soon lose their prickly characteristics when dropped into boiling water. When they are young, the water in which they have been washed is sufficient for cooking if they are placed in a tightly covered pot or pan.

The bitterness to which some object in the older plants can, as with the dandelion, be removed by parboiling, although that way you lose a lot of vitamins, minerals, and character.

©AJA

PRICKLY PEAR *(Opuntia)*

FAMILY - Cactus *(Cactaceae)*

OTHER NAMES - Indian Fig, Tuna, Prickly Pear Cactus, Plains Cactus, Eastern Prickly Pear, Devil's Tongue, Western Prickly Pear, Beavertail.

DESCRIPTION - Prickly pears are the cactus plants with the flat stems. Those members of the same cactus family with round stems are known as chollas. Both species are jointed. Whereas the prickly pears are highly edible, any of the chollas I have sampled have been dry and fibrous.

The solitary flowers that appear on the padlike joints of the prickly pear are waxy. Appearing in the late springtime and the early summer, they lend a certain lush showiness dramatically to the dry regions where they unfurl with reddish or yellowish splendor.

They finally develop into little, usually thorny knobs, ranging from the size of prunes to that of large lemons. Actually, the generally spine-armored skin of this fruit of the cactus is so unlikely to be mistaken for anything else that any difficulties lie not in identifying but in harvesting. It's wise in most cases to go about this with leather gloves and a sharp knife.

The ripened colors of these Indian figs, as they are also known, range from yellowish-green and purplish-black to the most delicious of them all, the large red fruits of the big *Opuntia megacantha* of the continental Southwest.

The perennial prickly pear is a fleshy stemmed succulent either without leaves or with tiny, usually slimly pointed leaves that soon fall off to keep from wasting the plant's water supply. This water content is further protected by an impermeable hide, like a thickly waxed leather, through which evaporation takes place extremely slowly, enabling these cacti to spread and grow tall in arid regions. Barbed spines, lifting from bristly pads, further protect them.

DISTRIBUTION - The cactus family, growing thickest of all in Mexico, is native only in the Americas. In the United States and Canada the prickly pear grows from Vancouver and some of the Gulf islands and the dry interior of British Columbia south to California and, in the East, from New England to Florida.

Large stands of prickly pear grow around some of the Southwest's missions where the Spanish padres planted them both for their protection as well as for their succulency. They are also grown, more or less on their own, for cattle feed and in thick green strips by makers of such retailed products as cactus candy.

EDIBILITY - A number of wildfolk could not survive if it were not for this desert plant. Doves and sapsuckers are among the birds eating the seeds, also relished by some of the little desert mammals. Mountain sheep and deer, as well as cattle, disregard the thorns and browse on the prickly pear, also dethorned with blowtorches by some cattlemen for silage.

To enjoy the so-called Indian fig, cut off the ends of these fruits of the prickly pear, slice the hide lengthwise, and scoop out the pulp. Either that, or peel them. A few species, though, are smooth, while others are covered only with bristles that can be easily scraped away as with a bunched handful of grass. Pleasant raw, the ripe fruit can also be turned into candy or jelly.

The dried seeds are sometimes ground into flour or used to thicken soups. The newer, tenderer pads in particular are sweetly edible once they have been despined when necessary. Sliced, boiled, or roasted, and seasoned, they have proved to be valuable greens in lean times. Although this can be further cooked until it is a rich, dark, highly nutritious paste, some say it is at its best while still a sauce if first allowed to ferment slightly. They also make an interesting pickle.

A bitterish and somewhat sticky juice can be pressed or sucked from the insides of these prickly pear stems and used as emergency water.

© AJA

PURSLANE *(Portulaca)*

FAMILY - Purslane *(Portulacaceae)*

OTHER NAMES - Pusley, Low Pigweed.

DESCRIPTION - "I learned that a man may use as simple a diet as the animals, and yet retain health and strength. I have made a satisfactory dinner off a dish of purslane which I gathered and boiled. Yet men have come to such a pass that they frequently starve, not for want of necessaries but for want of luxuries."

Since Henry D. Thoreau noted this in his classic *Walden* at Concord, Massachusetts well over a century ago, purslane has been spreading into almost every American and Canadian city and town. The prostrate, succulent edible was native to India and Persia where it has been esteemed as a food since before the start of Christianity. An early immigrant to Europe, it has also been eaten there for centuries. It was introduced to this continent back in colonial times.

The reason for this amazing distribution is the purslane's incredible production of seeds, more than fifty-two thousand of which have been counted on a single common, ordinary plant; something that is all the more miraculous because of the fact that these wild edibles do not grow large.

The ground-embracing annual trails and crawls over many a garden, spreading broadly and sometimes forming mats although it infrequently reaches more than an inch or two into the air. Although generally spurned as a weed in Canada and the U.S., it is often the likeliest edible in the yard, especially because if you'll cut off just the tender leafy tips, they'll sprout again in short order, making it possible for just a few plants to keep you supplied with greens from June until October, unless frost intervenes.

The semisucculent pusley, as it is often called, has fleshy, paddle-shaped leaves that grow in rosettes, each with a tiny yellow flower. Scattered in nearly opposite positions, these narrow leaves grow from about ½ to 2 inches long, from plump, jointed, frequently forking stalks that, emanating from the middles of the edibles, have a pretty reddish or purplish-green cast to them, reminiscent of carved jadeite.

Opening only on bright sunshiny mornings, the little flowers become tiny specks of yellow at the forkings of the stems. Botanists call them sessile which is another way of saying that they are without stalks of their own, instead growing directly from the parent plants. Unfurling only under strong warm light, their five to seven petals and some eleven stamens, those parts giving rise to the male fertilizing cells, they evolve into minute round seed vessels whose tops when mature lift off like hats.

DISTRIBUTION – From the warmer parts of Canada to the southern states, it would be difficult to find a city or town with fertile sandy soil where purslane is not prevalent.

EDIBILITY - The small seeds of the purslanes are sought by birds and rodents, while fur and game animals eat the juicy plants.

Although purslane is over 92% water raw and over 94% water after being boiled and drained, a 100-gram edible portion contains 2,500 international units of Vitamin A raw and 2,100 cooked; whereas a similar weight of potatoes, to pick a common vegetable, has only a trace in either form. Potatoes have no more than .04 milligrams of riboflavin raw or baked in their skins, but purslane leaves including stems have .10 milligrams raw and .06 boiled and drained. If you're interested in dieting, it does all this while containing 21 calories to potato's 76 calories raw, 15 to 76 boiled whole. Raw purslane, too, boasts 25% more Vitamin C.

Because it grows so close to the ground, purslane should always be well washed, but its mildly acid taste and okralike mucilaginous quality make it an excellent candidate for use raw, cooked, pickled, or frozen. It is a salad and potherb favorite in many households, and many count on the body it gives to soups and stews.

The entire herb is good to eat, and Indians learned to use the minute black seeds which when utilized today are most often harvested, sieved, and mixed about half and half with regular wheat flour to give a hearty, unique substance to breadstuffs.

RASPBERRY and BLACKBERRY *(Rubus)*

FAMILY - Rose *(Rosaceae)*

OTHER NAMES - Cloudberry, Baked-Apple Berry, White-Flowering Raspberry, Purple-Flowering Raspberry, American Red Raspberry, Wild Red Raspberry, Dewberry, Thimbleberry, Western Thimbleberry, Swamp Blackberry, Salmonberry, Western Raspberry, Virgiania Raspberry, California Blackberry, Running Blackberry, Highbush Blackberry, Blackcap, Purple Raspberry, Black Raspberry, Creeping Blackberry, Mountain Blackberry, Tall Blackberry, Bake-Apple, Arctic Raspberry, Flymboy, Sand Blackberry, Rocky Mountain Raspberry, Flowering Raspberry, Wineberry, Nagoonberry.

DESCRIPTION - The most valuable wild fruit on this continent both in terms of money and of importance as a summer wildlife food, the raspberry-blackberry genus combines from some fifty to four hundred species in the United States alone, depending on whether the equally competent botanist doing the counting is a lumper or a splitter. The fact that some plants are thornless makes no difference in the general classifications, nor does the color, the so-called black raspberry being one of the more delicious of the tribe. Although there are differences in taste, all are good to eat, so as far as the amateur gourmet is concerned the precise identification can be a matter of no more than casual curiosity.

All plebes in good standing in the rose company, they provide closely and for the most part delectably related fruits in commonly differing reddish, tawny, black, and even bluish hues. Size and consistency vary also, but all are berries that are composed of numerous, small, usually juicy, pulp-filled ovals in the center of each of which is a hard seed, frequently not too noticeable when the fruit is devoured raw but becoming more predominant with cooking. The easiest way to separate them is through their similarity to domestic species.

The fruit, in particular, has a readily identified sameness to market products even when, as in the instance of the Far North's red nagoonberry or so-called wineberry, the erect stems are less than 6 inches long, lifting directly, first with dark rose to red flowers, from a spreading rootstock to ground level. More have greater familiarity with the white-flowered salmonberry or thimbleberry which, growing juicy red fruit on spineless stems, is seen on bushes from several to six feet tall.

Quickly picked in encouraging quantity, the mature blackberries and raspberries separate easily from their white-coned, five-tailed hulls, leaving a hollow entity in which each section has developed from its own ovary, forming a loosely adhering whole.

DISTRIBUTION - The genus is common along the northern rim of the continent and, in fact, throughout the world although the heaviest distribution is in the north temperate zone. Species, growing from the deepest valleys to mountainsides 1½ miles higher, reach all the way to the Mexican border.

The majority of the common species prefer moist, relatively open areas. Others, with a preference for shade, are typical woodland natives. Wild raspberries, dewberries, and blackberries frequently enliven roadsides, fence rows, field borders, abandoned meadows, and deserted farmyards.

EDIBILITY - Wildlife from the smallest towhee to the largest wild turkey, and from the chipmunk to the grizzly, make the fruit and sometimes the stems of the raspberry-blackberry family their foremost summer food. Despite the thorns or fuzz on many of the species, moose, deer, elk, caribou, and mountain sheep and goat browse on the stems and foliage wherever they can reach them.

The fresh fruit is an extremely rich source of the antiscorbutic Vitamin C. When frozen immediately after gathering and kept hard until ready to eat, it retains much of this vitamin. One sample of *Rubus chamaemorus* kept iced from harvesting in the autumn to April of the succeeding year was found to contain 356 milligrams of the ascorbutic acid per 200 grams, approximately a cup. This is from 2½ to 3 times that contained in an orange. On the other hand, when these berries are kept in a warm place and allowed to mold and ferment as is sometimes done, the Vitamin C it totally obliterated.

The tender, young, peeled sprouts and twigs are also pleasant and nutritious to eat when you're outdoors and hungry.

Beside the usual kitchen uses, blackberries and raspberries lend themselves to superior cordials and wines. A refreshing non-alcoholic beverage can be made from them, too, by letting the ripe fruit stand in vinegar for a month, then straining, sweetening to taste, and diluting with iced water.

Top—Raspberries; Bottom—Blackberries

ROCK TRIPE *(Umbilicaria)*

FAMILY - Rock Tripe *(Umbilicariaceae)*

OTHER NAMES - Blistered Rock Tripe, Tripe, *Tripe de Roche.*

DESCRIPTION - Likely the most widely known of the wild foods of the Far North is the lichen called rock tripe, whose growth reaches down into our southern states. Rock tripe resembles a leathery, dark, up-curling, ruffly edge lettuce leaf, up to some three inches across, attached at its lower middle to a Precambrian rocky surface. Unless the day is wet, rock tripe is apt to be rather dry. It can be eaten raw, especially in small amounts, but you'll probably prefer it boiled to thicken soups and stews.

Rock tripe is one of the lichens that manufacture soil by disintegrating rock, so it is apt to be rather gritty. Wash it as well as possible, preferably soaking it in at least two changes of water for several hours to help rid it of its purgative, bitter character. The flavor can be improved if you roast it in a pan, before the campfire or in a partially open oven, until it is dry and crisp.

One of the rock tripes, *Umbilicaria muhlengergii,* that ranges fram the Far North into the mountains of the eastern U.S., is a large, irregularly pocked, plant showing no difference in any such distinct members as stem, leaves, and root and, indeed, looking much like a large inverted leaf that is a brownish green atop and darker beneath.

The similar *U. vellea,* seen further North and in the higher eastern U.S. mountains, is greenish-grey above, where there is a bit of a bloom on the more sheltered species, and brown to almost black below.

Common, too, from the North to the eastern United States is *U. dillenii,* a brownish-green above and blackish beneath, which, the largest of the group, is occasionally almost as big as a mature man's hand.

DISTRIBUTION - Rock tripe extends across the top of Alaska and Canada, across the Dominion, and down into the eastern U.S. mountains to the Southern States.

EDIBILITY - Sir John Franklin, Sir John Richardson, and other early Arctic explorers and their Canadian voyageurs, as well as other Far Northern adventurers during the early exploring and trapping days, lived on rock tripe for months with hardly any change in diet. It is exceedingly rich in starches, vitamins, and minerals.

First soaked for several hours if possible to remove the purgative and bitter properties, rock tripe can be simmered slowly for an hour or so, or until tender, whereupon it will impart a gumbolike thickness to stew or soup. Depending on the main ingredients, this may be short in taste, but it will be surpassingly long in nourishment.

©AJA

ROSE *(Rosa)*

FAMILY - Rose *(Rosaceae)*

OTHER NAMES - Wild Rose, California Wild Rose, Sweetbrier, Fendler Rose, Japanese Rose, Cinnamon Rose, Red Rose, Ash-Leaved Rose, Moss Rose, Prickly Rose, Nutka Rose, Neechee, Wood Rose, Common Wild Rose, Wild Brier, Brier Hip.

DESCRIPTION - When you inspect a blossom of the fast and valuable rose family, you discover there are five wide petals. Inside these is a ring of numerous stamens, the organs bearing the grains of pollen. These stamens often bend close to the petals. Underneath all this you find a quintet of green-pointed sepals, the outer of two series of flower leaves which are united at their bases to make a green tube.

There are differences in sizes, colors, and scents, but the above holds true of all flowers in the huge, usually deliciously edible rose family which in addition to such well-known fruits as strawberries, blackberries, dewberries, and raspberries include such common trees as the peaches, cherries, plums, apples, pears, and the prolific hawthorns.

The roses proper vary and hybridize so divergently, as you can tell from the tamed varieties in your garden, that it is difficult, as well as unnecessary for purposes of edibility, to differentiate among the different varieties.

The wild roses the majority of us know most familiarly are shrubs from several to a dozen feet tall with branched, brambled stems. The usually pinkish flowers, sometimes more white or red, are ordinarily a fragrant one to three inches across, customarily bursting forth on young branches angling from older stalks. The compound leaves, with members extending from either side of a common stem, are sawtoothed.

The flowers develop into scarlet and orangish seed pods up to an inch in diameter, usually called hips or haws, that are smoothly round and contracted to a prominent, shriveling, five-leaved neck on top. This fruit, with its core of small seeds, clings to the plants all winter, well into the spring when, about May, the roses commence to bloom anew.

DISTRIBUTION - These prickly beauties thrive from the Aleutians, as far west as Unalaska, throughout most of the rest of the State, east to the northern Atlantic coast, south throughout Canada and the United States wherever the soil is sufficiently moist. Some 35 or more species abound in this country, particularly by roadsides and fences, along streams, and in open woods, fields, and meadows where they often form cloth-catching thickets that are sanctuaries for such wildfolk as rabbits, game birds, and songsters.

EDIBILITY - Grouse, pheasants, prairie chickens, and quail are among the upland game birds eating the fruit and buds of the wild rose. Songbirds such as the thrush seek the haws. Game from squirrels and rabbits to the bears seek part of their nourishment from the fruit, stems, and foliage. Antelope, moose, deer, elk, and mountain sheep and goat browse on the plants despite their thorns.

People throughout the world have long relished both the fragrance and the rich edibility of wild roses. On this continent the tender young shoots, the fruit, the flowers, and the leaves were all eaten by the Indians, the latter in particular being brewed into a tea. Tea is also sometimes brewed from the well-washed roots, as well as from the flowers.

Rose hips, with their delicate applelike flavor, are both a pleasant free food and a potent source of the scurvy-preventing-and-curing Vitamin C. Just 3 of them contain as much of this antiscorbutic as an orange. Human requirements of this vitamin, which the body cannot store, are estimated by the nutrition experts to be 60 to 75 milligrams a day. Yet tests in Idaho found from 4,000 to nearly 7,000 milligrams of ascorbic acid per pound of raw pulp. The raw juice, to isolate that, is from 6 to 24 times richer in Vitamin C than the orange juice for which Americans and Canadians spend millions of dollars each year.

The skin and pulp of rose haws is also used in making jams, jellies, and syrups. The remaining seeds are also valuable, being rich in Vitamin E which is sometimes extracted by grinding, boiling, and straining, then using the vitamin-replete fluid in place of the water called for in recipes for jellies, syrups, and jams.

Not only are the young shoots and the flower stems good to eat, but the petals themselves are delectable if the bitter white or green bases are first snipped off. Dark red roses are the strongest tasting, the flavors becoming more subdued through the light pinks.

Too, the flowers make a pleasant tea, each heaping teaspoon of dried petals, twice that amount if they are fresh, being covered with a cup of boiling water, then steeped for five minutes. A bit of added sweetening brings out more of the fragrance. Leaves, roots, and the haws themselves are also efficaciously used for tea.

Julep is translated as rosewater in Persian, and one refreshing way to make this is to soak fresh rose petals with an equal amount of cool water, then to point up the flavor with lemon juice and honey.

ROSEROOT *(Sedum)*

FAMILY - Sedum *(Crassulaceae)*

OTHER NAMES - Scurvy Grass, Stonecrop, Rosewort.

DESCRIPTION - Roseroot is one more of the wild grasses that is known to some as scurvy grass because of the often life-saving quantities of abscorbic acid it has provided for gold diggers, explorers, trappers, sailors, settlers, and other adventurers on this continent's frontiers. Quickly recognized, it becomes unmistakably so when you scrape or cut the big fleshy roots, as these then give off a pleasing odor reminiscent of attar of roses.

The leaves, too, are fleshy and are crowded along the numerous stems which rise from about four to fourteen inches high, depending on the habitat. These leaves, which grow alternately to one another, crowd together. Usually a whitish or pinkish green, they are either oval or oblong, while some have sawtoothed, others smooth, edges.

Dense tufts of purplish-red to yellow flowers are arranged in flat heads at the tips of the branches. Each of the throngs of little blossoms has four narrow petals. These blooms produce red and purple seed-filled capsules, each with four or five prongs.

DISTRIBUTION - Found in rocky ground, on cliffs and ledges, in moistly rich mountain soil, and on the tremendous northern tundras, roseroot is seen from Alaska, the Yukon Territory, and British Columbia across Canada to Labrador and Newfoundland, south to the mountains of the Carolinas.

EDIBILITY - The succulent fleshy stems and leaves, best before the flowers burst forth at the branches' summits, are used raw in often mixed salads in early summer and, especially later, are also cooked as a green vegetable. The big rough roots are eaten, too, particularly where these valuable wild edibles are abundant.

©AJA

RUM CHERRY *(Prunus)*

FAMILY - Rose *(Rosaceae)*

OTHER NAMES - Wild Black Cherry, Capuli, Black Cherry, Cabinet Cherry, Sweet Black Cherry, Wild Cherry.

DESCRIPTION - The rum cherry is the only native species of this estimable edible wild growth which reaches the size of a large tree, sometimes attaining heights in excess of one hundred feet with trunks four and five feet through.

Too, it is possible to distinguish it at any time of the year by its irregularly cracking bark. This is nearly black on older trees and rough with irregular, thick scales that have a tendency to curl upwards along their edges. The bark on young trunks is shiny, reddish-to-olive brown, and predominantly marked with horizontally elongated, breathing pores that appear at a casual glance to be white lines.

The inner bark has an almondish odor and characteristically bitter taste due to the presence of poisonous hydrocyanic acid.

Furthermore, when in bloom the edible can be picked out from the other wild cherries in that its white flowers droop in cone-shaped spikes, appearing in May and June while the tree, which may be little larger than a shrub, is still leaving.

The fruit is a drupe in that, like the plum and peach, it consists of skin-enclosed pulp, surrounding a single seed. Ripening to a bright black or dark purple in August and September, it varies in size and quality from tree to tree. Usually about the size of garden peas, it grows even larger in Mexico where, the only native wild cherry to be had there, it finds its way to markets as *capulinos*.

The leaves vary from narrow ovals to oblong lancehead shapes, with widely rounded or wedge-formed bases and long-pointed tips. Measuring from about two to five inches in length by about one-third that width, they have edges that are minutely toothed with incurving and somewhat blunt teeth. Thick and firm, they are a shiny dark-green above, lighter and smooth underneath. The stems, seldom more than an inch long, have twin reddish glands at their tops.

Commonly some 45 to 55 feet high, with trunks 1½ to 3 inches through, the rum cherry has irregularly oblong tops when it grows in the open, although in forests it shoots up tall and straight with lofty, comparatively small crowns. The hardy strong, moderately heavy, beautifully close-grained wood is valuable for panels and furniture, both solid and as a much less expensive veneer, both all the more desirable because of the way it accepts a high polish, while neither splitting nor warping.

DISTRIBUTION - The rum cherry, whose range alone among the native wild cherries reaches through Mexico into South America, grows from the Maritime Provinces to Florida, west to North Dakota, Texas, and Arizona. Thriving best in moist and fertile deep soil, it also springs up in the dry gravelly and sandy uplands.

EDIBILITY - Game birds and songsters feast on rum cherries summers and autumns when they ripen, and even before, and animals feed on the fruit that falls to the ground. Bear gorge themselves on all they can reach. Moose, deer, elk, and mountain sheep are among the big game adding the foliage, twigs, and the aromatic if bitter bark to their meals. Deer mice and chipmunks deem the pits a favorite repast, the latter storing them in quantity for the periods during which they rouse and eat in the wintertime.

Their richly bittersweet, winy juiciness makes rum cherries popular raw wherever they grow, particularly among small boys. They get their name, incidentally, from the way the simmered and sweetened juice was added to raw liquors to smooth and thriftily stretch them. They are still used in various combinations with ardent spirits.

Rum cherries make rich dark jelly when combined with apples, or they will jell alone with added pectin. Sauces, pies, sherbets, and flavoring juices are also successfully concocted from them in the kitchen.

©AJA

SALSIFY *(Tragopogon)*

FAMILY - Composite *(Compositae)*

OTHER NAMES - Goatsbeard, Oyster Plant, Vegetable Oyster, Purple Oyster Plant, Yellow Salsify, Meadow Salsify.

DESCRIPTION - The distinctive part of the salsify's single-headed blossom, which is mainly composed of a large yellow or purple wheel of many rayflowers (superficially like an aster, daisy, or sunflower) is that the narrow, green, long-pointed, petal-like bracts that extend outward beneath the heads are often longer than the golden petals themselves. The wild salsify flowers during June and July the second year. The blossoms usually close afternoons.

The large, white, round seed-heads that develop when these flowers mature, usually during August, are even more noticeable than the blossoms themselves. Resembling giant ripened dandelion tops, two to three inches in diameter, they are composed of long, matured seed stalks. At the summit of each is a fluffy tuft resembling an umbrella that has been turned inside, or perhaps a goat's beard. These seed heads give the wild edibles their name of goatsbeard, their scientific cognomen coming from the Greek *tragos,* goat, and *pogon,* beard.

The milky juiced plants grow from about one to four feet high, depending on such factors as latitude and soil. The numerous leaves, particularly along the lower portions, are up to about a foot long, narrow, alternate, and grasslike. They clasp the smooth stems, which in such a species as the *Tragopogon porrifolius* are hollow.

The tapering roots, that grow vertically downward, are long, white, and fleshy.

DISTRIBUTION - Several species of salsify thrive from coast to coast in the northern U.S. especially, more sparsely throughout the rest of the country, and in southern Canada.

EDIBILITY - Scrubbed and scraped, the roots of the salsify taste to some a bit like parsnips, to others more like oysters. They become overly pithy once the tall, leafy flowering stem develops the second year, but before then they are so good that salsify is grown commercially both in this country and Europe. Usually boiled in two changes of water, they are also sliced raw into salads when very young. Later, roasted and ground, they provide another coffee substitute.

The tender young leaves are also edible. In fact, the entire root crown cut off about two inches below ground level and, including the bases of the stems and leaves, affords a fine cooked vegetable springs and summers.

Indians used the coagulated sap of a number of the *Tragopogons* as gum, regarding it as a remedy for indigestion.

©AJA

SASSAFRAS *(Sassafras)*

FAMILY - Laurel *(Lauraceae)*

OTHER NAMES - Ague Tree, Tea Tree, Mitten Tree, Cinnamonwood.

DESCRIPTION - Just one species of the familiarly fragrant sassafras is native to North America, but this has long been so popular that its roots made up part of the first cargo ever shipped back from Massachusetts to Europe.

The alternate, untoothed leaves are characteristic, appearing in three forms usually on the same tree: a thumb and mitten, three fingers with the largest in the middle, and smooth egg-shaped. All growing on stems ordinarily less than an inch long from green, many times branched, occasionally hairy twigs, these leaves are hairless to velvety downy beneath and some two to nine inches long.

The bark in the mature trees is furrowed and reddish-brown. The very limber twigs and young shoots are bright green and mucilaginous. The leaves, aromatic when crushed, oxidize in the fall to magnificent reds and oranges. Greenish-golden flowers, which have a spicy fragrance, appear with the leaves in the spring, the sexes on separate trees, those with the male fertilizing cells usually being the more prevalent.

Birds, attracted in part by the rich, spicy aroma of twigs, bark, and fruit, flock to the dark blue drupes of berries when, almost ½ inch across, they ripen on their picturesquely thick red stems in the fall.

DISTRIBUTION - Our small to medium-size trees grow from New England to Ontario, Iowa, and Kansas, south to Florida and Texas.

EDIBILITY - The kingbird, phoebe, and crested flycatcher, all belonging to the flycatcher family and living mainly on insects, vary their diets with sassafras berries. Bobwhites and wild turkey are among the game birds eating the fruit, also sought by many songbirds. Black bears, beavers, and cottontails eat fruit, bark, and wood, while the white-tailed deer browse on the twigs and foliage.

If one breaks off a brittle green-barked twig of sassafras and chews it, the taste of the deliciously flavored, mucilaginous bark, reminiscent of its pleasantly fragrant aroma, is unmistakable.

Sassafras tea, famous for centuries on this continent where in the South particularly many individuals still drink it as a spring tonic, can be made by dropping a handful of preferably young roots into a pot with cold water and boiling them until the rich red color that you've learned by experience you like best is achieved. Second and third extractions can be made from the same roots.

For drying and storing some of the makings, use just the bark of the young roots. This can be utilized, too, like spice. Older roots can be used also, but for tea it is best to scrape off the usually hard, rough covering first. Many like this beverage sweetened. Only moderate amounts should be drunk, in any event, as an overdose of the oil may have a narcotic effect. But you can imbibe too much ordinary tea, too.

With the assistance of lemon juice, sugar, and commerical pectin, spicy jellies are made of strong Sassafras teas. The dainty green winter buds are delicious, and later the young leaves will add flavor to a salad.

In the South, soups are flavored and thickened by the dried leaves, the veins and hard portions of which are first discarded. If you like the wholesome thickness and smoothness of gumbos, why not try this for yourself? The easiest way to go about it is by drying the young tender stems and leaves, grinding them to a fine powder, passing this through a sieve to remove the hard parts, and pouring the remainder into a large saltshaker for everyone at the table to use according to his own pleasure.

194

©AJA

SCOTCH LOVAGE *(Ligusticum)*

FAMILY - Parsley *(Umbelliferae)*

OTHER NAMES - Sea Lovage, Wild Celery.

DESCRIPTION - Scotch or sea lovage, one more of the wild celeries, has long been eaten by the Alaskan natives and was early discovered on our northeastern shores by the seafaring Scots who were used to eating it in the Hebrides and other seacoast sections of their homeland.

Growing with triple-topped stems up to about three feet tall, rising from a deep, stout root, it is composed of long-stalked leaves. Each leaf terminates in three leaflets which, oval-shaped, are shiny, roughly toothed, and about one to three inches long. The bottoms of the leafstalks, broad and sheathing, have a reddish or purplish cast.

Slim, bending stems, some of them taller than the leaves, support flat-topped, umbrellalike clusters of white or pinkish flowers. These develop into tannish, rather juiceless, oblong fruits some ½ inch long.

The entire plant has an aromatic fragrance to it.

DISTRIBUTION - Scotch lovage is found along the sandy and gravelly seashores from the Aleutians to southeastern Alaska and, in the other direction, along the Bering Sea and Bering Straits. You can find it, too, in similar habitats from Labrador, down along the Maritimes and New England, to New York.

EDIBILITY - Good sources of Vitamins A and C, the leaves and stalks, collected before the plant flowers, are usually eaten raw. They are also used with cooked fish. Leaves and stalks can be utilized, too, as a cooked domestic celery substitute. The young shoots are occasionally candied.

©AJA

SCURVY GRASS *(Cochlearia)*

FAMILY - Mustard *(Cruciferae)*

OTHER NAMES - Spoonwort.

DESCRIPTION - Radishes, cabbages, and turnips also belong to this *Cruciferae* family, so named because four petals of their flowers form a cross. There are six stamens, which bear the pollen grains, and a single pistil, the central organ containing the ovules. From each of these pistils develops a flattish, oval-shaped pod that becomes filled with tiny seeds.

The delicate, little, white blossoms grow in long clusters at the ends of branching stems, themselves leaved, which grow from rosettes of older leaves. The leaves are simple, without lobes or other subdivisions, and are succulent, fleshy, and nearly veinless. The upper ones have no stalks. The lower leaves, which have brief stems, are up to an inch long, some with and others without teeth, broad-based, and spoon-shaped.

Scurvy grass has a strong, distinguishing, horseradishlike odor and flavor.

DISTRIBUTION - Scurvy grass grows abundantly in sandy, rocky, and mountainous habitats and along the sea coast, especially in wet places from Labrador and Newfoundland across northern Canada to the entire Alaskan coast, from Southeastern Alaska, the Aleutians, and along the Arctic shores.

EDIBILITY - Scurvy and the debilitating condition leading to it, all due to the lack of Vitamin C which the human body cannot store, has killed more hundreds of thousands of people than can ever be reckoned, for it is a subtle slayer whose intricacies even today are widely misunderstood.

Scurvy, it is recognized now, is a vitamin-deficiency disease. If you have it or are becoming more and more unable to combat infection by its onset, eating a little Vitamin C will cure you. Indeed, a small regular intake of Vitamin C will keep you from all such trouble in the first place. Fresh vegetables, fruit, fish, and meat will both prevent and cure scurvy. So will the long-misused lime and lemon juice but, no matter how sour, only if they, too, are sufficiently fresh. The Vitamin C in all these is lessened and eventually destroyed by age, by oxidation, and incidentally by salt.

Scurvy grass, of which there are several species belonging to the mustard family, was one of the first wild greens used by explorers, seamen, prospectors, and frontiersmen across the northern portions of this continent to fight scurvy; hence the name. It so happens, also, that other greens throughout North America were similarly used and named, this general practice being one reason for the use of distinguishing Latin names in this book.

Scurvy grass is not only pleasant to eat in spring and early summer, but young lower leaves can also be found in the fall. Although it has a pleasant cress flavor both raw and briefly simmered in a small amount of water, it provides its maximum amounts of ascorbic acid raw.

SERVICEBERRY *(Amelanchier)*

FAMILY - Rose *(Rosaceae)*

OTHER NAMES - Saskatoon, Shad, Shadberry, Shadblow, Shadbush, Juneberry, Indian Pear, Sugar Pear, Sweet Pear, Grape Pear, *Poires*, Sugar Plum, Western Serviceberry, Currant Tree.

DESCRIPTION - The serviceberries' white, daintily long-petalled blossoms are among the first spring flowers among our native shrubs and trees. Although they burst forth in March in the South, along the North Atlantic Coast their blossoming coincides with the spawning of the shad, regarded next to the Pacific Salmon as the most important species inhabiting the waters of North America, who then ascend the freshwater streams for propagation.

Growing with five white, slim, usually prettily contorted petals, serviceberry blossoms are often so profuse that they silhouette the shrub snowily against hillsides and darker growth. They appear in briefly elongated clusters, each flower with some twenty stamens, while the leaves are starting to expand.

Thriving both as low and tall shrubs and as small trees, this member of the rose family has smoothly greyish bark and unusually flexible limbs that are usually not broken even when the fruit is roughly gathered, as by bears.

The alternate green leaves, most of them up to an inch or two long, are elliptic to almost round. Some are pointed. Others have blunt tops. Most have rounded bases, and toothed edges are common along the upper or entire rims. The leaves paint the woodlands a beautiful rusty red in the autumn.

The blueberrylike fruit, reddish when young, becomes dark purple to almost black when ripe. Darker than blueberries, the serviceberries are also larger and plumper, some of those at our log-cabin site in northern British Columbia getting to be ½ inch in diameter. Both have the same sort of distinctive, five-toothed indentations puckering their summits.

Ten soft seeds are sometimes annoying in their largeness, but they add an almondlike piquancy to the flavor, especially when the berries are dried or cooked.

DISTRIBUTION - Scattered throughout Alaska all the way across the continent to damp Newfoundland, serviceberries grow southward in the United States to Mexico. They prefer moist habitats and open situations, such as the rims of woods and sparsely vegetated swamps, although bushy varieties enliven dry, stony banks, slopes and hillsides. They are usually slow in reseeding after fires.

EDIBILITY - Animals large and small, from chipmunks and squirrels to bears, cram down all the serviceberries they can eat. Grouse, pheasant, and such songbirds as the cardinal and robin also relish this fruit. Moose, elk, mule and white-tailed deer, and even the mountain sheep and goat browse on the twigs and foliage.

Although the fruit is wholesomely edible raw, it is sweetish and rather insipid until cooking brings out the almondlike deliciousness of the seeds. Some acid, like a little lemon juice, points up the flavor even more. Serviceberries thus make superior pies, muffins, flapjacks, jams, jellies, sauces, preserves, and wines.

The Indians used to dry them in cakes for winter and trail rations. Thousands of bushels of the dried fruit were also pounded into pemmican, which when genuine is still the best natural concentrated food ever.

Such true pemmican—by weight ½ well-dried lean meat and ½ rendered fat—contains nearly every necessary food ingredient with the exception of Vitamin C. Eating a little fresh food, such as several rose hips daily, will supply the Vitamin C necessary to prevent scurvy. It takes five pounds of fresh lean meat to make one pound of jerky suitable for pemmican.

To make pemmican, shred jerky by pounding. Cut raw animal fat into walnut-size pieces, and melt the fat from these in a pan over a slow fire, not letting the grease boil up.

When the grease is all out of the lumps, discard these and pour the hot fat over the shredded jerky, mixing the two together until you have about the consistency of ordinary sausage. Any dried fruit is added for flavor only. Pack the pemmican in waterproof bags. The Indians used skin bags.

© AJA

SHEPHERD'S PURSE (Capsella)

FAMILY - Mustard *(Cruciferae)*

OTHER NAMES - Pickpocket, Mother's Heart, Pepper and Salt, Lady's Purse.

DESCRIPTION - This is one of the commonest of our wayside edibles, having accompanied Europeans in all their navigations, establishing itself with wayfaring persistency wherever they have settled long enough to till the soil. It flourishes most of the growing year in all parts of the world except the tropics, even in the Arctic, and being so pleasant an addition to the table is a good and easy plant to know.

The flowers, which are not particularly attractive, grow near together on stalks close to the tip of the stem. Very small, each has two pairs of opposite petals, characteristic of the mustard family. Because the blossoms lowest on the stalk open first, flowers are blooming while there is still a cluster of green buds at the tip.

Tiny yellow stamens are in the center of these four petals, below which are a quartet of small green sepals. Once the blossom has withered, the seed vessel clinging to the center of the stalk increases in size until it resembles a jewel-like emerald heart with a hard little mass in its middle. These flattish, triangular, heartlike seed pods are more noticeable than the preceding blossoms. When mature, the seed pouches burst open readily.

· The leaves at the base of each shepherd's purse, growing in a rosette, are dandelionlike, being long and narrow with edges that are deeply indented, almost to the center vein. The leaves higher on the flower stem are formed like arrowheads, their bottoms clasping the stalk tightly.

DISTRIBUTION - Following civilization through most of the world, this alien now grows throughout most of Canada and the United States, beginning its activity especially where the ground has been disturbed.

EDIBILITY - Grouse, larks, and the cheery little goldfinches are among the birds making a practice of eating the seeds of the shepherd's purse.

The young leaves are enjoyed in salads and later as a potherb. The seeds can be gathered and ground into a nutritious meal.

SILVERWEED *(Potentilla)*

FAMILY - Rose *(Rosaceae)*

OTHER NAMES - Argentine, Goose Tansy, Good Tansy, Wild Tansy, Wild Sweet Potato, Fivefingers, Goose Grass, Cramp Weed, Moor Grass, Cinquefoil, Silver Cinquefoil.

DESCRIPTION - Silverweed, with its vividly golden blossoms, gets its name from the whitish undersides of the green-topped leaves of one of its more widespread species, *Potentilla anserina*. A close relation, *P. egedei*, common along the northern coasts of both the Atlantic and Pacific Oceans, has much duller underneaths.

The important *anserina*, or argentine as the French Canadians call it, is a perennial herb whose distinctive long runners protect it from being destroyed by overgrazing, rooting and leaving as they do at their joints. Hence, when the more mature portions die or are eaten, the younger ones that have developed along the runners become parent plants in their own right.

The bright yellow flowers, appearing about May and continuing until nearly August up and down the continent from the valleys to some 8,500-feet elevations, have the appearance of lone roses. Growing showily on singular stalks, they have five petals, some of the blossoms being nearly an inch across. Each has about two dozen stamens or more. They develop into what resemble dry strawberries.

The featherlike leaves, lustrously silver beneath and verdant above, grow in tufts directly from the roots. Smooth along their tops, they are woolly with matted bristles beneath. These leaves are compound, with the leaflets arranged on either side of a single stalk.

The roots are long and narrow, the fleshier and therefore the more valuable of them being found beneath the older, bigger plants. A reddish dye, incidentally, can be extracted from them.

DISTRIBUTION - These nutritious members of the rose family, also abounding in both Europe and Asia where they are likewise recognized as foods, grow from the Aleutians to Newfoundland, south along the New Jersey Coast in the East and to the Mexican border in the West. Preferring damp to wettish soil, even though it may be salty, they are seen along lake, river, and ocean shores, around water holes where the rest of the vegetation has been grazed off, and in open country.

EDIBILITY - Historically, during times of famine, silverweed roots have sometimes sustained groups of people for weeks and even months. The North American Indians know them well.

Boiled or roasted, these starchy roots have been compared in taste to especially choice parsnips with overtones of sweet potatoes, although like other wild edibles they have a flavor all their own. They retain even more subtlety of flavor when steamed.

One of the wilderness teas is made by steeping a teaspoonful of the fresh green leaves in a cup of boiling water. This was sometimes drunk cold, one or two cupfuls a day, to relieve diarrhea.

©AJA

SLIPPERY ELM *(Ulmus)*

FAMILY - Elm *(Ulmaceae)*

OTHER NAMES - Moose Elm, Red Elm, Gray Elm, Rock Elm.

DESCRIPTION - A medium-size tree, generally some forty to seventy feet tall with a trunk diameter of from one to three feet, the slippery elm is well known to many boys who chew its intriguing bark. This tree may have a single or a divided trunk. Spreading branches provide broad, open, flattish crowns. The common name, as might be expected, comes from the pleasantly, somewhat slimy, mucilaginous, sweet-tasting inner bark, now widely chewed for the pure joy of it but once eaten as a scurvy preventative.

No other elm, one of this continent's favorite shade and ornamental trees, has rough, hairy twigs or red, downy buds. The bark is distinctive, too.

The sharply toothed leaves, scratchy above and downy beneath, grow on short, hairy, stout stems. Sprouting from woolly, blunt, egg-shaped buds, these leaves become unsymmetrical, four to eight inches long, and from two to three inches across the middle where they are generally widest. Dark green and dull, lighter on their under portions, they become magnificent masses of golden yellow in the fall. The leaves, incidentally, seem rough when stroked in any direction, whereas those of our other elms are rough only in one direction.

The flowers burst out in short-stemmed clusters early in the springtime. The outcomes are winged, flattish, brief-stemmed seeds.

The bark is either greyish or a dark reddish-brown, becoming divided by shallow fissures and mottled by large, loose scales. As the bark thickens on old trunks, the vertical furrows separate broad ridges which finally break away as big loose plates. The hairy twigs turn out to be mucilaginous when chewed.

In the wintertime, the slippery elm may be recognized by its slender twigs that are fatter, however, than those of the American elm. These are colored an ash grey to pale brownish-grey and are harshly rough and hairy. The leaf buds at this time of year are particularly dark brown, ovoid, and blunt.

DISTRIBUTION - The slippery elm, which likes soil that is heavily charged with lime, grows from the valley of the St. Lawrence River to the Dakotas, south to Texas, the Gulf of Mexico, and sunny Florida.

EDIBILITY - The fresh green seeds which mature long before most such food is available are relished by many birds, once being a favorite spring staple of the erstwhile passenger pigeons. The white-tailed deer browses on the twigs and foliage.

Pour a cup of boiling water over a teaspoon of the shredded inner bark of the slippery elm. Cover and allow to steep until cool. Then add lemon juice and sweetening to taste, and you'll have some of the famous slippery elm tea of pioneer days, still highly regarded as a spring tonic and as a plain pleasant drink in some parts of the country.

The inner bark of branches, trunk, and roots is extremely mucilaginous. Thick and fragrant, it is still widely gathered in the spring when, because of the rising sap, the trees peel more easily. The whitish inner bark can then be dried as in a garret or warm, half-open oven, then powdered as in the kitchen blender.

It has demulcent and emollient, as well as nutritive, properties. Medically, it is still used for dysentery, diseases of the urinary passages, and bronchitis. For external application, the finely ground or powdered bark is mixed with enough hot water to make a pasty mass and used as a poultice for inflammations, boils, and the like, and also in the form of both rectal and vaginal suppositories. More simply, the previously described tea is sometimes used for coughs due to colds, one or two cupfuls a day, several cold sips at a time.

The Indians also used this inner bark for food, some of them boiling it with the tallow they rendered from buffalo fat. It will also provide nourishment today, either raw or boiled.

©AJA

SOW THISTLE *(Sonchus)*

FAMILY - Composite *(Compositae)*

OTHER NAMES - Milk Thistle, Prickly Sow Thistle, Spiny-Leaved Sow Thistle, Common Sow Thistle, Field Sow Thistle, Hare's Lettuce, Beach Lettuce.

DESCRIPTION - A cousin of both the dandelion and the thistle *(Cirsium)* and called a thistle by some botanists, the sow thistle is distinguished from this latter group by the bitter white sap that is distributed throughout the plant and by the fact that its heads are made up entirely of rayflowers—the long, flat, daisylike extensions of the corolla.

These clusters of yellow blossoms look like small dandelions, a resemblance that is heightened when they mature into seeds tipped with silky, long, white hairs. Before these are scattered by the winds, the tops of these plants look like nodding little mobiles of cotton balls.

The leaves of the various species vary some. Those of the *Sonchus asper,* for example, are curled and particularly spiny, their lobed bases folding over the smooth stalks. Sharply pointed ears where the leaves clasp the smooth stalks mark the *S. oleraceus.* The *S. arvensis* has a sharply toothed but otherwise rather dandelionlike leaf, embracing a hairy stalk.

DISTRIBUTION - These immigrants from Europe are found in usually damp soil about fields, farms, gardens, waste places, roadsides, barnyards, rights of way, and mountains throughout temperate Canada and the U.S.

EDIBILITY - The goldfinches, those cheerful little relatives of the caged canary, are among the birds feasting on the heads of the sow thistles.

The North American Indians soon learned to use sow thistles as greens. They make a good salad plant when very young and later a better-than-average potherb. As with the dandelion, some relish the bitter flavor, while others prefer to discard the first boiling water. Because of an abundance of soluble vitamins and minerals, only a minimum amount of water should be used in any case, and the boiling should be brief.

SPICEBUSH *(Benzoin)*

FAMILY - Laurel *(Lauraceae)*

OTHER NAMES — Wild Allspice, Benjamin Bush, Spicewood, Snapwood, Downy Spice, Feverbush, Feverwood, Common Spicebush, Souther.

DESCRIPTION - Two species of these aromatic-leaved shrubs, typical of the undergrowth in flood-plain forests, swampy woods, and in moistly rich bottom lands, are native to the United States.

The spicebush is a spicy-scented shrub, from some 4 to 15 feet high, with darkly smooth bark and slim, brittle twigs, several branches commonly developing from the same set of roots to form rounded thickets. Its richly emerald leaves change to gold in the autumn. Growing alternately, they are elliptically oval to oblong, smooth, even-edged, thinly textured, conspicuously veined, pointed, and from three to five inches long.

The thick clusters of numerous yellow flowers, whose spicy fragrance precedes the leaves from March to May, grow like those of the related sassafras with one sex to a shrub. The blossoms are petalless, but they have a six-lobed calyx. Arranged in rows of three, the stamens number nine. The pistil develops from July to September into an oily, aromatic, bright red, oval berry, actually a one-seeded drupe, somewhat less than ½ inch long.

DISTRIBUTION - The northern species of spicebush is found from Maine to Michigan, south to Kansas and Georgia. A similar species, but with downy branches and leaves, thrives in the southern States.

EDIBILITY - The wood, hermit, grey-cheeked, and the veery thrushes really go to town with these reddish fruits, each with its one large seed, eaten only sparingly by such other birds as pheasants, bobwhites, flycatchers, catbirds, kingbirds, and robins. Whitetail deer, cottontails, and opossums also eat the fruit as well as the twigs.

There is even a spicebush butterfly, common in the Atlantic States and the Mississippi Valley, whose larva feeds on this shrub as well as sassafras. The butterfly, also distinguished by a red spot on each back wing, is large and greenish black. Each front wing has a row of yellow dots near its edge, while each back wing is marked with a similar row of blue-green dots and a like-colored band across the middle.

Incidentally, our early surveyors such as George Washington regarded the presence of spicebushes in the undergrowth as signifying good agricultural land.

The young leaves, twigs, and bark of the spicebush provide another of the wild teas much used on this continent, especially in the early days when remoteness and wars made oriental blends scarce and expensive commodities. They still provide a pleasant drink, particularly if you happen to prefer your tea with cream and sweetening.

A handful of young twigs, leaves, or bark simmered for 15 minutes in a quart of water is the formula. Some used the berries for this purpose, too. Dried and powdered, these also provide a substitute for allspice. If you become parched while outdoors, chewing a bit of the pleasantly flavored young bark is an enjoyable way to start the saliva flowing again.

©AJA

SPRING BEAUTY *(Claytonia)*

FAMILY - Purslane *(Portulacaceae)*

OTHER NAMES - Groundnut, Fairy Spuds.

DESCRIPTION - The spring beauty, one of the prettier flowers that bloom early in the springtime, is often seen in beautiful, bountiful patches, although sometimes you find only a few scattered around the base of a tree or along a bank, in which case you'll likely be reluctant to disturb any great proportion of them except in an emergency. Every plant generally has several blossoms, opening at different times. Although these expanses bloom in the lowlands as early as the first part of April, in the higher mountains they may be seen flowering as late as mid-August.

Five pink or white petals, with numerous darker rose veins branching toward the center of the bloom, characterize the lovely spring beauty. Attracting numerous bees, a minute sack of nectar lies sweetly at the base of each petal. A quintet of golden-headed stamens rises in a ring in the center of each blossom, enclosing a seed vessel. Two modified, green, leaflike sepals extend below the bright petals.

The slender stalk that supports each flower droops before the petals open, then straightens proudly to lift the dainty luxuriance into the sunlight. Once the blossom withers, the graceful stem sags at ease once more, the seed cell hanging precisely as the bud did before.

Inconspicuous except when in flower, each spring beauty has up to some sixteen long, narrow, pointed leaves, mostly growing opposite one another in sets of two on the single stalk. There is also usually an odd basal leaf.

DISTRIBUTION - About fifty generally closely related species occur around the world, three growing in this continent's Arctic where their leaves and roots are prized by the Eskimos, both raw and cooked. Commonly Alpine plants found in wet places, these members of the purslane family are seen in moist valleys and along sandy and gravelly seashores, near the edges of woods, and almost two miles high in the mountains, especially in meadows and below steaming snowbanks. Children admire their prettiness in the springtime from Alaska to Nova Scotia, south to Florida, Texas, and California.

EDIBILITY - Mountain sheep, deer, elk, and moose browse on the leaves and flowers of the spring beauty when they first appear. Rodents eat the bulbs, for which the gigantic grizzlies also hungrily dig.

The leaves can be enjoyed as an early-season, vitamin-rich nibble raw, added advantageously to salads, or briefly cooked as greens.

It is for the starchy roots, however, that this wild edible is most famous. These small, potatolike tubers, ranging in diameter from ½ to 2 inches, usually lie several inches below the ground level and take a bit of digging, although where they are abundant just a few minutes with a pointed stick will amass a respectable meal. Primarily roundish, they become more and more irregular in shape the bigger they grow.

A brush makes cleaning easy, although this is not too critical a task as they are boiled in their jackets. Drop into salted boiling water and simmer up to about 15 minutes, only until a fork will pierce the larger ones easily. Then just peel and eat, perhaps with butter or margarine and a little salt. They can also be prepared the other ways regular potatoes are handled, although more of the goodness is retained if they are cooked with the jackets on. To me they have the flavor of especially choice little potatoes with overtones of cooked chestnut.

Spring Beauty. Left—*Claytonia virginica;* **Right—***Claytonia lanceolata.*

STRAWBERRY *(Fragaria)*

FAMILY - Rose *(Rosaceae)*

OTHER NAMES - Wild Strawberry, Scarlet Strawberry, Virginia Strawberry, Wood Strawberry, European Wood Strawberry, California Strawberry, Earth Mulberry, Beach Strawberry, Yukon Strawberry, White Strawberry.

DESCRIPTION - This most delectable of all berries, wild or tame, is known to everyone because of its similarity to the far larger but always infinitely less sweet domesticated varieties. The fruit is usually the familiar red, an exception being a strain of wild white strawberries, also delicately sugary and delicious, that grows in New York, Pennsylvania, and West Virginia.

Ripe from June to August depending on the elevation and latitude, wild strawberries are mostly tiny and grow in loose clusters close to the sheltering ground. I've enjoyed them all over the continent, except in the deserts, and the largest I have picked have been some inch long, growing in Southeastern Alaska. This same juicy fruit, *Fragaria chiloensis,* is also found in the Aleutians, on the Seward Peninsula, and along the Gulf of Alaska. Yet even as nearby as the dry hillsides of the upper and central Yukon River in the interior of this 49th State, the plants are more slender and the berries of more usual minuteness, with tighter clinging hulls.

In fact, the difficulty of disengaging the hulls of wild strawberries is the most time-consuming part of the joy of gathering these wilderness delicacies everywhere, particularly when they are not fully ripe.

It all starts with the five-petaled flower, the members of this frequently having notched outer edges. Underneath the five parts of these sweet-smelling blossoms are five leaflike sepals, each pointed, and five bracts—the modified leaves, actually the reproductive spore cases, at the base of the flower cluster. To save a lot of picking over, it is best to take the time initially to separate the berries from the hulls. When you're feasting as you harvest, the easiest way to rid an individual berry from a tenacious calyx is just to bite the fruit from it.

Twenty or more stamens lift in a dense ring around the seed vessels of each blossom, being united so fast to the sepals that they do not fall off when the white petals wither. Once the flower shrinks and shrivels, the receptacle under the central seeds starts to swell, expanding finally into a luscious berry. The minute yellowish or brownish seeds still cling to the outside of this, in such a variety as the *Fragaria virginiana* being sunk in pits that indent the fruitlike berries. Actually, strawberry fruits are the tiny surface seeds. What we enjoy are actually the enlarged flower containers.

The dark green leaves of the typical wild strawberry grow separately from the roots. Each is made up of three roughly toothed leaflets, further armed with soft hairs.

DISTRIBUTION - Wild strawberries perfume the air from Alaska, the Yukon, and the Northwest Territories to Mexico, thriving nearly everywhere except in arid areas.

EDIBILITY - Grouse, prairie chickens, pheasants, and quail, along with a host of songbirds among which the robin is especially ravenous, seek the luscious strawberry. Hare, rabbits, possums, chipmunks, and squirrels dine on both fruit and the tenderer leaves. White-tailed and mule deer are among the hoofed browsers nuzzling the plants.

Wild strawberries make shortcakes, tarts, sauces, jellies, jams, and preserves whose flavor and sweetness is difficult to approach with any other fruit, wild or tame. Not only are they delectable raw, but in home desserts it is unnecessary to cut them up first as a sprinkling of sugar soon draws out their unexcelled juices.

They are unusually nutritious in that they are rich in such necessary food ingredients as quickly assimilated iron, potassium, sulphur, calcium, sodium, silicon, and the related malic and citric acids. A part of a cup, the proportion depending on the environment and the season, equals the Vitamin C content of an orange.

The leaves not only make a tasty tea, but they can provide one that is unusually rich in the scurvy-preventing-and-curing C Vitamin. For refreshing enjoyment, cover two full handfuls of the sawtoothed, fresh, green leaves with a quart of boiling water, allow to steep five minutes, and then serve either plain or with a bit of fresh lemon juice and a trifle of sweetening. For free medicinal quantities of Vitamin C, immerse newly picked, green, young strawberry leaves with boiling water, cover, and drink cold the next day.

If you've ever outdoors and hungry and if the strawberry crop about you is limited, remember that the stems and stalks of this ever-popular perennial are also tasty.

© AJA

STRAWBERRY SPINACH *(Chenopodium)*

FAMILY - Goosefoot *(Chenopodiaceae)*

OTHER NAMES - Indian Strawberry, Strawberry Blite, Blite.

DESCRIPTION - Strawberry spinach is similar to its close relative, lamb's quarter, the primary difference existing in the pulpy red masses of soft bright fruits which make this wild edible so easily recognizable and which, when you're in the north woods in the fall, often stain your footwear like dye.

The annual thrusts itself erect, with either a single or branching smooth stem, from about 4 to 24 inches tall. It has irregular, triangular leaves with wavy or coarsely toothed edges.

Round heads of flowers grow in the angles between leaves and stalk and in spikes at the upper end of the stem. These become showily red and berrylike, hence the majority of the names.

DISTRIBUTION - One of the most striking native wild edibles in clearings, woods and waste areas, the strawberry spinach is common across Alaska and Canada, southward into the northern States.

EDIBILITY - The young leaves are good in salads when tender, and as a spinachlike potherb when older, being an excellent source of Vitamins A and C.

The fruit, although rather flat and tasteless, is nutritious both raw and cooked.

©AJA

SUMAC *(Rhus)*

FAMILY - Cashew *(Anacardiaceae)*

OTHER NAMES - Staghorn Sumac, Lemonade Tree, Vinegar Tree, Smooth Sumac, Scarlet Sumac, Dwarf Sumac, Shining Sumac, Mountain Sumac, Hairy Sumac, Velvet Sumac, Fragrant Sumac, Virginian Sumac, Winged Sumac.

DESCRIPTION - The rapidly growing staghorn sumac, also called the lemonade tree and the vinegar tree, is one of the larger members of the cashew family, commonly reaching a height of from ten to twenty feet. It is quickly recognized in any season because of the close resemblance of its stout and velvety twigs to deer antlers while these are still in velvet.

Incidentally, there's another identifying factor. Cut any of these twigs, and a gummy, white sap will flow out that'll immediately turn black on the knife blade.

The bark of these shrubs or small trees, which often form thickets, is smooth. The satiny and frequently streaked wood, sometimes used commercially for such small objects as napkin rings and picture frames, is greenish to orange in color.

The fernlike leaves, about 14 to 24 inches long, are composed of 11 to 31 pointed leaflets, each 2 to 5 inches long. Dark green and smooth above, pale and occasionally softly hairy beneath, these flame into brilliant red in the autumn.

The tiny, tawnily green flowers grow in loosely stemmed clusters, one sex to a plant. The male clusters are sometimes 10 to 12 inches long. The extremely dense female blossoms are smaller, producing compact bunches of berries. They are erect and so startlingly red that I've come upon a lone clump suddenly in the frosty woods and thought it was a scarlet tanager.

The hard red fruits are thickly covered with bright red hairs. These hairs are tart with malic acid, the same flavorsome ingredient found in grapes. Since this is readily soluble in water, the sumac berries should be gathered for beverage purposes before any heavy storms if possible.

By the way, the berries of the poisonous sumacs are white and drooping. However, there are other sumacs in the United States and Canada with red berries, similar to those of the staghorn sumac, that provide a refreshing substitute for pink lemonade. All these red-fruited species are harmless.

One of them is the smooth or scarlet sumac, *Rhus glabra,* which grows from the Maritimes to Minnesota, south to Louisiana and Florida. This closely resembles the staghorn sumac except that it is entirely smooth, with a pale bluish or whitish bloom coating the plump twigs.

Another is the dwarf, shining, or mountain sumac, *Rhus copallina,* which grows from New England and Ontario to Texas and Florida. Although similar to the aforementioned species, it can be distinguished from all other sumacs because of the peculiar winglike projection along the leaf stems between the leaflets.

DISTRIBUTION - Sumacs grow all over southern Canada and the U.S. Three of the more common ones in the East, staghorn sumac, smooth sumac, and dwarf sumac, are usually small trees, the other species being mainly shrubs. The sumacs prefer open, sunny, moist situations; in pastures, meadows, orchard edges, and along fences, roads, and stream rims. Shade kills them.

EDIBILITY - Ruffed grouse, ring-necked pheasants, band-tailed pigeons, prairie chickens, and bobwhite and mountain quail eat the fruit of the sumacs—which stays on the shrubs and trees late into the winter and so is available when other, perhaps more desirable, foods are lacking—and will often stay near a copse of sumacs until the clusters of red berries are gone. A wide variety of songbirds feast on the fruit which is rich in Vitamin A. In addition, rabbits and hares, as well as moose, deer, and mountain sheep feed on the bark, twigs, and fruit of these wild edibles.

Sumac "lemonade" is just the thing to take the edges off a hard afternoon. Pick over a generous handful of the red berries, drop them into a pan and mash them slightly, cover with boiling water, and allow to steep away from any heat until this is well colored. Then strain through two thicknesses of cloth to remove the fine hairs. Sweeten to taste, then serve the so-called Indian lemonade hot or cold. The berries are best for this in late summer and early fall. Incidentally, the fruit of the staghorn sumac is less tart than that from the other similar edibles.

Some Indian tribes like this acid drink so much that they dried the small, one-seeded berries and stored them for winter use. Many colonists followed suit.

©AJA

Staghorn Sumac *(Rhus typhina)*

SUNFLOWER (Helianthus)

FAMILY - Composite (Compositae)

OTHER NAMES - Common Sunflower, Tall Sunflower, Giant Sunflower, Marigold of Peru, Prairie Sunflower, Weak Sunflower, Saw-Toothed Sunflower, Ten-rayed Sunflower, Thin-leaved Sunflower, Swamp Sunflower, Pale-leaved Wood Sunflower, Little Sunflower, Aspen Sunflower, Stiff-Haired Sunflower, Showy Sunflower, Wild Sunflower, Woodland Sunflower, Western Sunflower.

DESCRIPTION - Native to the Americas and probably getting its start in Peru, the sunflower is now the state flower of Kansas. Its name, more descriptive than most, comes from two Greek nouns, *helios*, the sun, and *anthus*, flower. Not only do the golden blossoms resemble an idealized sun, but they turn naturally toward this star's brightness.

All relatively tall, these annuals and perennials range from three to a dozen feet in height. The wild blossoms, in which a center of yellow and purplish-red to brown so-called disk flowers are ringed by an array of bright yellow ray flowers, are seldom more than several inches broad, reverting quickly to type when a tame variety with a blossom head perhaps a foot across escapes from cultivation. The ray flowers are neuter, incidentally, the disk blossoms fertile.

The brilliant rays, many times spectacularly turning fields and hillsides into nearly solid golden stretches, ordinarily run in number from about 10 to 25. Although the majority of the edibles bloom in July, August, and September, a few are seen brightly blossoming in the early springtime.

Some of the usually branching wild sunflower plants are smooth, while others are hairy. The leaves, which also vary, are both opposite and alternate, being characteristically narrowish, long, sawtoothed, and rough.

DISTRIBUTION - Nearly two-thirds of the sunflowers that cheer the world, about sixty species, grow in southern Canada and in the U.S. Although they are to be found in every state, they spring up in greater numbers in the West, from British Columbia and Alberta southward. Although some are woodland plants, the majority prefer sunny, open spots.

EDIBILITY - These attractive woody plants are of especial value to wildlife on the plains and other expanses of the continental West. The long list of game birds seeking the large nutritious seeds are the snipe, doves, grouse, partridges, pheasants, and several species of quail. Songbirds and small mammals, from the pleasant little goldfinches of both the East and West to lemmings and prairie dogs, also break open the hard shells to get the soft seeds inside. Deer, moose, antelope, and even muskrats eat the plants.

Indians used them everywhere, but it was on the prairies that they proved most beneficial to the tribes, there often taking the place of corn.

However, sunflowers had, and have, many other uses. For instance, the Indians discovered they could crush and boil the seeds, then skim a particularly nourishing oil from the surface. This was used at mealtimes and in cooking. Incidentally, it was also perhaps this continent's first hair oil.

The often first-roasted seeds are also cracked and their insides devoured by the public everywhere, especially abroad. In fact, during a recent cruise around the world we found a number of shops with signs by their doors prohibiting the entry of anyone eating sunflower seeds.

These seeds can be shelled in quantity if first broken up, as with a rolling pin or food chopper, then scattered in a large water-filled container and strenuously stirred so as to bring all the kernels in contact with the fluid and to break the surface tension, upon which they will sink. The floating shells that remain can be roasted and used as a wild coffee if you want, a use to which the entire roasted seeds are sometimes put. The nuts can be briefly dried and roasted, as in an open oven pan, and used in any recipe calling for nuts. Or the entire mass of kernels can be ground and pounded into a fine meal, Indian style.

In Lewis and Clark's Journal during July of 1805 when they were near the start of the Missouri River in western Montana, they speak of the Indians, most especially those who did not cultivate maize, parching sunflower seeds and then pounding them between two stones until they were reduced to a fine meal.

"Sometimes," the Journal continued, "they add a portion of water and drink it thus diluted. At other times they add a sufficient proportion of marrow-grease to reduce it to the consistency of common dough and eat it in that manner. This last composition we preferred to all the rest, and thought it at that time a very palatable dish."

© AJA

SWEET FERN *(Myrica) (Comptonia)*

FAMILY - Sweet Gale *(Myricaceae)*

OTHER NAMES - Wild Tea.

DESCRIPTION - Whenever anyone in the U.S. and Canada sees what is apparently a fern growing as a low bush with a woody stalk and leaves, the viewer is looking at our sweet fern whose fragrant leaves were used even before the American Revolution for brewing one of the wild teas.

This sweetly scented shrub, sometimes reaching a height of five feet, has fernlike leaves that give it its name. These are deeply sectioned, nearly to the midrib, into many rounded sections. They are slender, greyish, delectably fragrant, dryish, and long.

The buds have four or more scales, the apparent end buds being false. The twigs, aromatic when bruised, are generally hairy.

Distinctive when in foliage, in winter it is our only aromatic wild plant among those with three bundle scars—the small, somewhat round dots within the leaf scar that are caused by the breakage of the duct bundles originally leading into the leafstalk—with false end buds and with genuine buds that have over four scales apiece.

The April to June feminine blossoms grow in egg-shaped catkins. The resulting bristly, round burs envelop hard, shiny, brown, little nuts. If you don't mind getting your thumbnail yellow, these are easily exposed and enjoyed, especially during June and early July while they are still tender.

DISTRIBUTION - These shrubs, found in open fields and on upland slopes where trees are infrequent or absent, often form solid stands. They are found to a lesser degree in open woods. The sweet fern grows from Canada's Maritime Provinces to Saskatchewan, down through the Appalachian Mountains to North Carolina and west to Minnesota.

EDIBILITY - White-tailed deer browse on this tea substitute in the Alleghenies, as do cottontails. Ruffed grouse and prairie chicken are among the upland game birds eating the buds, catkins and foliage.

The nutlets are a woodland nibble.

The dried aromatic leaves of the sweet fern, a teaspoon to each cup of boiling water, make a very pleasant tea. When you use them fresh, just double the amount of makings.

We've also brewed this in the sun by filling a clear quart bottle with cold water, adding 8 teaspoons of the shredded fresh leaves, covering the glass with aluminum foil, and setting it in the sunlight. The several times I tried this in New England, about three midday hours were needed before the brew became sufficiently dark. Made this way, wild teas have none of the bitterness of acrid oils extracted by other methods. You can then strain it, dilute it to individual taste if you want, and serve like regular tea with ice.

©AJA

SWEET FLAG *(Acorus)*

FAMILY - Arum *(Araceae)*

OTHER NAMES - Calamus, Myrtle Flag, Sweet Rush, Sweet Grass, Sweet Cinnamon, Sweet Root, Flagroot.

DESCRIPTION - The sharp, thin, narrow, swordlike leaves of the sweet flag grow stiffly up to about four or five feet tall. They sheathe one another tightly at the base, often below the surface of the ground or mud. Stout, horizontal roots with the unmistakable gingery taste spread from them in closely intertwining mats. This is a close cousin of our friend the jack-in-the-pulpit which also belongs to the worldwide arum family.

The flower stalk, two-edged and bladelike, grows about the same length as the leaves. Partway up it the fingerlike, tapering, yellow-green spadix, several inches long and reminiscent of the "jack" of the jack-in-the-pulpit, grows off at an angle. This becomes closely crowded with minute yellowish-green blossoms that turn into dry, berrylike fruits in the fall. There is no spathe as such, the extending leaflike continuation of the flower stalk being actually a spathe.

The pleasantly aromatic fragrance of the bruised foliage of the sweet flag, and of its underground portions which grow fleshily in tangled clumps often several feet in extent, distinguish it from the poisonous wild iris or blue flag, *Iris prismatica*. The rootstocks of the wild iris, which grows throughout the eastern half of the U.S. from Texas northward, have a strong and disagreeable flavor. The sweet flag is a considerably larger plant. Also, the edible sweet flag has glossy, yellowish-green leaves, whereas those of the harmful wild iris are both dull and bluish-green. There is no likelihood of confusion when the wild iris is bearing its typical iris blossoms.

DISTRIBUTION - Preferring marshes, swamps, damp grasslands, and areas along rivers and more stagnant waters, the sweet flag now grows throughout southern Canada and the lower 48 states.

EDIBILITY - Candied sweet flag has somewhat the same aromatic pungency of candied ginger which is now difficult to obtain, even in the Orient. To make your own candy, once regarded as a country aid to digestion, cut the tender bases of the stalks into very thin slices. Parboil them in several changes of water to moderate the strong taste.

Then simmer, stirring frequently, barely covered with a syrup composed proportionately of two cups of sugar to every cup of water until most of the sugar has become absorbed. Drain, dry apart from one another on waxed paper or foil for several days, roll in granulated sugar, and pack what you don't devour on the spot into tightly closing jars.

The fleshy rootstalks were often used for this purpose back in the days of wood fires, but they usually need to be kept on the back of a warm stove for several days to become sufficiently tender.

Raw sweet flag is excellent in the springtime, when the partially grown flower stems are edible and the interiors of the young stalks, crammed with half-formed leaves, are sweet and tasty enough to be taken home for salads.

The spicy fragrance of the sweet flag's leaves were a major reason why our pioneer ancestors chose to spread them cleanly on the floors of their cabins. They are also natural insecticides, a property that is concentrated in the dried and powdered roots of the plant.

TOOTHWORT *(Dentaria)*

FAMILY - Mustard *(Cruciferae)*

OTHER NAMES - Cut-Leaved Toothwort, Two-Leaved Toothwort, Slender Toothwort, Crinkleroot, Pepper-Root, Spring Blossom, Lady's Smocks, Milkmaids, Pepperwort, Large Toothwort.

DESCRIPTION - These slender members of the mustard family get their names of pepper-root and pepperwort from the fact that their edible roots have a deliciously pungent bite similar to that of watercress, lending impromptu savor to many an otherwise simple meal in the cool recesses of the forest. In some localities, such as along the Coast Range in the West, they are among the first daintily shy flowers of the spring. The cognomen toothwort arises from the scales or teeth on the long, fleshy underground portions.

From the underground stem of the species known as *Dentaria laciniate,* producing roots on its lower portion, lift erect bottom leaves that are deeply indented and toothed. A whorl of three compound leaves stem, too, from the flowering stalks, 8 to 15 inches tall, each of these leaves being divided into a trio of slim, sharply cut segments. Broad clusters of white or pale amethyst flowers are borne, also, each March to May blossom being about 2/3 inch across, with a regular combined calyx and corolla of four short sepals and, mustardfashion, four separate petals.

The closely related *D. diphylla,* known also as crinkleroot and pepperwort, has, instead, a pair of almost opposite stem leaves, each cut into three wide, toothed leaflets. The basal leaves are similar but with long stems. The whitish flowers seem pinkish when withering.

Large toothwort, *D. maxima,* differs from the first mentioneᵤ of the family by having its three leaves branching from the stalk at differing levels. The flowers, when they are not white, are more of a purple.

Slender toothwort, *D. heterophylla,* with its pink blossoms, is characterized by a pair of small stem leaves, each divided into a trio of either toothed or smooth-edged lanceheadlike parts very much different from the broad, long-stemmed bottom leaves.

The flowers of all these have six stamens and a single pistil that develops into characteristic mustardlike seedpods. The long, fleshy roots are either crisp or brittle, with a mustard pepperiness that makes one or two, among the hundreds that frequently grow together, desirable as a relish or a nibble.

DISTRIBUTION - Toothworts grow from Ontario, Quebec, and the Maritimes south to Kentucky, South Carolina, Indiana, Ohio, and California.

EDIBILITY - The roots make very palatable additions to most sandwiches, whose salt brings out their flavor. Chopped, they add pungency to salads. Or just scrape or grate several of these sharply flavored, fleshy rootstocks, mix with vinegar, and set on the table in a little covered pot.

Toothwort (*Dentaria laciniate*)

WATER CRESS *(Nasturtium)*

FAMILY - Mustard *(Cruciferae)*

OTHER NAMES - Pepperleaf, Water Nasturtium, Scurvy Grass.

DESCRIPTION - The usually prostrate and often floating plant thrives in cold water and wet places, growing in mats or clumps, characterized by innumerable, little, white, threadlike roots. The roots are tough and should in the main be left, in any event, so that the cress can continue to spread.

The minute white flowers, arranged in their mustardlike crosses, many of them extending from the stem joints and all blossoming on a succession of tiny stocks attached to a longish stalk, are usually inconspicuous. They develop needlelike pods from about ½ to 1 inch long which, if still tender to the bite, are tasty, too.

Dense green leaves, dark and shiny, with smooth but wavy edges, grow with three to eleven smooth and roundish segments, the biggest of which is at the end.

Depending on the location, water cress flowers from May to August.

DISTRIBUTION - Water cress is common throughout Canada and the United States, growing in every state and throughout the world, especially in this Northern Hemisphere. A native of Europe, it is cultivated there and in this country, often escaping to the wilds. You can even buy the seeds and, following the directions on the packet, start your own patch.

EDIBILITY - Pungently tasty both cooked and in its native state, it is generally preferred raw. However, briefly simmered leaves, stems, flowers, and young pods are not only hard to beat among the boiled greens, but a handful of them adds zest to most other edible greens.

Boiling, too, does away with the danger of contamination. The familiar plant prefers clean, clear, cold water, but you can't always be sure that those pools, trout streams, expanses of mud, and even springs are pure. In case of doubt, it is a sensible precaution to soak the well-washed leaves and tender shoots in water in which halazone tablets have been dissolved, using two of the little white pellets to a quart of water and letting everything stand half an hour before rinsing the cress. A bottle of one hundred halazone tablets can be obtained from almost any drug or sporting goods store for about fifty cents. These work by releasing purifying chlorine gas and should, therefore, be fresh. Keep tightly closed in a dark, dry place.

A tangy and interesting supplement to any salad, water cress, stimulating the appetite, is also a prime appetizer and will enliven hors d'oeuvres. Enjoy its characteristic peppery flower in sandwiches, too, where it has been relished as long as these food snacks have been known.

A memorable, nutritious, vitamin-and-mineral-swarming tea can be made by covering a teaspoon of the leaves or roots with a cup of boiling water and steeping for five minutes.

WILD APPLE *(Malus) (Pyrus)*

FAMILY - Rose *(Rosaceae)*

OTHER NAMES - American Crab Apple, Southern Crab Apple, Prairie Crab Apple, Biltmore Crab Apple, Lance-Leaved Crab Apple, Iowa Crab Apple, Wild Crab Apple, Common Apple, American Crab, Wild Crab, Fragrant Crab, Garland Crab, Oregon Crab Apple, Narrow-Leaved Crab Apple, Wilding Tree.

DESCRIPTION - "The Time for wild apples is the last of October and the first of November," wrote an early expert on the subject, Henry D. Thoreau. "They then get to be palatable, vivacious and inspiring, for they ripen late.

"To appreciate the wild and sharp flavors of these October fruits, it is necessary that you be breathing the sharp October or November air. The outdoor air and exercise which the walker gets gives a different tone to his palate, and he craves a fruit which the sedentary would call harsh and crabbed.

"This noblest of fruits must be eaten in the fields, when your system is all aglow with exercise," Thoreau added, "when the frosty weather nips your fingers, the wind rattles the bare boughs or rustles the few remaining leaves, and the jay is heard screaming around. What is sour in the house a bracing walk makes sweet. Some of these apples might be labeled, 'To be eaten in the wind.' "

Everyone knows the apple. Even though your yellow-green find may be little more than an inch in diameter, and hard and sour to boot, very few fruits are as quickly gathered, and their tartness and firmness lend themselves to some of the best apple dishes you have ever eaten. The flowers of the apple are perhaps the most beautiful of any tree. The scent of both them and the later developing fruit has a piquancy unequalled in the most costly perfume.

Most of the early American settlers had a dog on their doorstep and an apple tree beside their cabin. Frequently the tree was a wild crab apple.

North America's wild apple, commonly known as a wild crab apple, seldom is more than twenty feet high, with a contorted and rigid crown which is useful in identification. The leaves, which grow alternately on these small trees, are single in form, with sawtoothed and sometimes lobed edges, and with a compound network of fibrous veins on either side of a central vein.

The lateral branches are ordinarily short and stubby, spurlike, and slow-growing, often being tipped with a short, rigid, spikelike point. The flowers and fruit grow on some of these spurlike lateral branches.

In fact, the chief charm of these trees lies in the magnificent color and fine smell of these fragrant blossoms, which resemble those of our orchard apples but are more deeply tinted with crimson and also even more sweetly agreeable in scent. They are perfectly formed, with a quintet of pink or whitish petals and a large number of stamens.

These blossoms develop into five-celled ovules or cores, closely connected and cartilaginous in texture, containing the delicately tasty seeds. The whole becomes enclosed by the fleshy calyx, the portion of the apple we eat. This entire body may be a small, yellowish-green fruit, no more than 1 or 1½ inches in diameter and dangling on a slim stem of about the same length, ripening about October but often hanging on the tree far into the winter. In fact, even when they fall they seldom rot until spring, although they do lose much of their greenish hue but not their bitterish taste.

DISTRIBUTION - Scattered by such wildlife as birds, by Johnny Appleseed (actually the pioneer preacher named John Chapman) who travelled some one hundred thousand miles between Massachusetts and Missouri planting seeds and seedlings, and by casual eaters who toss the cores where they finish with them, wild apples and crab apples now grow all over southern Canada and in every State of the Union including Alaska.

EDIBILITY - Such animals as deer and foxes, as well as raccoons, bears, coyotes, opossums, and rabbits, are fond of wild apples. Squirrels, though, usually discard the fleshy portions in favor of the seeds. Grouse, pheasants, prairie chickens, and quail are among the birds eating fruit, seeds, and buds.

The Iroquois, employing wild apples and maple syrup, made an applesauce that was all the more flavorsome because the fruit was used unpeeled. Too, if you can beat the deer and other forest folk to them, you can sometimes come upon wild apples plump and sweet enough with what Thoreau called the "wild flavors of the Muse" to bake.

"Who knows," he added, "but that this chance wild fruit, planted by a cow or a bird on some remote and rocky hillside, may be the choicest of its kind. It was thus the Porter and the Baldwin grow. Every wild apple shrub excites our expectation thus, somewhat as every wild child it is, perhaps, a prince in disguise."

©AJA

WILD CELERY *(Angelica)*

FAMILY - Parsley *(Umbelliferae)*

OTHER NAMES - Seacoast Angelica, Purple-Stemmed Angelica, Alexanders Angelica, Angelica.

DESCRIPTION - This wild celery grows with hollow, leafy, hairless, erect stems from one to about eight feet high that, in the *Angelica lucida* variety, are coarse with many oil tubes. The inflated bases of the leaves, which grow in groups of three leaflets, are longer than they are broad, thick, and roughly and unevenly toothed. The small flowers have five white or greenish petals, many of them being clustered umbrellalike at the tops of the stalks.

In the *Angelica atropurpurea* type, the hollow stems, from four to nine feet long, are smooth and purplish. The leaves, again divided into three parts, may also have further divisions of three and five segments. They are egg-shaped to obliquely oblong, of similar length to the above, and also coarsely toothed. The small, greenish-white flowers grow in almost globe-shaped clusters, some three to six inches in diameter. This whole edible is agreeably aromatic.

DISTRIBUTION - The plants grow along the seacoast and mountain streams, in moist fields, rich low grounds, ditches, and swamps from the Aleutians to Labrador, south to Illinois, West Virginia, and Maryland.

EDIBILITY - The tender and juicy young leaf stems and peeled stalks are eaten raw, as in salads. When older, they somewhat resemble stewed domestic celery when boiled, perhaps in two waters, either alone or with fish.

Wild Celery (Angelica atropurpurea)

WILD COFFEE *(Triosteum)*

FAMILY - Honeysuckle *(Caprifoliaceae)*

OTHER NAMES - Feverwort, Fever Root, Tinker's Weed.

DESCRIPTION - Wild coffee has rather hairy stems up to three or four feet in height. The opposite leaves in *Triosteum aurantiacum,* which taper to their bases, often encircle the stalk. The leaves of the *T. perfoliatum,* which have wings that meet and surround the stalk, are paired.

The bell-shaped flowers, the petals being clung to by five long leaflike sepals, are yellowish or greenish to a dull purplish-brown. The reddish or orange berries, which are egg-shaped to nearly spherical and about ½ inch long, grow in the latter summer and in the fall in tiny, hairy clusters in the joints between the leaves and the stalks. Each contains three large and bony seeds.

DISTRIBUTION - The three species of this wild coffee grow in open woods, thickets, and on stony slopes from the Maritimes, Quebec, Ontario, Wisconsin, and Minnesota, south.

EDIBILITY - Dried, roasted, and ground, these berries can be used instead of store coffee. Put into fresh cold water, using two level teaspoons for every cup of water. Amounts may be varied, of course, for a stronger or weaker brew. Watch it carefully. As soon as it boils up once, lift it off the heat to take on body for five minutes. Then settle the grounds, if you want, with a couple of tablespoons of cold water and start pouring. Cream and sweetening may be added.

Wild Coffee (*Triosteum perfoliatum*)

WILD CUCUMBER *(Streptopus)*

FAMILY - Lily *(Liliaceae)*

OTHER NAMES - Liver Berry, Scoot Berry, Twisted Stalk, Clasping Twisted Stalk, Cucumber Root, White Mandarin.

DESCRIPTION - When you catch the reflection of a wild cucumber with its dangling red berries in a trout-swirled pool on a cool autumn morning, it is one of the most beautiful sights in the woods.

This wild perennial grows with branched stems from about 1 to 4 feet tall from thick, fibrous, horizontal roots in moist woods. The distinctive thing to look for is a definite kink in each flower or berry stem near its middle, the reason for the name twisted stalk.

The bell-shaped flowers, greenish-white or pinkish, droop separately from single, long, slender stems arising from the angles between the leaves and the main stalks. In *Streptopus amplexifolius,* the species being considered, they have smooth, unbroken edges.

The robustly clasping leaves of the wild cucumber are extremely smooth, their underneaths being floured with a whitish bloom. These leaves, which are taper-pointed, are egg-shaped, growing alternately directly from the tall stalks. Longer than they are wide, broadest toward the base, they are some two to five inches in length and strongly veined.

The individualistic berries, one to a leaf-stalk angle, are small and pulpy and, when ripe, range from a yellowish white to orange or light red.

DISTRIBUTION - Common from Alaska down through British Columbia to California, the wild cucumber is also found in woods and cool damp thickets from Iowa, Illinois, Michigan, Ontario, New York, Connecticut south. Other species of the genus are widely distributed in Europe and Asia.

EDIBILITY - Grouse are among the birds eating the berries.

These berries, known in some parts as liver berries and as scoot berries in deference to their cathartic qualities, have a cucumberlike flavor and were eaten sparingly by some of the Indians.

The tender young shoots and leaves make a particularly cooling and pleasing salad.

©AJA

WILD GINGER *(Asarum)*

FAMILY - Birthwort *(Aristolochiaceae)*

OTHER NAMES - Sturgeon Potato, Hot Potato, Asarabacca, Snakeroot, Heartweed, Canada Snakeroot, Indian Ginger, Sierra Wild Ginger, Vermont Snakeroot.

DESCRIPTION - The two beautiful, heart-shaped leaves of each wild ginger plant, deeply indented where their broad bases meet the softly hairy, long stalks that lift directly from the ground, rise upon the rims of many a shaded stream, almost as if they enjoy the gossiping of the brook as it gurgles past. Greyly green and velvety with short hairs, the twin leaves are each some three to seven inches broad, dark green above and lighter green below. When crushed, they emit a spicily pleasant fragrance. Their two stout, fuzzy stalks are some four to eleven inches long.

A warm hue appears between each pair of still undeveloped leaves in the early springtime. Presently a strange, dull bud protrudes its long tip on a separate small stem from their middle. The shy flowers eventually blossom in May, often so close to the ground that the purplish-brown blossom with their three long prongs are sometimes nearly invisible on the forest floor.

The flower cup, creamy within, is formed by three long-pointed sepals. There is some difference among the blossoms of the separate species, but with the *Asarum canadense,* for instance, there are no petals. There is, however, a set of a dozen stamens and an ovary with six chambers and a six-lobed stigma, the part of the pistil which collects the pollen and upon which they germinate. The cup part of this nodding blossom is about an inch wide, but the three long pointed lobes give the whole the somewhat hobgoblin aspect of a lurking spider. Seeds are eventually developed and nurtured until they ripen.

The gingerlike pungency of the rootstocks is responsible for some of the more common names, their proclivity to creep horizontally along and near to the surface of the ground for others.

DISTRIBUTION - Wild ginger grows all the way across southern Canada and the northern United States, down into California and Nevada in the West and into Tennessee and North Carolina in the East.

EDIBILITY - The long slim roots of wild ginger, often gathered and well scrubbed in the spring although actually they remain pungent throughout the year, can be sliced and used like regular ginger roots in cooking, in slightly larger amounts as they are not quite as potent.

Too, the pioneers often dried these roots, ground them into a powder, and used this like the commercial spice they then resemble. Once regarded as effective in treating whooping cough, this is still commonly used in parts of eastern Canada as a remedy for flatulency. If you'd like to try it, just add ½ teaspoon of the powdered or granulated root to a cup of boiling water. Sip this, about two tablespoons at a time, as often as necessary.

Candied wild ginger still comes close to being some woodsmen's favorite sweet. Wash the roots well and then cut them into short pieces. Simmer these until tender, barely covered with liquid made by dissolving two cups of sugar in each cup of water. Then drain, cooking the fluid longer if it still does not seem to be quite thick enough.

You can keep the wild ginger in the syrup, but many prefer to bottle each separately, first letting the pieces dry on waxed paper or foil for several days and then rolling them in granulated white sugar.

Wild Ginger (*Asarum canadense*)

WILD LETTUCE (Lactuca)

FAMILY - Composite *(Compositae)*

OTHER NAMES - Chicory Lettuce, Canada Wild Lettuce, Horseweed.

DESCRIPTION - This milky juiced plant also resembles the dandelion in its blossoms. These are comparatively small, pale, and insignificant, however, growing in narrow, long clusters atop the edible which if undisturbed may at maturity be as tall as a basketball player's reach. Each blossom head boasts from a dozen to some twenty small flowers. Colors range for the most part among yellows and bronzes.

Deeply indented like those on the dandelion, the lower leaves, shiny green atop and whitish beneath, wrap their bases about the stalk. The upper leaves, on the other hand, are frequently only slightly wavy along their edges and are shaped more like slender lanceheads. Like the clasping basal stem leaves, the hollow, generally smooth stalks have a milky cast to them.

DISTRIBUTION - About a dozen species of wild lettuce are common in the moist, rich soil of yards, fields, roadsides, and open thickets from British Columbia to Newfoundland, south through the United States.

EDIBILITY - These delicious and vitamin-teeming relatives of domesticated lettuce are avidly sought by horses, hence one of their names. Deer and other game also seem to find the delicately flavored greens especially toothsome, even when they're too old for the table. Ring-necked pheasants are among the birds seeking the seeds. The selective prairie dogs enjoy the foliage.

Anyone relishing the slightly bitter flavor of dandelions will enjoy wild lettuce as a potherb. Otherwide, drain off the first water in which it is boiled. The stems and leaves are tender enough to cook until the wild food is some 16 inches tall. Small, tender plants are excellent raw.

©AJA

WILD ONION *(Allium)*

FAMILY - Lily *(Liliaceae)*

OTHER NAMES - Wild Garlic, Wild Leek, Wild Chive, Field Garlic, Swamp Onion, Sierra Garlic, Sierra Onion, Nodding Wild Onion, Meadow Garlic, Tree Onion, Siberian Chive, Shortstyle Onion.

DESCRIPTION - For the most part, wild onions have slender, quill-like leaves, similar to those of domestic species. They grow from layered bulbs. Flowers appear on otherwise naked shafts, arising like the ribs of an inverted umbrella. The one and only characteristic on which to depend, though, is the characteristic onionlike odor.

An exception in the leaf department is *Allium tricoccum* whose flat leaves, some one to three inches broad, nod in the breezes from the Maritime Provinces to Iowa and Minnesota, south to the Carolinas. When Pére Marquette and his band journeyed from Green Bay, Wisconsin, to near our present Chicago—whose name is taken from the Indian word *shikata,* meaning place where wild onions are strong-smelling—it may have been these wild leeks that were his main food.

Other authorities, though, suspect it was *Allium canadense,* a peculiarity of which is that it bears a head of bulbs in place of flowers, that Marquette and his followers ate. This meadow garlic, as it is also called, grows from the Maritimes to Florida, west to Minnesota and Texas.

Although you probably won't like all the breed—especially not the strong-tasting field garlic, *A. vineale,* which is an immigrant from Europe and which is beloved by cows in the East to the detriment of the flavor of their milk—wild onions are all good to eat. They are usually moistest and fleshiest in the spring and early summer. Then the best way to find out your likes and dislikes is by trying them. Often you can use the entire plant.

However, have nothing whatsoever to do with any plants, wild or otherwise, that resemble the onion but do not have its familiar odor! Some bulbs whose appearance is superficially like that of onions are among our most concentrated poisons. Your nose will be your own best protector.

It has been found that odors that sometimes linger on the breath after one has eaten onions, chives, leeks, and garlic are entirely the result of solid particles remaining in the mouth. Brushing the teeth and tongue and rinsing the mouth after eating will do away with any fear of offending.

DISTRIBUTION - Wild onions, including the leeks, the chives, and the garlics, grow all over North America except in the far northern regions.

EDIBILITY - Ground squirrels are among the animals hunting out the wild onion. So are prairie dogs.

The Indians ate grouse, duck, quail, plover, and other wild eggs whenever possible, often cooking them with wild onions. Eggs and this wild vegetable still really go together.

Wild onions simmered until tender in a small amount of lightly salted water, then drained and topped with butter or margarine, or for a change mayonnaise or sour cream, are fine fare. Save the liquid for soup or for other cooking. In fact, the wild onion group can be used throughout the spectrum of their domestic counterparts. The milder of them are delicious raw.

Some are particularly potent in Vitamin A.

© AJA

Left—Onion *(Allium stellatum)*; **Center—Leek** *(Allium tricoccum)*; **Right—Garlic** *(Allium canadense).*

WILD PLUM (Prunus)

FAMILY - Rose (*Rosaceae*)

OTHER NAMES - Beach Plum, Wild Red Plum, Wild Yellow Plum, Chickasaw Plum, Porter Plum, Wild Goose Plum, Flatwoods Plum, Canada Plum, American Wild Plum, Horse Plum, California Plum, Sierra Plum, Pacific Plum, Mountain Cherry, Sand Plum, Allegheny Sloe, Bullace Plum, Sloe Plum, Munson Plum, Graves, Thorny Plum, Thornless Plum, August Plum, Hog Plum, Sloe, Indian Cherry.

DESCRIPTION - The wild plums are close cousins of the several wild cherries, considered at length elsewhere in this volume, but in general are fleshier fruits with more flattened stones. Many wild plums bear thorns, where the wild cherries are always thornless. The fruit of the plums is covered with a whitish powder and is encircled around its long axis by a line. Cherries lack such a powdery bloom and such encircling lines. Their seeds are nearly spherical. Plums also differ from wild cherries in that the twigs lack true end buds. It is unfortunate that in many parts of the continent the wild plums are subject to fungus infections and to caterpillar infestations, both of which greatly reduce the crops.

One of the more important varieties is the so-called beach plum, *Prunus maritime*, whose growth and fruiting habits vary, a common trait in seedling plants. It resembles a bush more frequently than a tree. Some bushes sucker freely from the roots, producing dense thickets. The root systems, as necessitated by the usual dry and bleak habitat, are coarse, rangy, and deep.

The fruit, which ordinarily varies between ½ and an inch in diameter, differs in color from red through blue and purple to almost black. Yellow-fruited bushes are occasionally found. The natural home of the beach plum is in sandy, light soils and even in the pure sand of wind-sculptured dunes. Most beach plums blossom profusely each year but proceed to fruit only once every three or four years. One reason for this is that they depend on cross-pollination. The weather, often very foggy or rainy, dark, cold, and windy during blooming, may greatly reduce or even stop insect flight so that there is no transfer of pollen among the self-sterile plants. Too, it may slow the growth of the pollen tubes so that fertilization fails.

Specifically, the beach plum is a sprawling shrub up to about six feet in height. It does not have thorns, although the oval leaves, hairy underneath, are sharp with sawtoothed edges. Twigs and buds are velvety, end buds being absent. The innumerable white flowers burst out before the leaves begin to appear. The fruit, which occupies many thrifty families day after day and finds its way onto wayside stands, ripens during the sweltering weather of August and September.

Another wild plum that is often seen in country markets is the *Prunus americana*, formerly a great favorite among the Indians. Its numerous branches, whose twigs are thornlike, have rough, thick barbs. The oval or oblong leaves, ending in long tapering points, are sharply sawtoothed like those of the beach plum. The frail white blossoms, again showing up before the leaves in early springtime, are extremely fragrant. The red and sometimes yellow plums, appearing in late summer, are about ⅞ inch in diameter, tough-skinned, pulpy, and usually sweet.

In northern California and southern Oregon many families make annual pilgrimages to wild plum orchards in and around the mountains and bring home luscious bushels of richly mottled yellow, red, and purple fruit, especially in the northern parts of the range. Here the trees and shrubs are from three to ten feet tall, with ash-grey bark and occasionally spiny branches. The flowers, again showing before the leaves from March to May, are white, fading to rose. By August and September, the branches are often loaded with the handsome fruit, its colors duplicated in the brilliant autumn foliage.

The Canada plum, which finds its way from New England and the Great Lake States into the southern Dominion, is a small tree some 20 to 24 feet high, often with generally football-shaped leaves, coming to abrupt points, some three to five inches long and one to 2½ inches across. These have fine, double-toothed, blunt edges. The fruit, a vivid orange-red, grows an inch long.

DISTRIBUTION - Some 15 species of wild plums abound through the United States and southern Canada, growing from Alaska and California to the Great Lakes and the eastern seaboard, where the fragrant white flowers of the prolific beach plum brighten the springtimes along the beaches and sand dunes and on the coastal plains from Nova Scotia and New Brunswick to Virginia and inland, as around the Great Lakes.

EDIBILITY - Wildlife does not use the wild plum as freely as it does the wild cherries, foxes being the most avid diners. On the other hand, scattered thickets afford invaluable shelter for birds and small game.

The fruit varies considerably, some of it being delicious straight off the twigs. The chief value of much of the rest is in incomparable jellies, jams, and other kitchen delights.

Along Cape Cod in Massachusetts there are so many dozens of home stands selling wild plum jelly that I started to enjoy this at an early age. There are two secrets for making this delicacy successfully. First, pick the plums while they are still on the unripe side. Second, unless you have special equipment, make only small batches at once, about three quarts at a time being plenty.

You can also use wild plums to mellow gin, a process especially favored by some of the colonists because it thriftily stretched available supplies of the ardent spirits.

244

© AJA

WILD RICE (*Zizania*)

FAMILY - Grass *(Gramineae)*

OTHER NAMES - Indian Rice, Water Oats, Water Rice.

DESCRIPTION - Growing as it does from about four to ten feet tall, with a stout stalk some ½ inch in diameter at its base, this prime human and waterfowl fodder can scarcely be mistaken for anything else, especially as it thrives most luxuriantly on mucky or silty bottoms in shallow water where there is enough circulation to prevent stagnation.

Wild rice is a large, coarse, plume-topped grass whose leaves are long and slim, averaging between one and three feet in length, and close to ½ or 1½ inches in width. The elongated, branched, broomlike flower cluster is from one to two feet long. The lower parts of this are generally spreading and bear those flowers whose organs carry the microspores, the pollen grains. The erect upper branches are rich with the ovales. The slender seeds, when they grow, become dark and rodlike, about ¾ inch long, expanding in husks that are stiffly tipped with a hairlike growth.

These husks are loose upon maturity, however, and not hard to get off. The secret is to spread the rice in a warm shelter, as on newspapers in the attic, until it is dry. Then parch it in a moderately warm oven for an hour or so, reaching in a hand and mixing it occasionally so that it will dry evenly without burning. The husks can then be freed by beating or, if you've only a small quantity, by rubbing the seeds between the palms. The easiest way I know to blow away the chaff is by pouring the dark grains back and forth between two containers in a stiff breeze. Store in a dry place in closed receptables.

A trickier consideration is to harvest the crop during the latter half of the summer or in the early fall where, depending on the local climate, it will be ripe. The mature seeds soon separate from the plants. However, they stick on far too tenaciously for easy gathering while yet green. The Indian method of getting in wild rice is still a good one. This consists of spreading a large canvas over the bottom of a canoe, paddling among the plants, bending the stalks over the craft, and beating the seeds out on the tarpaulin with a stick. Or you can use a bare, dry canoe and merely empty that each time.

In fact, there is only one drawback to enjoying this very real delicacy, unless you harvest it yourself for free, and that is the surprising expensiveness of the purple-black seeds with their smoky sweetness, such fine eating with game and poultry and even by itself as cereal or such. By the way, if the home-gathered wild rice is not well washed in cold water before using, it is apt to have too much of this smoky flavor.

DISTRIBUTION - This Indian rice, as it is sometimes called, grows in two native varieties in the East from around the Canadian border to the Gulf of Mexico. Its stands, however, are rather localized and insignificant south of the coastal lands of the Carolinas, although it does grow down the Atlantic rim and throughout Florida.

The famous waterfowl food thrives most abundantly in the northern States from Maine to the eastern edge of the prairies and in freshwater marshes along the Atlantic Seaboard. On the other hand, wild rice has been successfully introduced in other parts of the country where, when there is deep soft mud and slowly moving water, satisfactory crops come up year after year.

EDIBILITY - Black, baldpate, canvasback, bufflehead, ring-necked, pintail, mallard, redhead, both greater and lesser scaup, teal, and the beautiful wood ducks are among the waterfowl vying with such other game birds as the goose for this best of all the native cereal grains growing wild in the United States and Canada. Numerous shorebirds, marshbirds, and songbirds also share the seeds.

Although it is ordinarily too precious to be used indiscriminately, it will improve any recipe calling for domestic rice. You can even pop it, placing a small amount of your best, freshly gathered, still unwashed seeds in a fine sieve, immersing this in deep hot fat until the kernels pop, draining on paper towels, salting, and serving hot, perhaps with some cool wild fruit juice.

WILLOW (Salix)

FAMILY - Willow *(Salicaceae)*

OTHER NAMES - Pussy Willow, Black Willow, Drummond's Willow, Shining Willow, Snow Willow, Glossy Willow, Glaucous Willow, Blue Willow, White Willow, Weeping Willow, Crack Willow, Felty-Leaved Willow, Beaked Willow, Bebb Willow, Ward Willow, Harbison Willow, Coastal Plain Willow, Tall Prairie Willow, Canada Willow, Quebec Willow, etc.

DESCRIPTION - The names could go on and on, for there are over one hundred different bushes, shrubs, and trees of the willow family growing in all parts of North America. It takes an expert to distinguish the numerous species of willows. On the other hand, the average individual can tell a willow from other trees without too much difficulty which is the important thing, for all willows can furnish life-sustaining food in an emergency. For example, everyone who has traveled outdoors in the early spring must have seen the pussy willow, nothing other than the developing flower tassels of this branch of the family which also includes the poplars, which themselves have edible inner bark as discussed elsewhere.

The willow has alternately, or rarely opposite, one-piece leaves with sawtoothed or smooth edges. Most of our species have long and narrow leaves with short stems, although a few are oblong or shaped like lanceheads. A number have persistent and many times leaflike appendages at the bases of the leaves. In other willows these stipules, as they are called, are tiny and often fall away upon maturity.

The twigs are slim, flexible, and round, often being brittle at the base. The buds are ordinarily very flat on the side next to the twig and outwardly rounded on the other side, usually pressing closely to the twig and being covered with a single bud scale. The large majority of the willows are shrubby, although a few become small and others large trees. The bark of many species is bitter with the drug salicin, used medically to reduce fever as well as for other purposes. Other barks are surprisingly sweet.

The flowers appear in the early springtime, either before or with the developing leaves. Male and female blossoms appear on different trees, each with a nectar-secreting gland to facilitate reproduction by insects. Both these staminate and pistillate flowers grow in catkins. In no other family do both kinds of blossoms appear on drooping tassels.

The seeds are extremely light, produced in tremendous numbers and provided with a dense cover of long hairs which encourage their dispersal by the winds. Too, not only do the willows reproduce freely, in many wet situations forming thickets to the exclusion of almost all other woody growth, but they live for long periods even after they seem to be dying, repairing damaged parts with surprising rapidity.

DISTRIBUTION - Willows grow all over the United States and Canada, from the Arctic Coast to Mexico.

EDIBILITY - Willows provide the favorite browse of many moose, elk, deer, and the like, as well as the nibbling rabbit. Several species of grouse, as well as other birds, look to tender willow buds and twigs for food. Often the first spring source of Vitamin C, especially in the Far North and the high mountains, willow sprouts provide the main subsistence of ptarmigan.

The outer bark of the new shoots is stripped off and the inner portions eaten raw with some varieties. In others, the outer bark is cut off and removed and the thin inner layer scraped off with knives and eaten. Eskimos call this *Keeleeyuk,* which literally means *the scrape,* and in such a variety as the *Salix alaxensis* it is amazingly sweet.

Young willow leaves, when they are not too bitter, are eaten in emergencies. The young underground shoots of any of the small, creeping willows found on the Arctic tundra and on the mountains can be peeled and eaten raw. Everywhere the inner bark is edible, raw, cooked in strips like spaghetti, or dried and powdered into flour.

Too, half-digested willow tips in the stomachs of the deer family, tasting like salad with vinegar, were and are regarded as delicacies by some of our aborigines.

© AJA

WINTERCRESS *(Barbarea)*

FAMILY - Mustard *(Cruciferae)*

OTHER NAMES - Scurvy Cress, Belle Isle Cress, Yellow Rocket, Bitter Cress, Upland Cress, Wild Mustard, Herb of St. Barbara.

DESCRIPTION - The distinctive thing about wintercress is that it grows vigorously during the warm days of winter and may be found, gathered, and eaten whenever the ground is free of snow. In fact, if you know where it is thriving, you can even scrape away the snowfall to get at it. Its Latin name *Barbarea* takes note of the fact that the young leaves and stems are generally ready for the table when St. Barbara's Day comes every December 4.

Actually, if the rosettes of long, smooth, dark green leaves are not harvested when they first shove up directly from the perennial and biennial roots during winter and early spring, they become too bitter to enjoy. Wintercress reaches this state when it blossoms, although the acridness is modified once more with the frosts of fall.

In the meantime, the young blossoms can be enjoyed like broccoli. Best to eat in the bud stage, these developing clusters of tiny, four-petaled, golden flowers, each resembling a small Maltese cross, indicate that these edible herbs belong among the numerous native and European species of mustard that enhance this continent.

The bright little blossoms, opening in groups between the stalks and the upper leaves and at the tops of the stems, mature into narrow, plump-stalked, four-sided pods up to three inches long that become filled with pungent seeds. The smooth stalks, ordinarily growing one to two feet high, support an abundance of shiny, long, green leaves that have none of the hairiness of some of the other mustards.

There are two closely related, look-alike cousins, *Barbarea vulgaris* and *Barbarea verna,* which share the same seasons, are equally choice on the table, and which often grow side by side.

Before the days of man-made vitamins, wintercress was important when the first signs of scurvy, such as a scratch which was slow in healing, appeared. In fact, many on tight budgets could save money by eating it today, as the leaves are about three times as plentiful in ascorbic acid as the stores' often expensive orange juice. As for the buds, they have even higher percentages of this vital Vitamin C.

DISTRIBUTION - Found on the banks of streams, in swamps, on wet rocky ground and beaches, along roadsides, and on disturbed land where the rosettes of glossy, dark green leaves are one of the first available new year's greens, wintercress has long been important in Alaska from where it grows eastward and southward across Canada and the United States, particularly in the East where three of this country's four species thrive.

EDIBILITY - Doves and grosbeaks are among the birds eating the seeds.

The greens, picked before the plant blossoms or after the initial frosts of autumn, are good either as salad plants or as pot-herbs. Anyone objecting to their radishlike bitterness can drain off the first boiling water, then simmer in fresh water until tender.

The buds, along with no more than a few of the opened blossoms, simmer into a broccolilike savoriness, the important thing being not to cook them to mushiness.

Wintercress (*Barbarea vulgaris*)

WINTERGREEN (Gaultheria)

FAMILY - Heath *(Ericaceae)*

OTHER NAMES - Creeping Wintergreen, Teaberry, Checkerberry, Western Wintergreen, Ground Holly, Mountain Tea, Boxberry, Spicy Wintergreen, Partridgeberry, Woodsman's Tea, Ground Berry, Salal.

DESCRIPTION - Wintergreens are creeping little woodland perennials whose evergreen leaves are often coolly shaded by conifers above. Small, oval, shiny, these remain on the plants all winter, growing up from the ground on short stems, seldom longer than five or six inches, at whose tops they are generally clustered. When rubbed between the fingers, they give off the familiar wintergreen fragrance.

They are paler on their underneath portions, becoming leathery with age. Tiny teeth, each tipped with a bristle, ring them inconspicuously. The young leaves are lighter and often more yellowish, sometimes with a reddish tinge, than the glossy dark green most of them later attain. Later in the year many of them are as red as the aromatic red berries they then harbor. When such leaves are used for the tea for which they are famous, they give a healthy ruddy hue to the beverage.

This miniature member of the heath family is a trailing plant whose shrubby, thin stems weave through or beneath woodland soil, moss, and conifer needles, putting up occasional leaving and blossoming sprigs that, unless you examine them closely, seem like separate entities.

Little bell-like flowers appear whitely and solitarily in the angles between leaves and stems from June to September. Each tiny, frosty blossom, given its bell-form by the fusion of five petals, encloses ten stamens and one ovule-bearing pistil. The five-lobed bells become fleshy, evolving into firm berrylike fruit that hang redly, in all their delicate goodness, on the tiny evergreens all winter.

Salal, *Gaultheria shallon,* is the tall, coarse wintergreen of the Pacific Coast. The aromatic berries of this shrub, found from Alaska to California, were also widely used by the Indians although they are less spicy than the eastern species.

DISTRIBUTION - The eastern wintergreen *(G. procumbens)* which I still enjoy with particular nostalgia, its being the first edible wild plant I ever remember gathering, grows in often rough mountainous forests from Newfoundland to the Great Lakes, south to Mississippi, Alabama, and Georgia.

EDIBILITY - Grouse, turkeys, bears and deer make use of the wintergreens as food.

Large amounts of wintergreen leaves used to be harvested about October, dried, and then packed for shipping. Before the volatile oil was distilled off, they were soaked in water for at least 24 hours, which should give you an idea if you ever want to render some of your own. If just the flavorful liquid is going to be used, without any further processing, it will be stronger and more palatable if allowed to stand in a covered, impervious receptacle, such as a glass bowl, for several days until it begins to bubble. For tea, then just strain and heat in a covered teapot.

Wintergreen leaves lose their aroma so rapidly that they cannot be successfully dried for winter use like most wild tea plants. If you live where they grow, this is no problem as they remain evergreen even beneath the snow. Don't be afraid of putting in too many when brewing fresh tea. Tearing them into fine bits will provide more flavor, which can be made even more satisfying for many with cream and sweetening.

The twigs and inner bark of the black birch largely replaced wintergreen for obtaining the popular flavor commercially, and now synthetics have taken the place of even these.

The firm berrylike fruit, which clings to the plants all winter, is tasty and sustaining raw and when sometimes used for pies or such retains maximum flavor when crushed by hand or blender, then added to the cooked ingredients and served.

YELLOW WATER LILY (Nuphar)

FAMILY - Water Lily *(Nymphaeaceae)*

OTHER NAMES - Pond Lily, Yellow Pond Lily, Cow Lily, Water Lily, Pond Collard, Wokas, Spatter-dock, Bonnet.

DESCRIPTION - Nearly every freshwater fisherman, canoeist, and other frequenter of the farther places knows the bright golden, waxy flowers and the broad green leaves of the yellow pond lily whose floating beauty enhances many of the ponds, shallow lake rims, and other quiet waters of the United States and its northern neighbor.

Blossoming during the vacation months of June, July, and August, the showy prettiness of these yellow flowers provides a tranquil background to the noisiness of frogs, while the shady green coolness of the large leaves serves as excellent trout and bluegill cover.

The vividly yellow flowers are from two to some six inches across with from a dozen to a dozen-and-a-half petals, backed up with from eight to twelve sepals. Centered in each flower are numerous reddish stamens, bright in season with yellowish pollen. The flowers later develop many large seeds which somewhat resemble kernels of popcorn and which are known and widely available in their habitats, so densely are marshes sometimes peopled with these picturesque lilies.

The prominent oval to roundish leaves are from several inches to a foot long and about three-fourths as wide. Some loom erect out of the water. They are rather deeply cleft where they join the stems and are blunt along their tops.

The cool stems, slippery and often slimy to the touch, move upward from the tops of spongy, large, starch-filled roots that thrive for the most part far enough below the water surface to be snugly below the frost line. They are scaly and also yellowish.

DISTRIBUTION - The yellow pond lily, as it is also widely known, enlivens fish-filled waters from Alaska to Labrador, south to California and the Gulf of Mexico. There are five species in this country.

EDIBILITY - Mallard, ring-necked, and wood ducks eat the seeds to some extent, as do cranes and rails. Beavers, muskrats, and porcupines like the plants. It is in the homes of these former two that squaws used to gather many of the roots they used, diving for others.

The roots are richest in starch from autumn to early spring and, along with the seeds, were an important Indian food. These roots can be advantageously roasted or boiled, after which they peel easily. The sweetish interiors are usually cut up in soups and stews. Especially during famines, the aborigines dried and ground them for flour.

The roundish seed vessels become filled in late summer and in the autumn and are easily gathered, fried, and shelled. Cook, butter, and salt like popcorn. They swell but do not crack like the latter and can also be enjoyed with milk or cream as a breakfast cereal. The Indians sometimes went one step further and ground the poppings for more meal.

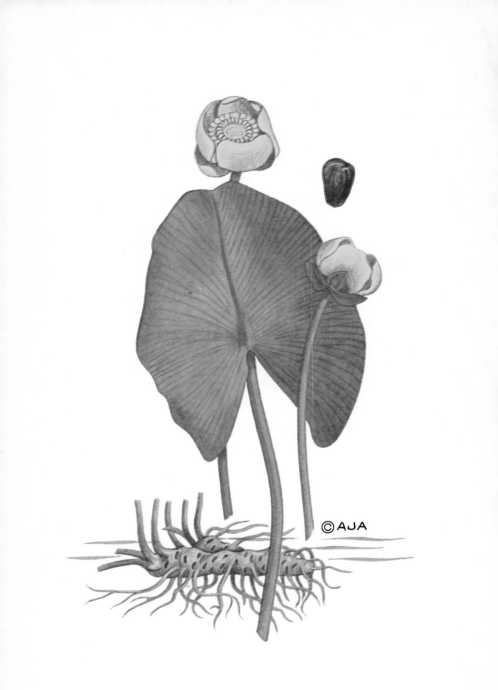

©AJA